T0356396

NONMONOTONIC REASONING WITH DEFEASIBLE RULES ON FEASIBLE AND INFEASIBLE WORLDS

Dissertations in Artificial Intelligence

Artificial Intelligence (AI) is one of the fastest growing research areas in computer science with a strong impact on various fields of science, industry, and society. This series publishes excellent doctoral dissertations in all sub-fields of AI, ranging from foundational work on AI methods and theories to application-oriented theses.

Volume 355

Previously published in this series:

Vol. 354 Lisa Grumbach, Flexible Workflows – A Constraint- and Case-Based Approach
Vol. 353 Leonid Berov, From Narratology to Computational Story Composition and Back – An Exploratory Study in Generative Modeling
Vol. 352 Kai Sauerwald, Semantics of Belief Change Operators for Intelligent Agents: Iteration, Postulates, and Realizability
Vol. 351 Peter Bourgonje, Shallow Discourse Parsing for German
Vol. 350 Steven Kutsch, Knowledge Representation and Inductive Reasoning using Conditional Logic and Sets of Ranking Functions
Vol. 349 Markus Schwinn, Ontologie-basierte Informationsextraktion zum Aufbau einer Wissensbasis für dokumentgetriebene Workflows
Vol. 348 Pascal Welke, Efficient Frequent Subtree Mining Beyond Forests
Vol. 347 Johannes Hellrich, Word Embeddings: Reliability & Semantic Change
Vol. 346 Mark Wernsdorfer, Symbol Grounding as the Generation of Mental Representations
Vol. 345 Alexander Steen, Extensional Paramodulation for Higher-Order Logic and its Effective Implementation Leo-III
Vol. 344 Jan Ole Berndt, Self-Organizing Multiagent Negotiations – Cooperation and Competition of Concurrently Acting Agents with Limited Knowledge
Vol. 343 Emmanuelle-Anna Dietz Saldanha, From Logic Programming to Human Reasoning: How to be Artificially Human
Vol. 342 Marc Finthammer, Concepts and Algorithms for Computing Maximum Entropy Distributions for Knowledge Bases with Relational Probabilistic Conditionals
Vol. 341 Jasper van de Ven, Supporting Communication in Spatially Distributed Groups – Privacy as a Service for Ambient Intelligence
Vol. 340 Nina Dethlefs, Hierarchical Joint Learning for Natural Language Generation
Vol. 339 Jens Haupert, DOMeMan: Repräsentation, Verwaltung und Nutzung von digitalen Objektgedächtnissen
Vol. 338 Mari Carmen Suárez-Figueroa, NeOn Methodology for Building Ontology Networks: Specification, Scheduling and Reuse
Vol. 337 Nicola Pirlo, Zur Robustheit eines modellgestützten Verfolgungsansatzes in Videos von Straßenverkehrszenen

ISSN 0941-5769 (print)
ISSN 2666-2175 (online)

Nonmonotonic Reasoning with Defeasible Rules on Feasible and Infeasible Worlds

Exploring a Landscape of Inductive Inference Operators

Jonas Philipp Haldimann

Knowledge Based Systems, FernUniversität in Hagen, Germany

IOS Press

ISBN 978-1-64368-529-8 (print)
ISBN 978-1-64368-530-4 (online)
Library of Congress Control Number: 2024942278
doi: 10.3233/DAI355

Dissertation, approved by FernUniversität in Hagen
Date of the defense: 29 April 2024
Supervisor: Prof. Christoph Beierle

ORCID page of the author: https://orcid.org/0000-0002-2618-8721

Publisher
IOS Press BV
Nieuwe Hemweg 6B
1013 BG Amsterdam
The Netherlands
https://www.iospress.com/contact

PRINTED IN THE NETHERLANDS

Foreword

Ever since the emergence of Artificial Intelligence as a research field, the modelling of intelligent behaviour has been a central topic in this area. Using classical logics for representing the knowledge and beliefs of an intelligent agent suffers from the fact that all inferences drawn remain valid under any additional information, i.e., the set of conclusions grows monotonically with the amount of available information. In realistic situations, however, conclusions for making decisions and for planning actions must be taken in the presence of uncertain and incomplete information. This leads to the requirement that previously obtained inferences may have to be withdrawn in the light of new information, and nonmonotonic logics provide the capability to model such a behaviour. In particular, given a belief base consisting of a set of defeasible conditionals of the form "*If A, then usually B*", an inductive inference operator completes any such conditional belief base and maps is to a full nonmonotonic inference relation that can represent an agent's epistemic state.

The dissertation presented by Jonas Haldimann is located in the area of nonmonotonic reasoning from conditional belief bases. While in classical logic there is a unique notion of deductive inference, in nonmonotonic reasoning there is no inference method that is generally accepted as "best". Instead, there are various postulates that describe desirable properties of nonmonotonic reasoning, and there are many inference methods that differ in which of the postulates they satisfy. In his thesis, Haldimann explores and evaluates several inductive inference methods. Among these are the well-known p-entailment, which coincides with inferences based on system P, and system Z, which coincides with rational closure. A special focus is on the only recently introduced system W which extends both rational closure and c-inference. Haldimann shows that system W fully satisfies syntax splitting and also conditional syntax splitting, and he develops several upper and lower approximations of system W.

For all addressed inference operators, Haldimann examines whether they are able to deal with, or how they can be extended to deal with contradictions that may arise from a belief base and can lead to the complete implausibility of possible worlds, an aspect that has often been neglected before. For these investigations, the central notions of strong and weak consistency of conditional belief bases and the concepts of feasible and infeasible worlds are introduced, allowing for a precise and conclusive formalization of nonmonotonic inferences even in the presence of local inconsistencies. All considered inductive inference operators and their extended versions are inserted in a comprehensive landscape showing the arising interrelationships among them.

Overall, Jonas Haldimann has presented a very successful dissertation; all theoretical results are convincingly and rigorously proven and placed in the scientific context. In the area of logic-based knowledge representation, he has delved deeply into challenging problems of nonmonotonic reasoning from conditional belief bases and has achieved insightful and significant results that mark considerable scientific progress.

Hagen, May 2024 Christoph Beierle

Abstract

For an intelligent agent in a complex environment it is important to draw conclusions from incomplete and uncertain information. One established way to represent uncertain beliefs are *conditionals* $(B|A)$ formalizing defeasible rules of the form "if A then usually B". Semantic structures for conditional beliefs are often built upon propositional interpretations which are called *possible worlds.* To formalize the process of inference we use the notion of *inductive inference operators* by Kern-Isberner, Beierle, and Brewka that map a set Δ of given conditionals (called a *belief base*) to an inference relation containing all inferences an agent draws from Δ. Investigating how an agent should draw inferences from defeasible rules is part of the research field of *nonmonotonic reasoning*, which is a sub-field of *knowledge representation and reasoning* and *artificial intelligence.*

In literature different definitions of consistency have been used. We contrast two notions of consistency that we call *weak* and *strong* consistency. A main topic of this thesis is inductive inference from weakly consistent belief bases. We observe that weakly consistent belief bases can require some worlds to be completely infeasible in the induced inference relations while strongly consistent belief bases allow every world to be at least somewhat feasible.

Among the postulates put forward for nonmonotonic inference, there are postulates that deal with *syntax splittings*, the idea being that if a belief base contains completely independent information on different topics, then inference operators should treat these two parts independently. The syntax splitting postulates that were previously introduced assume all belief bases to be strongly consistent. We introduce extended versions of these syntax splitting postulates that *also* cover inference from weakly consistent belief bases.

Another focus of this thesis is investigating the properties of the recently defined inductive inference operator *system W*. We evaluate system W with respect to different postulates for inference relations; and we show that system W fully complies with syntax splittings and even the more general *conditional* syntax splittings.

The inductive inference operators system W and c-inference were initially defined only for strongly consistent belief bases. We extend both inference operators to cover also weakly consistent belief bases and thus to handle inference with infeasible worlds. We evaluate the extended versions of system W and c-inference with respect to their properties, and especially we show that extended system W and extended c-inference still comply with syntax splitting.

We also investigate relationships among inductive inference operators. We propose operations that generate inductive inference operators from given inference operators, and use these to introduce approximations of system W. We investigate the relations among inductive inference operators like (extended) c-inference, (extended) system Z, (extended) system W, approximations of system W, and lexicographic inference, leading to a landscape of inductive inference operators and their interrelationships. Additionally, we give characterizations of inductive inference operators that extend *rational closure* in terms of properties on their underlying semantic structures.

Zusammenfassung

Für einen intelligenten Agenten in einer komplexen Umgebung ist es wichtig, Schlussfolgerungen aus unvollständigen und unsicheren Informationen zu ziehen. Eine gängige Methode zur Darstellung unsicheren Wissens sind *Konditionale* $(B|A)$, die unsichere Regeln der Form „wenn A dann normalerweise B“ formalisieren. Semantische Strukturen für konditionales Wissen basieren häufig auf aussagenlogischen Interpretationen, die als *mögliche Welten* bezeichnet werden. Um den Prozess der Inferenz zu formalisieren, verwenden wir den Begriff der induktiven Inferenzoperatoren von Kern-Isberner, Beierle und Brewka, die eine Menge Δ von gegebenen Konditionalen (*Wissensbasis* genannt) auf eine Inferenzrelation abbilden, die alle Inferenzen enthält, die ein Agent aus Δ zieht. Die Untersuchung der Frage, wie ein Agent Schlussfolgerungen aus unsicheren Regeln ziehen sollte, ist Teil des Forschungsgebiets *nichtmonotones Schließen*, das ein Teilgebiet von *Wissensrepräsentation und Verarbeitung* und *künstlicher Intelligenz* ist.

In der Literatur wurden verschiedene Definitionen von Konsistenz verwendet. Wir stellen zwei Begriffe von Konsistenz gegenüber, die wir als *schwache* und *starke* Konsistenz bezeichnen. Ein Hauptthema dieser Arbeit ist die Inferenz aus schwach konsistenten Wissensbasen. Wir beobachten, dass schwach konsistente Wissensbasen erfordern können, dass einige Welten in den induzierten Inferenzrelationen völlig unplausibel sind, während stark konsistente Wissensbasis erlauben, dass jede Welt zumindest etwas plausibel ist.

Unter den Postulaten, die für nichtmonotone Inferenz aufgestellt wurden, gibt es Postulate, die sich mit *Syntax-Splittings* befassen. Die Idee dahinter ist, dass, wenn eine Wissensbasis völlig unabhängige Informationen zu verschiedenen Themen enthält, Inferenzoperatoren diese beiden Teile unabhängig voneinander behandeln sollten. Die bisher eingeführten Syntax-Splitting-Postulate gehen davon aus, dass alle Wissensbasen stark konsistent sind. Wir führen erweiterte Versionen dieser Syntax-Splitting-Postulate ein, die auch die Inferenz aus schwach konsistenten Wissensbasen abdecken.

Ein weiterer Schwerpunkt dieser Arbeit ist die Untersuchung der Eigenschaften des kürzlich definierten induktiven Inferenzoperators *System W*. Wir evaluieren System W im Hinblick auf verschiedene Postulate für Inferenzrelationen und zeigen, dass System W Syntax-Splittings und sogar die allgemeineren konditionalen Syntax-Splittings berücksichtigt.

Die induktiven Inferenzoperatoren System W und c-Inferenz wurden ursprünglich nur für stark konsistente Wissensbasen definiert. Wir erweitern beide Inferenzoperatoren so, dass sie auch schwach konsistente Wissensbasen abdecken und somit auch Inferenz mit unplausiblen Welten ermöglichen. Wir evaluieren die erweiterten Versionen von System W und c-Inferenz im Hinblick auf ihre Eigenschaften und zeigen insbesondere, dass erweitertes System W und die erweiterte c-Inferenz immer noch Syntax-Splittings berücksichtigen.

Außerdem untersuchen wir die Beziehungen zwischen induktiven Inferenzoperatoren. Wir schlagen Operationen vor, die induktive Inferenzoperatoren aus gegebenen Inferenzoperatoren erzeugen, und verwenden diese, um Approximationen für System W zu erstellen. Wir untersuchen die Beziehungen zwischen induktiven Inferenzoperatoren wie (erweiterter) c-Inferenz, (erweitertem) System Z, (erweitertem) System W, Approximationen von System W und der lexikografischen Inferenz, was zu einer Landschaft induktiver Inferenzoperatoren und ihrer Beziehungen untereinander führt. Darüber hinaus geben wir Charakterisierungen von induktiven Inferenzoperatoren, die *Rational Closure* erweitern, durch Eigenschaften der ihnen zugrunde liegenden semantischen Strukturen an.

Acknowledgements

I enjoyed the past years I worked in Hagen, and I am very grateful to everyone who contributed to that.

I want to thank Christoph Beierle for advising, mentoring, and supporting me in many ways during the last five years. From him I learned so much about conducting research and scientific writing. I am grateful for all our discussions, the collaboration on the many papers we wrote together, and the incredible amount of feedback I got from him. I hope we work together on many future projects!

I want to thank Gabriele Kern-Isberner for the many papers we wrote together, the challenging discussions, and for introducing me to the area of KRR when I was a student at TU Dortmund University.

I want to thank my colleagues Kai Sauerwald and Steven Kutsch, who welcomed me when I started at the Knowledge Based Systems Group in Hagen, and Martin von Berg who joined the group later, for the many interesting discussions, their support, and for answering all my questions. I enjoyed working with you! I want to thank the student assistants I had the pleasure to work with, Jonas Aqua, Philip Heltweg, Arthur Sanin, Leon Schwarzer, and Aron Spang, for the collaboration. I want to thank the people from the Information Engineering Group at TU Dortmund University, Jesse Heyninck, Diana Howey, Andre Thevapalan, Meliha Sezgin, and Marco Wilhelm for our journal club meetings. I want to thank the people from the Artificial Intelligence Group, Lars Bengel, Lydia Blümel, Isabelle Kuhlmann, Jandson Ribeiro, Kai Sauerwald (again!), Kenneth Skiba, and Matthias Thimm for the discussions and for welcoming me to their social events.

And I want to thank my family, Petra, Ralf, and Max, without whom I could not have accomplished any of this.

This work was supported by the DFG through grant BE 1700/10-1 awarded to Christoph Beierle within the SPP 1921 "Intentional Forgetting in Organizations".

Contents

Chapter 1

Introduction

One large sub-area in artificial intelligence [RN20] is *Knowledge Representation and Reasoning* (*KRR*). KRR deals with the question of how an intelligent agent should represent and process symbolic beliefs. Among other things, this includes dealing with the change of beliefs in the light of new inputs, as well as reasoning with given beliefs. In real world applications, many beliefs are defeasible, i.e., they are believed to hold in most, but not all situations. Reasoning with defeasible beliefs is one of the challenges in KRR. This thesis addresses topics in the area of inductive inference from a set of *defeasible rules*, i.e., the process of drawing inferences from a set of rules that allow for exceptions.

1.1. Context

For an intelligent agent it is important to have the ability to draw conclusions from incomplete information. In real world applications this reasoning has to deal with uncertainty: the agent is usually not certain about everything she believes, and even rules that hold most of the time have exceptions. This is the field of nonmonotonic reasoning: an agent draws plausible conclusions, but additional information might cause the agent to revoke a conclusion she previously drew.

There are different approaches for representing and reasoning with uncertain beliefs. Approaches like probabilistic logic [Nil86; Pea89; Hal90], possibilistic logic [DLP91], and fuzzy logic [Zad65; Zim01] use numbers to express how likely or unlikely a proposition is. Other approaches like default logic [Poo88; Rei80] or answer set programming [Gel08] use rules with additional, nonmonotonic preconditions for their applicability. Another well established way to represent uncertain beliefs are defeasible rules "if A then usually B". These rules, also called conditional beliefs, qualitatively express a meaningful connection between A and B that is considered to be plausible, probable, typical, possible, etc. Because such rules are defeasible, they allow for exceptions. Defeasible rules are quite versatile, e.g., they allow expressing that a statement B plausibly holds by saying "if $\top$ then usually B" where $\top$ is a statement that is always true. Formally, such a rule "if A then usually B" can be captured by a *conditional* [Ada75; Nut80; NC02; DP94] $(B|A)$ connecting the two logical propositions A and B.

Reasoning with defeasible rules has a long tradition in KRR, and over the years, various semantics, methods, and postulates have been suggested (e.g., [Ada75; Leh89; KLM90; Pea90; LM92; Leh95; BEK16; KBB20; GG21]). Furthermore, reasoning with defeasible rules is connected to belief change, another important topic in KRR. This connection can be made, e.g., via the "Ramsey-Test" [Ram31; Sta81].

In this thesis, we investigate nonmonotonic reasoning based on the framework of Kraus, Lehmann, and Magidor [KLM90]; in particular we focus on the class of *preferential* inference relations. An inference relation captures all defeasible inferences that an agent can derive from his current beliefs, and preferential inference relations [KLM90] are those inference relations that satisfy a set of postulates called *system P* [Ada75; KLM90].

In addition to the description of preferential inference relations with postulates, [KLM90] provides a characterisation of inference relations by structures called *preferential models*. A preferential model orders a set of states according to their plausibility compared to each other and assigns a logical interpretation to each state. In this context, the interpretations are also called *worlds*. Preferential models can be used as models for defeasible rules, and it was shown that every preferential inference relation is modelled by a preferential model [KLM90]. But preferential models are not the only structures that are used to model defeasible rules. Other structures that can be used are, for example, ranking functions [Spo88] or ordering relations over a set of worlds [KM92]. Common to all of these structures is that they express how plausible the considered worlds are compared to each other. In this thesis, we will mostly use preferential models, ranking functions, and strict partial orders on a set of worlds to model defeasible rules.

The process of deriving an inference relation from a given set of conditionals is formally captured by *inductive inference operators* [KBB20] that map a set of given conditionals (called a *belief base*) to an inference relation. Thus, the notion of inductive inference operators clearly separates the conditional rules that are initially given as a set of conditionals *(the belief base)* and the conditional beliefs in the resulting inference relation. Many of the older approaches to inference, like p-entailment [KLM90] or system Z [Pea90] can be considered as inductive inference operators. Other examples of inductive inference operators are c-inference [BEK16] that is based on c-representations [Ker01; Ker04] and exhibits many desirable properties, and system W [KB22] that extends both c-inference and rational closure.

Among the more recent postulates put forward for nonmonotonic inference, there are the postulates that deal with *syntax splittings*. The idea of syntax splittings was originally developed by Parikh [Par99] and describes that a belief set contains completely independent information on different topics; based on that, Parikh proposed a postulate for belief revisions stating that for a belief set with a syntax splitting a revision should treat these two parts independently, as far as possible. The notion of syntax splitting was later extended to other representations, and [KBB20] introduced syntax splitting postulates for inductive inference operators. By requiring inference operators to focus on the relevant part of a belief base, they allow the agent to forget about the irrelevant parts during reasoning; hence syntax splitting plays an important role in the field of *intentional forgetting* [BT19; Bei+19; EK19; HKB20; HBK21].

While the focus of most of the approaches mentioned above is on handling of defeasible rules, some of these approaches also support so called *strict* beliefs that require a proposition to hold without exception. For a preferential model for example, a world that is not assigned to any state will not be considered feasible under any circumstances, thus strict beliefs can be represented by pre-selecting the worlds that are used in the preferential model [KLM90]. Ranking functions can assign the rank ∞ to mark formulas as impossible. But while some inference operators like p-entailment can handle infeasible worlds, other approaches like c-inference and system W are (initially) not designed to do this. This can be a drawback, because infeasible worlds can be required not only by explicitly modelled strict beliefs, but also by combinations of defeasible conditionals that can occur after merging belief bases with purely defeasible beliefs.

1.2. Research Questions and Main Contributions

The investigation and results in this thesis address the following five research questions. In the following, we will explain each question and summarize the main contributions made in this thesis towards answering it.

Q1: How can an agent handle plausible inference from belief bases that are not strongly consistent?

Informally, a belief base is *consistent* if it does not contradict itself. Being consistent is usually a prerequisite to drawing sensible inferences from it. But while many publications use the term "consistent", there is no single definition that is generally agreed upon. We identify two different notions of consistency that are used in literature, and give definitions for both of them in a common framework. To distinguish these two notions in our work we call one of them *strong* consistency (used for example in [GP96]) and the other, more general notion *weak* consistency (used for example in [CMV19]).

While some inference operators can draw inferences from weakly consistent belief bases, other inference operators require strongly consistent belief bases. What is the key to handling belief bases that are not strongly consistent?

In this thesis we contrast the two notions of consistency. We observe that weakly consistent belief bases can require worlds to be completely infeasible while strongly consistent belief bases only allow all worlds to be at least somewhat plausible. To model belief bases that are weakly consistent but not strongly consistent it is necessary to have some worlds that are not considered feasible under any circumstances. We introduce the terms *feasible* and *infeasible worlds* to distinguish worlds that are somewhat plausible and those that are completely implausible, and we observe how infeasible worlds are marked in models like ranking functions and preferential models. Furthermore, for strict partial orders (SPO) on worlds we introduce the notion of a *full SPO on worlds* that can only model defeasible beliefs and thus only strongly consistent belief bases, and the more general *limited SPO on worlds* that distinguishes feasible and infeasible worlds and can also model all weakly consistent belief bases.

Q2: What are adequate syntax splitting postulates for reasoning with infeasible worlds?

The syntax splitting postulates for inductive inference operators introduced in [KBB20] assume belief bases to be strongly consistent.

We elaborate the subtleties of dealing with infeasible worlds and introduce extended versions of these syntax splitting postulates that cover inference from weakly consistent belief bases, while at the same time staying consistent with the postulates from [KBB20] for strongly consistent belief bases.

Q3: What properties does system W have, especially with respect to syntax splitting?

While it is known that the only recently introduced system W has the remarkable property of extending both c-inference and system Z, here we evaluate system W with respect to common postulates like *Semi-Monotony*, *Rational Monotony*, or *Weak Rational Monotony*. We show that system W behaves quite well with respect to syntax splitting and prove that it satisfies both the syntax splitting postulates and the more general conditional syntax splitting postulates. Furthermore, we investigate the effect of syntax splittings on the preferred structure on worlds underlying the inference relations induced by system W, showing how we can decide this ordering relation on worlds while considering each part of the syntax splitting separately.

Q4: How can we extend system W and c-inference to belief bases that are not strongly consistent?

System W and c-inference are inductive inference operators that were defined for strongly consistent belief bases. We extend both inference operators and their underlying semantic structures to cover also weakly consistent belief bases and thus to handle inference with infeasible worlds. We evaluate the extended versions of system W and c-inference with respect to postulates like *Semi-Monotony*, *Rational Monotony*, or *Weak Rational Monotony*. Especially we show that extended system W and extended c-inference still comply with syntax splitting.

Q5: How do different inductive inference operators relate to each other?

We propose operations that generate inductive inference operators from given inference operators. Using these, we introduce approximations of system W that are either extended by system W or extending system W.

While in general, different inductive inference operators induce different inference relations, one way to relate inference operators is by establishing subset-relations on the induced inference relations. In this thesis we investigate the relations among inductive inference operators like (extended) c-inference, (extended) system Z, (extended) system W, approximations of system W, and lexicographic inference, leading to a comprehensive landscape of inductive inference operators and their interrelationships.

Finally, we give characterisations of inductive inference operators that extend the inference operator *rational closure* in terms of properties on their preferential models.

1.3. Structure of this thesis

This thesis is structured as follows. In Chapter 2 we recall the preliminaries on conditional logic, we formalize and contrast the notions of strong and weak consistency for belief bases, and we consider the operations marginalisation and combination of ranking functions. In Chapter 3 we first recall the notion of inductive inference operators as well as the definitions of the inference operators from the literature that occur in this thesis. We also discuss syntax splitting postulates for inductive inference operators. The properties of system W, especially with respect to syntax splitting and conditional syntax splitting, are considered in Chapter 4. Chapter 5 covers the results on reasoning with infeasible worlds and introduces the extended versions of system W and c-inference. In Chapter 5 we also investigate the properties of extended system W and extended c-inference. In Chapter 6 we establish the relationships among the mentioned inference operators and introduce various approximations of system W. Chapter 7 describes the characterizations of rational closure-extending inductive inference operators before we conclude in Chapter 8.

1.4. Previous Publications

During my time at the FernUniversität in Hagen as a doctorate student I contributed to publications on different topics. Large parts of the results covered in this thesis were previously published in one of those publications.

The topic of this thesis, nonmonotonic reasoning with conditionals, is also one of the main topics I worked on. Together with my supervisor Christoph Beierle I published on the properties of system W [HB22c], the compliance of system W with syntax splitting [HB22b], and system W's relation to other inductive inference operators [HB23a; HB22a]. We also contributed to publications on the implementation of system W [Bei+22] and showed that system W complies with *conditional syntax splitting* in [Hey+23]. In [Hal+23b] we discussed inference relations that are representable by strict partial orders on sets of worlds and characterized classes of inference operators that extend rational closure. In [Hal+23a; HBK23b; HBK24] we extended system W and c-inference to reasoning with infeasible worlds.

In addition to that, I worked on several other topics that are not covered by this thesis. Together with colleagues, I investigated properties of *Epistemic State Mappings*, which are mappings between different types of models of conditional beliefs [HK21; HBK23a], and we investigated and characterized *Conditional Descriptor Revision*, a kind of revision that revises ranking functions with beliefs on conditionals [Sau+20; Hal+21b; Hal+21a]. Furthermore, I contributed to multiple papers on normal forms for conditional knowledge bases (i.e., sets of condionals) [BH20a; BH20b; BHK21b; BH22a; BH22b; BHS23]. I also contributed to further research on syntax splitting that is not covered in this thesis. In [HKB20; HBK21] we investigate syntax splitting postulates for belief contractions. We showed that there are unique finest syntax splittings for ranking functions and total preorders on worlds [HB23b], and in [BHK21a; Wil+23] we investigate further notions of splittings that can be used to identify the parts of an agent's beliefs that are not relevant for the reasoning problem at hand.

Chapter 2

Conditionals, Consistency, and Marginalization

Before we go into details about inductive inference operators, we cover some preliminary topics. In Section 2.1 we recall propositional and conditional logic and introduce ranking functions as models for conditionals. We introduce the terms of strong and weak consistency for belief bases in Section 2.2. In Section 2.3, we recall the notions of marginalization and combination of ranking functions and show some related results.

The terms *strong* and *weak* consistency as well as the comparison of those two notions of consistency origin from [Hal+23a].

2.1. Background on Conditional Logic

In this section we briefly recall the background on conditional logic and the notations related to that.

2.1.1. Propositional Logic

A *(propositional) signature* is a finite set Σ of propositional variables. A propositional variable is also called *atom*; atoms and negated atoms are called *literals*. By combining the variables of a signature Σ with the usual logical connectives $\wedge, \vee, \neg$ we obtain the propositional language $\mathcal{L}_\Sigma$. An *interpretation* over a signature Σ is an assignment of every variable $a \in \Sigma$ to either *true* or *false*. The set of interpretations over a signature Σ is denoted by Ω_Σ. Interpretations are also referred to as *worlds* and Ω_Σ is called the *universe*.

Usually, atoms are denoted with lowercase letters $a, b, c, \ldots$ and formulas with uppercase letters $A, B, C, \ldots$. For brevity of notation, a negation $\neg A$ may be denoted by $\overline{A}$ and a conjunction $A \wedge B$ may be shortened to AB. As usual, $A \rightarrow B$ is shorthand for $\overline{A} \vee B$ and $A \leftrightarrow B$ is shorthand for $AB \vee \overline{A}\,\overline{B}$.

An interpretation $\omega \in \Omega_\Sigma$ is a *model* of a formula $A \in \mathcal{L}$ if A evaluates to *true* under ω. This is denoted as $\omega \models A$. The set of models of a formula (over a signature Σ) is denoted as $Mod_\Sigma(A) := \{\omega \in \Omega_\Sigma \mid \omega \models A\}$. A formula A *entails* a formula B if $Mod_\Sigma(A) \subseteq Mod_\Sigma(B)$. The Σ in Ω_Σ, $\mathcal{L}_\Sigma$ and $Mod_\Sigma(A)$ can be omitted if the signature is clear from the context or if the underlying signature is not relevant.

A *complete conjunction* over a signature Σ is a conjunction of literals such that each atom in Σ occurs only once. Worlds will be denoted by complete conjunctions where an atom occurs in positive form iff it is mapped to *true*, and in negated form otherwise. For example, the world over $\Sigma := \{a, b, c\}$ that maps a to *true*, b to *false*, and c to *false* is denoted as $a\overline{b}\overline{c}$. By slight abuse of notation we sometimes interpret worlds as their corresponding complete conjunctions.

2.1.2. Conditional Logic

While propositional formulas can only represent unconditional statements, conditionals are used to express conditional statements. Assuming an underlying signature Σ, a *conditional* $(B|A)$ connects two formulas $A, B \in \mathcal{L}_\Sigma$ and represents the rule "If A then usually B". For a conditional $(B|A)$ the formula A is called the *antecedent* and B the *consequent* of the conditonal. The conditional language over a signature Σ is $(\mathcal{L}|\mathcal{L})_\Sigma := \{(B|A) \mid A, B \in \mathcal{L}_\Sigma\}$. A finite set of conditionals is called a *belief base*. Note that belief bases are also called *knowledge bases* in some of our earlier publications.

Conditionals are used with a three valued semantic [Fin37]. For a world ω a conditional $(B|A)$ is either *verified* by ω if $\omega \models AB$, *falsified* by ω if $\omega \models A\overline{B}$, or *not applicable* to ω if $\omega \models \overline{A}$.

There are many different models for conditionals and conditional belief bases such as ranking functions [Spo88], total preorders over Ω_Σ [DP97], or preferential models [KLM90]. Here, we want to introduce ranking functions as one popular model for conditionals.

Ranking functions (also called *ordinal conditional functions*, *OCF*) [Spo88] are functions that assign ranks to the worlds in Ω_Σ that express the world's plausibility. Formally, a ranking function is a function $\kappa : \Omega_\Sigma \to \mathbb{N}_0 \cup \{\infty\}$ that maps each worlds to a *rank* such that at least one world has rank 0, i.e., $\kappa^{-1}(0) \neq \emptyset$. The intuition is that worlds with lower ranks are more plausible than worlds with higher ranks; worlds with rank ∞ are considered infeasible. Note that in [Spo88] ranking functions are introduced in a more general way that maps worlds to ordinals instead of natural numbers or ∞.

A ranking function κ is lifted to formulas by mapping a formula A to the smallest rank of a model of A, or to ∞ if A has no models: $\kappa(A) := \min_{\omega \in Mod_\Sigma(A)} \kappa(\omega)$. Formulas or worlds with rank ∞ are called infeasible for κ. A ranking function κ being a model of a conditional $(B|A)$ is denoted as $\kappa \models (B|A)$ and defined by

$$\kappa \models (B|A) \quad \text{iff} \quad \kappa(A) = \infty \text{ or } \kappa(AB) < \kappa(A\overline{B}).$$

A ranking function κ is a model of a belief base Δ, denoted as $\kappa \models \Delta$, if it is a model of every conditional in Δ.

2.1.3. Ordering Relations and Minimal Elements

To model conditional beliefs we will use ordering relations on worlds later in this thesis. Here we want to briefly recall the notions of total preorders and strict partial orders. Let S be a set. A *total preorder* (*TPO*) on S is a total, reflexive, and transitive binary relation on S. A *strict partial order* (*SPO*) on S is an irreflexive, antisymmetric, and transitive binary relation on S. For a reflexive relation $\preceq$, we denote the strict part of $\preceq$ with $\prec$ defined as $a \prec b$ iff $a \preceq b$ and $b \not\preceq a$. For a strict (irreflexive) relation, we denote the reflexive extension of $\prec$ with $\preceq$ defined as $a \preceq b$ iff $a \prec b$ or $a = b$.

Orderings can be used to find the minimum of a set. For a set U with a canonical ordering $<$ (like, e.g., the set of natural numbers) and a set $S \subseteq U$ we use the following notations:

$$\min S := \{s \mid s \in S \text{ s.t. there is no } t \in S \text{ such that } t < s\}.$$

For a set U with a canonical ordering $<$, a set $S \subseteq U$, and a function $S \to U$ we use:

$$\min_{s \in S} f(s) := \{f(s) \mid s \in S \text{ s.t. there is no } t \in S \text{ with } f(t) < f(s)\}$$
$$\arg\min_{s \in S} f(s) := \{s \mid s \in S \text{ s.t. there is no } t \in S \text{ with } f(t) < f(s)\}$$

For a set S and an ordering $\prec$ on S we use the notation:

$$\min(S, \prec) := \{s \mid s \in S \text{ s.t. there is no } t \in S \text{ such that } t \prec s\}.$$

How SPOs on worlds can be used to model conditionals will be discussed later in Section 4.2 and Section 5.3.

2.2. Strong and Weak Consistency

There are different definitions of consistency of a belief base in the literature. A quite strong notion of consistency is used, e.g., in [GP96]; this notion is equivalent to considering a belief base consistent iff it is modelled by a ranking function with only finite ranks. Another, weaker notion of consistency is used in, e.g., [Gio+15; CMV19]; this weaker notion also considers belief bases consistent that require some worlds to infeasible. To distinguish the two different notions of consistency that both occur in this thesis we call the first notion *strong consistency* and the other notion *weak consistency.*

Definition 2.1 (strong and weak consistency). *A belief base Δ is called* strongly consistent *if there exists at least one ranking function κ with $\kappa \models \Delta$ and $\kappa^{-1}(\infty) = \emptyset$.*

A belief base Δ is weakly consistent *if there is at least one ranking function κ with $\kappa \models \Delta$.*

Thus, Δ is strongly consistent if there is at least one ranking function modelling Δ that considers all worlds feasible. The belief base Δ is weakly consistent if there is a ranking function considering at least one world feasible. Trivially, strong consistency implies weak consistency.

For every weakly consistent belief base (and therefore every strongly consistent belief base) there is a world that does not falsify any of the conditionals in it.

Lemma 2.2. *Let Δ be a weakly consistent belief base over signature Σ. There is at least one world $\omega \in \Omega_\Sigma$ that does not falsify any conditional in Δ.*

Proof. Let Δ be weakly consistent. By definition there is a ranking function $\kappa : \Omega_\Sigma \mapsto \mathbb{N} \cup \{\infty\}$ with $\kappa \models \Delta$. Because κ is a ranking function, there is an $\omega \in \Omega_\Sigma$ such that $\kappa(\omega) = 0$. Because $\kappa \models \Delta$ either falsifies no conditionals in Δ, or for every conditional $(B|A) \in \Delta$ with $\omega \models A\overline{B}$ there is a world ω' such that $\omega' \models AB$ and $\kappa(\omega') < \kappa(\omega) = 0$. The second case is not possible as 0 is the lowest rank. Therefore, ω does not falsify any conditional in Δ. □

Different from strongly consistent belief bases, weakly consistent belief bases can also contain conditionals of the form $(\bot|A)$ for formulas A with $A \not\equiv \bot$. While $(\bot|A)$ is still a defeasible conditional, it strictly requires that $\overline{A}$ holds in all worlds that are considered feasible. This way $A \mid\!\sim \bot$ expresses the "hard constraint" $\overline{A}$ [LM92]. Other publications call this a *strict belief* that $\overline{A}$ holds (see, e.g., [CS13]). A belief base can also require formulas to be infeasible without a conditional of the form $(\bot|A)$. For example, a belief base containing both the conditionals $(B|A)$ and $(\overline{B}|A)$ also requires A to be infeasible because the conditionals directly contradict each other for A. In general, every belief base that is not strongly consistent requires some worlds to be infeasible. Correspondingly, the ranking functions modelling belief bases that are not strongly consistent would need to assign rank ∞ to some worlds. Belief bases that are not even weakly consistent do not allow any world to be feasible – such belief bases contradict themselves on everything. A belief base that is not weakly consistent is not modelled by any ranking function because every ranking function requires at least one world to have rank 0.

2.3. Marginalization and Combination of Ranking Functions and Worlds

The worlds and ranking functions introduced in Subsection 2.1.2 are each defined with respect to an underlying signature Σ. For some applications, e.g., when working with syntax splittings, it is interesting to focus only on a specific sub-signature. To do this, we can *marginalize* worlds or ranking functions over Σ to a sub-signature $\Sigma' \subseteq \Sigma$. Marginalization keeps only the information on Σ' and discards the information connected to $\Sigma \setminus \Sigma'$. Note that a marginalization to Σ' is also referred to as Σ'-reduct in model theory [Del17].

Definition 2.3 (marginalization of a world [Del17])**.** *Let Σ be a signature and $\omega \in \Omega_\Sigma$. For $\Sigma' \subseteq \Sigma$ the* marginalization *of ω to Σ' is the world $\omega_{|\Sigma'} \in \Omega_{\Sigma'}$ that assigns the same truth values as ω to the atoms in Σ'.*

Definition 2.4 (marginalization of a ranking function [BK09; BK12]). *Let Σ be a signature and let $\kappa : \Omega_\Sigma \to \mathbb{N} \cup \{\infty\}$ be a ranking function. For $\Sigma' \subseteq \Sigma$ the* marginalization *of κ to Σ' is the ranking function $\kappa_{|\Sigma'} : \Omega_{\Sigma'} \to \mathbb{N} \cup \{\infty\}$ defined by $\kappa_{|\Sigma'}(\omega') := \min\{\kappa(\omega) \mid \omega \models \omega'\}$.*

Observe that in Definition 2.4 the function $\kappa_{|\Sigma'}(\omega') = \min\{\kappa(\omega) \mid \omega \models \omega'\}$ is indeed always a ranking function: if we let ω^0 be one of the worlds with $\kappa(\omega^0) = 0$ then $\kappa_{|\Sigma'}(\omega^0{}_{|\Sigma'}) = 0$.

Marginalization of a ranking function to a sub-signature Σ' does not affect the rank of a formula A that uses only atoms from Σ'.

Lemma 2.5. *Let $\kappa : \Omega_\Sigma \to \mathbb{N} \cup \{\infty\}$ be a ranking function, and let $\Sigma' \subseteq \Sigma$. Then, for any formula $A \in \mathcal{L}_{\Sigma'}$ we have that $\kappa(A) = \kappa_{|\Sigma'}(A)$.*

Proof. We can obtain the models of A with respect to Σ by extending the models of A with respect to Σ' by any possible valuation of $\Sigma \setminus \Sigma'$, i.e., $Mod_\Sigma(A) = \{\omega^a\omega^b \mid \omega^a \in Mod_{\Sigma'}(A), \omega^b \in \Omega_{\Sigma\setminus\Sigma'}\}$. By definition, we have that $\kappa_{|\Sigma'}(\omega') = \min\{\kappa(\omega) \mid \omega \in \Omega_\Sigma, \omega \models \omega'\} = \min\{\kappa(\omega'\omega^b) \mid \omega^b \in \Omega_{\Sigma\setminus\Sigma'}\}$. Therefore,

$$\begin{aligned}\kappa(A) &= \min\{\kappa(\omega^a\omega^b) \mid \omega^a \in Mod_{\Sigma'}(A), \omega^b \in \Omega_{\Sigma\setminus\Sigma'}\} \\ &= \min\{\kappa'(\omega') \mid \omega' \in Mod_{\Sigma'}(A)\} = \kappa_{|\Sigma'}(A).\end{aligned}$$

□

Analogously, marginalizing a ranking function to Σ' does not affect the acceptance of conditionals over Σ'.

Lemma 2.6. *Let $\kappa : \Omega_\Sigma \to \mathbb{N} \cup \{\infty\}$ be a ranking function and let $\Sigma' \subseteq \Sigma$. Then, for formulas $A, B \in \mathcal{L}_{\Sigma'}$ we have that $\kappa \models (B|A)$ iff $\kappa_{|\Sigma'} \models (B|A)$.*

Proof. Using Lemma 2.5 we have $\kappa(A) = \kappa_{|\Sigma'}(A)$ and $\kappa(AB) = \kappa_{|\Sigma'}(AB)$ and $\kappa(A\overline{B}) = \kappa_{|\Sigma'}(A\overline{B})$. Therefore, $\kappa \models (B|A)$ iff $\kappa_{|\Sigma'} \models (B|A)$. □

In the other direction, we might want to combine information on different (disjoint) signatures.

Definition 2.7 (combination of worlds, cf., e.g., [KB17]). *Let Σ_1, Σ_2 be disjoint signatures and $\omega_1 \in \Omega_{\Sigma_1}, \omega_2 \in \Omega_{\Sigma_2}$ be worlds. Then $\omega_1\omega_2$ denotes the world in $\Omega_{\Sigma_1\cup\Sigma_2}$ that assigns the same truth values as ω_1 to the atoms in Σ_1 and as ω_2 to the atoms in Σ_2.*

Definition 2.8 (combination of ranking functions [KB17]). *Let Σ_1, Σ_2 be disjoint signatures and let $\kappa_1 : \Omega_{\Sigma_1} \to \mathbb{N} \cup \{\infty\}$ and $\kappa_2 : \Omega_{\Sigma_2} \to \mathbb{N} \cup \{\infty\}$ be ranking functions. The combination of κ_1 and κ_2, denoted by $\kappa_\oplus := \kappa_1 \oplus \kappa_2$, is the ranking function $\kappa_\oplus : \Omega_{\Sigma_1 \cup \Sigma_2} \to \mathbb{N} \cup \{\infty\}$ that is defined by $\kappa_\oplus(\omega) := \kappa_1(\omega_{|\Sigma_1}) + \kappa_2(\omega_{|\Sigma_2})$.*

Obviously, $\oplus$ is commutative, i.e., $\kappa_1 \oplus \kappa_2 = \kappa_2 \oplus \kappa_1$.

Lemma 2.9. *Let Σ_1, Σ_2 be disjoint signatures and let $\kappa_1 : \Omega_{\Sigma_1} \to \mathbb{N} \cup \{\infty\}$ and $\kappa_2 : \Omega_{\Sigma_2} \to \mathbb{N} \cup \{\infty\}$ be ranking functions. Let $\kappa_\oplus = \kappa_1 \oplus \kappa_2$. For formulas $A \in \mathcal{L}_{\Sigma_1}, B \in \mathcal{L}_{\Sigma_2}$ it holds that $\kappa_\oplus(AB) = \kappa_1(A) + \kappa_2(B)$.*

Proof. Let $\Sigma := \Sigma_1 \cup \Sigma_2$. Because $A \in \mathcal{L}_{\Sigma_1}$ and $B \in \mathcal{L}_{\Sigma_2}$, we have that $Mod_\Sigma(AB) = \{\omega^1\omega^2 \mid \omega^1 \in Mod_{\Sigma_1}(A), \omega^2 \in Mod_{\Sigma_2}(B)\}$. Therefore, it holds that

$$\begin{aligned}
&\kappa_\oplus(AB) \\
&= \min\{\kappa_\oplus(\omega) \mid \omega \in Mod_\Sigma(AB)\} \\
&= \min\{\kappa_1(\omega^1) + \kappa_2(\omega^2) \mid \omega^1 \in Mod_{\Sigma_1}(A), \omega^2 \in Mod_{\Sigma_2}(B)\} \\
&= \min\{\kappa_1(\omega^1) \mid \omega^1 \in Mod_{\Sigma_1}(A)\} + \min\{\kappa_2(\omega^2) \mid \omega^2 \in Mod_{\Sigma_2}(B)\} \\
&= \kappa_1(A) + \kappa_2(B).
\end{aligned}$$

□

To undo the combination of two ranking functions by $\oplus$, we can use marginalization.

Lemma 2.10 ([KB17]). *Let Σ_1, Σ_2 be disjoint signatures and let $\kappa_1 : \Omega_{\Sigma_1} \to \mathbb{N} \cup \{\infty\}$ and $\kappa_2 : \Omega_{\Sigma_2} \to \mathbb{N} \cup \{\infty\}$ be ranking functions. Let $\kappa_\oplus := \kappa_1 \oplus \kappa_2$. Then $\kappa_{\oplus|\Sigma_1} = \kappa_1$ and $\kappa_{\oplus|\Sigma_2} = \kappa_2$.*

Proof. First we show that $\kappa_{\oplus|\Sigma_1} = \kappa_1$. Let ω^1 be any world in Ω_{Σ_1}. Let $\omega^2 \in \Omega_{\Sigma_1}$ such that $\kappa_2(\omega^2) = 0$. We have that

$$\begin{aligned}
\kappa_{|\Sigma_1}(\omega^1) &= \min\{\kappa(\omega) \mid \omega \in \Omega_\Sigma, \omega_{|\Sigma_1} = \omega^1\} \\
&= \min\{\kappa_1(\omega^1) + \kappa_2(\omega_{|\Sigma_2}) \mid \omega \in \Omega_\Sigma\} \\
&\overset{*}{=} \kappa_1(\omega^1).
\end{aligned}$$

Equation ($*$) holds because we can choose, e.g., $\omega = \omega^1\omega^2$, resulting in $\kappa_2(\omega_{|\Sigma_2}) = 0$.

$\kappa_{\oplus|\Sigma_2} = \kappa_2$ can be shown analogously. □

While Lemma 2.10 shows that the combination of ranking functions can be undone by marginalization to the respective sub-signatures, the reverse is not true. In general, if we marginalize a ranking function κ over Σ to disjoint sub-signatures Σ_1, Σ_2 that partition Σ, the original κ cannot be reconstructed from the marginals $\kappa_{|\Sigma_1}$ and $\kappa_{|\Sigma_2}$. This is because the information about the correlation between formulas in $\mathcal{L}_{\Sigma_1}$ and the formulas in $\mathcal{L}_{\Sigma_2}$ is not represented by either $\kappa_{|\Sigma_1}$ or $\kappa_{|\Sigma_2}$. However, reconstructing κ from $\kappa_{|\Sigma_1}$ and $\kappa_{|\Sigma_2}$ is possible if the information about each sub-signature Σ_1, Σ_2 are independent (cf. syntax splittings for ranking functions in [KB17]).

Chapter 3

Inductive Inference Operators

For an intelligent agent, it is important to be able to draw conclusions about her environment, and nonmonotonic reasoning with defeasible beliefs is an important part of KRR. In this chapter, we first recall the notion of an inference relation and the notion of an inductive inference operator which formalizes reasoning from a conditional belief base. We distinguish SCA-inductive inference operators that are only defined for strongly consistent belief bases and universal inductive inference operators that are defined for all belief bases. Then we present and discuss different inductive inference operators from literature. We recall the syntax splitting postulates from [KBB20] for SCA-inductive inference operators and, by working out the details needed for dealing with infeasible worlds, extend them for universal inductive inference operators.

Besides recalling results on established inference operators from literature (cf. the references), this chapter also contains the following own contributions. Proposition 3.15 originates from [HBK23b]. Lemmas 3.17 and 3.18 as well as *adapted* lexicographic inference were first introduced in [Hal+23a]. The belief base Δ_{ve} from Examples 3.48 and 3.49 is from [HB22c], and extended versions of splitting postulates for universal inductive inference operator were first introduced in [Hal+23a].

3.1. Inference Relations and System P

Having a set of conditional beliefs of the form *A entails B* enables a reasoning agent to draw appropriate conclusions in different situa-

(REF)	*Reflexivity*	for all $A \in \mathcal{L}$ it holds that $A \mid\!\sim A$
(LLE)	*Left Logical Equivalence*	$A \equiv B$ and $B \mid\!\sim C$ imply $A \mid\!\sim C$
(RW)	*Right weakening*	$B \models C$ and $A \mid\!\sim B$ imply $A \mid\!\sim C$
(CM)	*Cautious Monotony*	$A \mid\!\sim B$ and $A \mid\!\sim C$ imply $AB \mid\!\sim C$
(CUT)		$A \mid\!\sim B$ and $AB \mid\!\sim C$ imply $A \mid\!\sim C$
(OR)		$A \mid\!\sim C$ and $B \mid\!\sim C$ imply $(A \vee B) \mid\!\sim C$

Figure 3.1. The system P postulates for inference relations.

(AND)	$A \mid\!\sim B$ and $A \mid\!\sim C$ imply $A \mid\!\sim BC$

Figure 3.2. The postulate (AND) that can be derived from system P.

tions. This set of conditional beliefs is formally captured by a binary relation $\mid\!\sim$ on propositional formulas with $A \mid\!\sim B$ representing that A (defeasibly) entails B; this relation is called *inference* or *entailment relation*. As we consider defeasible or nonmonotonic entailment, it is possible that there are formulas A, B, C with $A \mid\!\sim B$ and $AC \not\mid\!\sim B$: Given more specific information, the agent might revoke a conclusion that she draw based on more general information.

There are many different sets of properties for inference relations, also called *postulates*, suggested in literature. A *preferential inference relation* is an inference relation satisfying the set of postulates called *system P* [KLM90] displayed in Figure 3.1. System P is often considered as minimal requirement for inference relations. The postulate (AND) [LM92] shown in Figure 3.2 can be derived from the system P postulates. Preferential inference relations can be equivalently characterized by a variant of system P where (CUT) is replaced with (AND).

The preferential models introduced by Kraus, Lehmann, and Magidor are a type of models for conditionals that are useful to represent preferential inference relations.

Definition 3.1 (preferential model [KLM90]). *Let Σ be a propositional signature. Let $\mathcal{M} := \langle S, l, \prec \rangle$ be a triple consisting of a set S of* states, *a function $l : S \to \Omega_\Sigma$ mapping states to interpretations, and a strict partial order $\prec$ on S. For $A \in \mathcal{L}_\Sigma$ and $s \in S$ we denote $l(s) \models A$ by $s \mid\!\equiv A$; and we define $[\![A]\!]_\mathcal{M} := \{s \in S \mid s \mid\!\equiv A\}$.*

$\mathcal{M}$ is a preferential model *if for any $A \in \mathcal{L}_\Sigma$ and $s \in [\![A]\!]_\mathcal{M}$ either s is minimal in $[\![A]\!]_\mathcal{M}$ or there is a $t \in [\![A]\!]_\mathcal{M}$ such that t is minimal in $[\![A]\!]_\mathcal{M}$ and $t \prec s$ (smoothness condition).*

(RM) *Rational Monotony* [KLM90] $A \mathrel{|\!\sim} B$ and $A \mathrel{|\!\not\sim} \overline{C}$ imply $AC \mathrel{|\!\sim} B$

Figure 3.3. Postulate *rational monotony* (RM) for inference relations.

Note that the smoothness condition is automatically satisfied for finite sets of interpretations. As this thesis only considers propositional logic with finite signatures, we can ignore this condition in Definition 3.1. Every preferential model induces an inference relation.

Definition 3.2 ([KLM90]). *A preferential model* $\mathcal{M} = \langle S, l, \prec \rangle$ *induces an inference relation* $\mathrel{|\!\sim}_{\mathcal{M}}$ *by*

$$A \mathrel{|\!\sim}_{\mathcal{M}} B \quad \textit{iff} \quad \min([\![A]\!]_{\mathcal{M}}, \prec) \subseteq [\![B]\!]_{\mathcal{M}}. \tag{3.1}$$

Two preferential models $\mathcal{M}$, $\mathcal{N}$ are called *equivalent* if they induce the same inference relation, i.e., if $\mathrel{|\!\sim}_{\mathcal{M}} = \mathrel{|\!\sim}_{\mathcal{N}}$.

One remarkable result from [KLM90] states that preferential models characterize preferential entailment relations: Every inference relation $\mathrel{|\!\sim}_{\mathcal{M}}$ induced by a preferential model $\mathcal{M}$ is preferential, and for every preferential inference relation $\mathrel{|\!\sim}$ there is a preferential model $\mathcal{M}$ with $\mathrel{|\!\sim}_{\mathcal{M}} = \mathrel{|\!\sim}$.

Furthermore, preferential models can be used as models for conditionals and belief bases.

Definition 3.3 ([KLM90]). *A preferential model* $\mathcal{M} = \langle S, l, \prec \rangle$ *models a conditional* $(B|A) \in \mathcal{L}_\Sigma$*, denoted as* $\mathcal{M} \models (B|A)$*, if*

$$\min([\![A]\!]_{\mathcal{M}}, \prec) \subseteq [\![B]\!]_{\mathcal{M}}.$$

$\mathcal{M}$ *models a belief base* Δ*, denoted as* $\mathcal{M} \models \Delta$*, if* $\mathcal{M}$ *models every conditional in* Δ.

Another postulate for inference relations is *rational monotony* (RM) (see Figure 3.3) [Pea90]. Inference relations that satisfy both system P and (RM) are also called *rational* [LM92].

Besides preferential models, also ranking functions induce inference relations. The inference relation induced by a ranking function κ is

$$A \mathrel{|\!\sim}_{\kappa} B \quad \text{iff} \quad \kappa(A) = \infty \text{ or } \kappa(AB) < \kappa(A\overline{B}). \tag{3.2}$$

The inference relation induced by any ranking function κ is preferential; a corresponding preferential model is, e.g., $\mathcal{M}_\kappa := \langle S, \mathrm{id}, \prec \rangle$

with $S := \{\omega \in \Omega_\Sigma \mid \kappa(\omega) < \infty\}$, the function id being the identity on S, and $\prec$ being an strict partial order on S defined by $\omega \prec \omega'$ iff $\kappa(\omega) < \kappa(\omega')$.

As the definition for $A \mid\!\sim_\kappa B$ coincides with $\kappa \models (B|A)$, the following is an immediate consequence of Lemma 2.6.

Lemma 3.4. *Let $\kappa : \Omega_\Sigma \to \mathbb{N} \cup \{\infty\}$ be a ranking function. Let $\Sigma' \subseteq \Sigma$ and let $\kappa' := \kappa_{|\Sigma'}$. Then, for formulas $A, B \in \mathcal{L}_{\Sigma'}$ we have that $A \mid\!\sim_\kappa B$ iff $A \mid\!\sim_{\kappa'} B$.*

Note that not only belief bases but also inference relations can require formulas to be infeasible. Corresponding to the conditionals of the form $(\bot|\overline{A})$ (see Section 2.2), an inference of the form $\overline{A} \mid\!\sim \bot$ requires that A holds in any feasible world [CS13].

In [LM92] formulas A with $A \not\mid\!\sim \bot$ are called "consistent" for $\mid\!\sim$; but to avoid too many different notions referred to by "consistency", in this thesis we will call such formulas *feasible* for $\mid\!\sim$. For example, a formula A is feasible for the inference relation $\mid\!\sim_\kappa$ induced by a ranking function κ iff $\kappa(A) < \infty$, and it is feasible for the inference relation $\mid\!\sim_\mathcal{M}$ induced by a preferential model $\mathcal{M} = \langle S, l, \prec\rangle$ iff $[\![A]\!]_\mathcal{M} \neq \emptyset$.

3.2. Inductive Inference Operators

Inductive inference is the process of completing a given belief base to an inference relation. This is formally captured by the concept of *inductive inference operators* introduced by Kern-Isberner, Beierle, and Brewka [KBB20]. The definition of inductive inference operators by Kern-Isberner, Beierle, and Brewka assumes all belief bases to be strongly consistent, but this requirement can be easily dropped. To distinguish the inference operators that are defined only for strongly consistent belief bases from those that are defined for all belief bases, we call the former *strong consistency assuming* or short *SCA* inductive inference operators inference operators and the latter *universal* inductive inference operators.

Definition 3.5 (SCA-inductive inference operator [KBB20]). *An* SCA-inductive inference operator *is a mapping $C : \Delta \mapsto \mid\!\sim_\Delta$ that maps every strongly consistent belief base to an inference relation such that direct inference (DI) and trivial vacuity (TV) are fulfilled, i.e.,*

(DI) *if $(B|A) \in \Delta$ then $A \mid\!\sim_\Delta B$, and*

(TV) *if* $\Delta = \emptyset$ *and* $A \mathrel{|\!\sim}_{\Delta} B$ *then* $A \models B$.

Definition 3.6 (universal inductive inference operator). *A* universal inductive inference operator *is a mapping* $C : \Delta \mapsto \mathrel{|\!\sim}_{\Delta}$ *that maps every belief base (even belief bases that are not weakly consistent) to an inference relation such that direct inference (DI) and trivial vacuity (TV) are fulfilled.*

Every universal inductive inference operator can be considered as an SCA-inductive inference operator by restricting it to only strongly consistent belief bases.

Note that the Definitions 3.5 and 3.6 do not assume an underlying fixed signature. Instead, an inductive inference operator covers inferences from belief bases over any signature.

While the notion of inductive inference operators was defined only recently, many older approaches to nonmonotonic inference like p-entailment, system Z, or lexicographic inference can be seen as inductive inference operators. The next sections in this chapter recall a selection of established inductive inference operators.

Postulates for inference relations can be canonically applied to inductive inference operators.

Definition 3.7. *Let* X *be a postulate or a set of postulates. An inductive inference operator* C *satisfies* X *if every inference relation* $\mathrel{|\!\sim}_{\Delta}$ *in the image of* C *satisfies* X.

E.g., C satisfies system P if every inference relation $\mathrel{|\!\sim}_{\Delta}$ in the image of C satisfies system P. An inductive inference operator satisfying system P is called a *preferential inductive inference operator*.

We can establish relations among inductive inference operators by comparing the induced inference relations.

Definition 3.8 (captures, strictly extends). *We say that an inductive inference operator* $C^1 : \Delta \mapsto \mathrel{|\!\sim}^1_{\Delta}$ captures *another inference operator* $C^2 : \Delta \mapsto \mathrel{|\!\sim}^2_{\Delta}$ *if for every belief base* Δ *it holds that* $C^2(\Delta) \subseteq C^1(\Delta)$. *The inductive inference operator* C^1 strictly extends C^2 *if* C^1 *captures* C^2 *and additionally there is a belief base* Δ^* *such that* $C^2(\Delta^*) \subsetneq C^1(\Delta^*)$.

This definition of C^1 capturing C^2 is equivalent to saying that C^1 captures C^2 if for every belief base Δ and formulas A, B we have that $A \mathrel{|\!\sim}^2_{\Delta} B$ implies $A \mathrel{|\!\sim}^1_{\Delta} B$. Then C^1 strictly extending C^2 is equivalent to requiring that additionally there is a belief base Δ^* and A, B such that $A \mathrel{|\!\sim}^1_{\Delta^*} B$ and $A \mathrel{|\!\not\sim}^2_{\Delta^*} B$.

3.3. p-Entailment

Kraus, Lehmann, and Magidor's p-Entailment [KLM90; LM92] is a universal inductive inference operator that is defined using preferential models.

Definition 3.9 (p-entailment, $\mathrel{|\!\sim}^p_\Delta$). *Let Δ be a belief base and $A, B \in \mathcal{L}_\Sigma$ be formulas. A p-entails B with respect to Δ, denoted as $A \mathrel{|\!\sim}^p_\Delta B$, if $A \mathrel{|\!\sim}_{\mathcal{M}} B$ for every preferential model $\mathcal{M}$ of Δ. P-entailment is the inductive inference operator mapping each belief base Δ to $\mathrel{|\!\sim}^p_\Delta$.*

Alternatively, p-entailment can be characterized via system P: from a belief base Δ we can derive $A \mathrel{|\!\sim}^p_\Delta B$ with p-entailment iff $A \mathrel{|\!\sim}^p_\Delta B$ can be derived from $\{X \mathrel{|\!\sim} Y \mid (Y|X) \in \Delta\}$ with the postulates in system P [KLM90]. Thus, p-entailment is the smallest inductive inference operator that satisfies system P: Every inductive inference operator that satisfies system P captures p-entailment, and there is no inductive inference operator that satisfies system P and is strictly extended by p-entailment.

When working with belief bases that are not strongly consistent the following postulate can be useful. It describes that the inferences of the form $A \mathrel{|\!\sim} \bot$ obtained by an inductive inference operator coincide with the inferences of this form obtained by p-entailment.

Postulate (Classic Preservation). *An inference relation $\mathrel{|\!\sim}$ satisfies (Classic Preservation) [CMV19] with respect to a belief base Δ if for all $A, B \in \mathcal{L}_\Sigma$*

$$A \mathrel{|\!\sim}_\Delta \bot \quad \textit{iff} \quad A \mathrel{|\!\sim}^p_\Delta \bot.$$

An inductive inference operator satisfies (Classic Preservation) if every belief base Δ is mapped to an inference relation that satisfies (Classic Preservation) with respect to Δ.

Finally, observe that weak consistency can be characterized by p-entailment.

Proposition 3.10. *A belief base Δ is weakly consistent iff $\top \mathrel{|\!\not\sim}^p_\Delta \bot$.*

Proof. We show both directions of the "iff".

Direction ⇒: Let Δ be weakly consistent. Then there is a ranking function κ with $\kappa \models \Delta$. This ranking function induces a preferential inference relation $\mid\!\sim_{\kappa}$ with $A \mid\!\sim_{\kappa} B$ for every $(B|A) \in \Delta$. Therefore, $\mid\!\sim^{p}_{\Delta}$ is a subset of $\mid\!\sim_{\kappa}$. Furthermore, there is at least one world ω with $\kappa(\omega) = 0$. Therefore, $\top \not\mid\!\sim_{\kappa} \bot$. In summary, $\top \mid\!\sim^{p}_{\Delta} \bot$.

Direction ⇒: Assume that $\top \not\mid\!\sim^{p}_{\Delta} \bot$, i.e., there is a preferential model $\mathcal{M} = \langle S, l, \prec \rangle$ of Δ such that $\min([\![\top]\!]_{\mathcal{M}}, \prec) \not\subseteq [\![\bot]\!]_{\prec}$. This means that there is at least one world $\omega^{min} \in \min([\![\top]\!]_{\mathcal{M}}, \prec)$. Because $[\![\top]\!]_{\mathcal{M}} = S$, the state $l(\omega^{min})$ is minimal in S with respect to $\prec$. Therefore, and because $\mathcal{M}$ is a model of Δ, ω^{min} cannot falsify any of the conditionals in Δ. Let κ be the ranking function defined by

$$\kappa(\omega) = \begin{cases} 0 & \text{if } \omega = \omega^{min} \\ \infty & \text{otherwise.} \end{cases}$$

All conditionals $(B|A)$ that are verified by ω^{min} are modelled by κ because $\kappa(AB) = 0$ and $\kappa(A\overline{B}) = \infty$. All conditionals $(B|A)$ that are not applicable for ω^{min}, are modelled by κ because $\kappa(A) = \infty$. Therefore, $\kappa \models \Delta$ and Δ is weakly consistent. □

If a belief base Δ is not weakly consistent, we can derive $A \mid\!\sim^{p}_{\Delta} B$ with p-entailment for all formulas A, B.

3.4. System Z

The *Z-partition* [Pea90] of a belief base Δ is an ordered partion of Δ that groups conditionals according to how "exceptional" they are. Pearl's *System Z* [Pea90] is an inductive inference operator that uses this Z-partition to rank worlds according their plausibility: worlds that falsify a very specific conditional are considered less likely than worlds falsifying no conditional or only a very general conditional. The inference relations yielded by system Z are then based on this ranking function.

Note that system Z is commonly defined as an SCA-inductive inference operator, i.e., it is usually only defined for strongly consistent belief bases.

Definition 3.11 (tolerance, Z-partition, $OP(\Delta)$). *A conditional* $(B|A)$ *is* tolerated *by a set of conditionals* $\Delta = \{(B_i|A_i) \mid i = 1, \dots, n\}$ *if* *there is a world* $\omega \in \Omega$ *such that* ω *verifies* $(B|A)$ *and* ω *does not falsify any conditional in* Δ, *i.e.,* $\omega \models AB$ *and* $\omega \models \bigwedge_{i=1}^{n}(\overline{A_i} \vee B_i)$.

The Z-partition $OP(\Delta) := (\Delta^0, \ldots, \Delta^k)$ *of a belief base* Δ *is the ordered partition of* Δ *that is constructed by letting* Δ^i *be the inclusion maximal subset of* $\bigcup_{j=i}^{n} \Delta^j$ *that is tolerated by* $\bigcup_{j=i}^{n} \Delta^j$ *until* $\Delta^{k+1} = \emptyset$.

It is well-known that the construction of $OP(\Delta)$ is successful iff Δ is strongly consistent, and because the Δ^i are chosen inclusion-maximal, the Z-partition is unique [Pea90].

Definition 3.12 (system Z, $\mathrel|\!\sim^{z}_{\Delta}$). *Let* Δ *be a belief base with* $OP(\Delta) = (\Delta^0, \ldots, \Delta^k)$. *The Z-ranking function* κ^z_Δ *is defined as follows: For each world* $\omega \in \Omega_\Sigma$ *let* Δ^j *be the last part in* $OP(\Delta)$ *that contains a conditional falsified by* ω. *Then let* $\kappa^z_\Delta(\omega) := j+1$. *If* ω *does not falsify any conditional in* Δ, *then let* $\kappa^z_\Delta(\omega) := 0$. *The inductive inference operator* system Z *maps* Δ *to the inference relation* $\mathrel|\!\sim^{z}_{\Delta}$ *induced by* κ^z_Δ.

System Z is a preferential inductive inference operator [Pea90], i.e., it satisfies system P. It also satisfies (RM), hence system Z is a rational inductive inference operator. The relationship between system Z and rational monotony is even closer: according to [Pea90], system Z can be seen as extension of p-entailment to acquire (RM) in addition to system P.

However, system Z suffers from the *drowning problem* [Pea90; Ben+93]. An inference relation suffers from the drowning problem if the inheritance of a property P from a superclass to a subclass is blocked because the subclass is exceptional with respect to another property Q: the first property P is "drowned" by the exceptionality with respect to Q. The drowning problem is usually illustrated with examples similar to the following.

Example 3.13 (adapted from [Bei+18]). *Let* $\Sigma := \{p, f, b, w\}$ *with the variable* p *for being a* penguin, *the variable* f *for* flying, *the variable* b *for being a* bird, *and the variable* w *for having* wings. *Consider the knowledge base*

$$\Delta^{drown} := \{(f|b),\ (\overline{f}|p),\ (b|p),\ (w|b)\}.$$

The conditional $(f|b)$ *encodes that birds usually fly, the conditional* $(\overline{f}|p)$ *encodes that penguins usually do not fly, the conditional* $(b|p)$

encodes that penguins are usually birds, and the conditional $(w|b)$ *encodes that birds usually have wings. With system Z we cannot entail* $p \mathrel{|\!\!\sim}^{z}_{\Delta^{drown}} w$, *i.e., that penguins have wings. The property of having wings is drowned by the penguin's exceptionality with respect to flying.*

System Z can be extended to cover belief bases that are not strongly consistent. In [GP90], system Z is defined in a more general way corresponding to a universal inductive inference operator. To distinguish the universal definition of system Z ([GP90], Definition 3.16) from the strong consistency assuming definition ([Pea90], Definition 3.12) we will call the former *extended system Z* in this thesis.

Definition 3.14 (extended Z-partition, $EP(\Delta)$ [GP90])**.** *The extended Z-partition* $EP(\Delta) := (\Delta^0, \ldots, \Delta^k, \Delta^\infty)$ *of a belief base* Δ *is the ordered partition of* Δ *that is constructed by letting* Δ^i *be the inclusion maximal subset of* $\bigcup_{j=i}^{n} \Delta^j$ *that is tolerated by* $\bigcup_{j=i}^{n} \Delta^j$ *until* $\Delta^{k+1} = \emptyset$. *The set* Δ^∞ *is the remaining set of conditionals* $\Delta \setminus (\Delta^0 \cup \cdots \cup \Delta^k)$.

The construction of $EP(\Delta)$ is possible for all belief bases and because the Δ^i are chosen inclusion-maximal, the extended Z-partition is unique. If Δ is strongly consistent, then for $EP(\Delta) = (\Delta^0, \ldots, \Delta^k, \Delta^\infty)$ we have $\Delta^\infty = \emptyset$ and $(\Delta^0, \ldots, \Delta^k) = OP(\Delta)$. If a belief base $\Delta = \{(B_1|A_1), \ldots, (B_n|A_n)\}$ is not weakly consistent, then we have $EP(\Delta) = (\Delta^0, \Delta^\infty)$ with $\Delta^0 = \emptyset, \Delta^\infty = \Delta$ and $A_1 \vee \cdots \vee A_n \equiv \bot$.

Proposition 3.15. *Let* $\Delta = \{(B_1|A_1), \ldots, (B_n|A_n)\}$ *be a belief base with* $EP(\Delta) = (\Delta^0, \ldots, \Delta^k, \Delta^\infty)$. *Then we have:*

(1.) Δ *is not weakly consistent iff* $\Delta^\infty = \Delta$ *and* $A_1 \vee \cdots \vee A_n \equiv \top$.
(2.) Δ *is weakly consistent iff* $\Delta^\infty \neq \Delta$ *or* $A_1 \vee \cdots \vee A_n \not\equiv \top$.
(3.) Δ *is strongly consistent iff* $\Delta^\infty = \emptyset$.

Using the extended Z-partition we can now define extended system Z.

Definition 3.16 (extended system Z, $\mathrel{|\!\!\sim}^{z+}_{\Delta}$ [GP90])**.** *Let* Δ *be a belief base with* $EP(\Delta) = (\Delta^0, \ldots, \Delta^k, \Delta^\infty)$. *If* Δ *is not weakly consistent, then let* $A \mathrel{|\!\!\sim}^{z+}_{\Delta} B$ *for any* $A, B \in \mathcal{L}_\Sigma$. *Otherwise, define the extended Z-ranking function* κ^{z+}_{Δ} *as follows: For* $\omega \in \Omega$, *if one of the conditionals in* Δ^∞ *is applicable to* ω, *then define* $\kappa^{z+}_{\Delta}(\omega) := \infty$. *If not, let* Δ^j *be the last part in* $EP(\Delta)$ *that contains a conditional falsified by* ω. *Then* *let* $\kappa^{z+}_\Delta(\omega) := j + 1$. *If* ω *does not falsify any conditional in* Δ, *then let* $\kappa^{z+}_\Delta(\omega) := 0$. Extended system Z *maps* Δ *to the inference relation* $\mid\!\sim^{z+}_\Delta$ *induced by* κ^{z+}_Δ.

In [GP90] belief bases that are not weakly consistent are not treated separately. Instead, for such belief bases all worlds are assigned rank ∞, which then leads to the full inference relation. The definition of a ranking functions that is used here requires at least one world to have rank 0. To stay compatible with this definition we deal with the case of not weakly consistent belief bases separately in Definition 3.16. Note that for a belief base Δ the induced κ^z_Δ is a model of Δ.

For strongly consistent belief bases Δ, extended system Z coincides with system Z, i.e., $A \mid\!\sim^z_\Delta B$ iff $A \mid\!\sim^{z+}_\Delta B$. Furthermore, extended system Z was shown to coincide with *rational closure* [Leh89] in [GP90].

Extended system Z still satisfies system P and (RM). It also satisfies (Classic Preservation).

The assignment of rank ∞ in an extended Z-ranking function is closely related to the inferences of the form $A \mid\!\sim^p_\Delta \bot$ with p-entailment.

Lemma 3.17. *For a weakly consistent belief base* Δ *and a formula* A *we have* $\kappa^{z+}_\Delta(A) = \infty$ *iff* $A \mid\!\sim^p_\Delta \bot$.

Proof. In the one direction, we have that $A \mid\!\sim^p_\Delta \bot$ implies $A \mid\!\sim^{z+}_\Delta \bot$ because system Z captures p-entailment. In the other direction, following [LM92, Lemma 30], we have $A \mid\!\sim^p_\Delta \bot$ only if $A \mid\!\sim^{z+}_\Delta \bot$. By looking at (3.2) we see that $A \mid\!\sim^{z+}_\Delta \bot$ iff $\kappa^{z+}_\Delta(A) = \infty$. □

We conclude this section with the following observation about the set Δ^∞ in the extended Z-partition.

Lemma 3.18. *Let* Δ *be a belief base with* $EP(\Delta) = (\Delta^0, \dots, \Delta^k, \Delta^\infty)$ *and let* $\omega \in \Omega$. *The world* ω *falsifies a conditional in* Δ^∞ *iff it is applicable for a conditional in* Δ^∞.

Proof. We prove both directions of the "iff".

Direction ⇒: Assume that ω falsifies at least one conditional in Δ^∞. Then this conditional is applicable for ω.

Direction ⇐: Assume that ω is applicable for at least one conditional $(B|A) \in \Delta^\infty$. There are two possible cases.

Case 1: ω *violates one of the other conditionals in* Δ^∞ In this case the lemma clearly holds.

Case 2: ω violates none of the other conditionals in Δ^∞ Towards a contradiction, we assume that ω also does not falsify $(B|A)$. If ω is applicable and does not falsify $(B|A)$ then ω must verify $(B|A)$. That implies that $(B|A)$ is tolerated by Δ^∞ which contradicts the construction of $EP(\Delta)$. □

In the next section we will consider another inductive inference operator that uses the Z-partition of a belief base.

3.5. System W

System W is an SCA-inductive inference operator that was recently introduced by Komo and Beierle [KB20; KB22] and is based on the Z-partition of a belief base. While system Z only considers what parts of $OP(\Delta)$ contain a falsified conditional, system W also takes into account the structural information which conditionals are falsified. The definition of system W is based on a binary relation called *preferred structure on worlds* $<^{\mathsf{w}}_{\Delta}$ over Ω_Σ induced by every strongly consistent belief base Δ.

Definition 3.19 (ξ^j, ξ, preferred structure $<^{\mathsf{w}}_{\Delta}$ on worlds [KB22]). *Let $\Delta = \{(B_1|A_1), \dots, (B_n|A_n)\}$ be a strongly consistent belief base with the Z-partition $OP(\Delta) = (\Delta^0, \dots, \Delta^k)$. For $j = 0, \dots, k$, the functions ξ^j and ξ map each world ω to the set of conditionals from the part Δ^j (or Δ, respectively) that are falsified by ω:*

$$\xi^j(\omega) := \{(B_i|A_i) \in \Delta^j \mid \omega \models A_i\overline{B_i}\}, \tag{3.3}$$
$$\xi(\omega) := \{(B_i|A_i) \in \Delta \mid \omega \models A_i\overline{B_i}\}. \tag{3.4}$$

The preferred structure on worlds *induced by Δ is given by the binary relation $<^{\mathsf{w}}_{\Delta} \subseteq \Omega \times \Omega$ defined by, for any $\omega, \omega' \in \Omega$,*

$$\begin{aligned} \omega <^{\mathsf{w}}_{\Delta} \omega' \text{ iff there exists an } m \in \{0, \dots, k\} \text{ such that} \\ \xi^i(\omega) = \xi^i(\omega') \quad \text{for all } i \in \{m+1, \dots, k\} \text{ and} \\ \xi^m(\omega) \subsetneqq \xi^m(\omega'). \end{aligned} \tag{3.5}$$

Thus, $\omega <^{\mathsf{w}}_{\Delta} \omega'$ if and only if ω falsifies strictly fewer conditionals than ω' in the last part of $OP(\Delta)$ where the conditionals falsified by ω and ω' differ. The relation $<^{\mathsf{w}}_{\Delta}$ is a strict partial order [KB22, Lemma 3].

Definition 3.20 (system W, $\mathrel{|\!\sim}^{\mathsf{w}}_{\Delta}$ [KB22]). *Let Δ be a strongly consistent belief base and A, B be formulas. Then B is a* system W inference *from A (in the context of Δ), denoted $A \mathrel{|\!\sim}^{\mathsf{w}}_{\Delta} B$, if for every $\omega' \in Mod_{\Sigma}(A\overline{B})$ there is an $\omega \in Mod_{\Sigma}(AB)$ such that $\omega <^{\mathsf{w}}_{\Delta} \omega'$. System W is the inductive inference operator mapping every strongly consistent Δ to $\mathrel{|\!\sim}^{\mathsf{w}}_{\Delta}$.*

In [KB22] it was shown that system W satisfies system P and that it avoids the drowning problem.

Example 3.21 (Example 3.13 continued). *Given the belief base Δ^{drown} from Example 3.13, with system W we can entail $p \mathrel{|\!\sim}^{\mathsf{w}}_{\Delta^{drown}} w$, i.e., that penguins have wings. Thus, system W avoids the drowning problem in this example.*

This thesis further investigates the properties of system W in Chapter 4.

3.6. Lexicographic Inference

Lexicographic inference by Lehmann [Leh95] is also based on the Z-partition of a belief base. It refines system Z by taking into account how many conditionals in each part of the Z-partition are falsified. The following definition of lexicographic inference is defined slightly different from (but still equivalent to) the original definition in [Leh95] and reuses some of the notations from Section 3.5 which are based on the notations in [KB22].

Definition 3.22 ($<^{lex}_{\Delta}$, lexicographic inference, $\mathrel{|\!\sim}^{lex}_{\Delta}$ [Leh95]). *The* lexicographic ordering *on two vectors in $\mathbb{N}_0^n$ is defined by $(v_1, \ldots, v_n) <^{lex} (w_1, \ldots, w_n)$ iff there is a $k \in \{1, \ldots, n\}$ such that $v_k < w_k$ and $v_j = w_j$ for $j = k+1, \ldots, n$.*

Let Δ be a belief base with $EP(\Delta) = (\Delta^0, \ldots, \Delta^k, \Delta^\infty)$ and ξ, ξ^i for $i = 0, \ldots, k, \infty$ be the functions mapping worlds to sets of falsified conditionals as introduced in Definition 3.19. The binary relation $<^{lex}_{\Delta} \subseteq \Omega_\Sigma \times \Omega_\Sigma$ induced by Δ is defined by, for any $\omega, \omega' \in \Omega_\Sigma$,

$$\omega <^{lex}_{\Delta} \omega' \quad \textit{iff} \quad (|\xi^1(\omega)|, \ldots, |\xi^k(\omega)|, |\xi^\infty(\omega)|) <^{lex} (|\xi^1(\omega')|, \ldots, |\xi^k(\omega')|, |\xi^\infty(\omega')|).$$

For formulas $F, G \in \mathcal{L}_\Sigma$ *define* $F <^{lex}_{\Delta} G$ *iff* $\min(Mod_\Sigma(F), <^{lex}_{\Delta}) <^{lex}_{\Delta} \min(Mod_\Sigma(G), <^{lex}_{\Delta})$*. Then* A *lexicographically entails* B *(in the context of* Δ*), denoted* $A \mathrel{|\!\sim}^{lex}_{\Delta} B$*, if* $AB <^{lex}_{\Delta} A\overline{B}$*. Lexicographic entailment maps each* Δ *to* $\mathrel{|\!\sim}^{lex}_{\Delta}$*.*

The inference relations induced by lexicographic inference satisfy system P and (RM) [Leh95], therefore it is rational.

If we restrict lexicographic inference to strongly consistent belief bases, it is an SCA-inductive inference operator. However, for belief bases that are not strongly consistent, lexicographic inference as defined by [Leh95] and presented in Definition 3.22 does not comply with (DI); and therefore is not a universal inductive inference operator.

Proposition 3.23. *Lexicographic inference violates (DI).*

Proof. Consider the belief base $\Delta := \{(b|a), (\overline{b}|a)\}$ over $\Sigma := \{a, b\}$. We have $EP(\Delta) = (\Delta^0, \Delta^\infty)$ with $\Delta^0 = \emptyset$ and $\Delta^\infty = \Delta$. This induces the ordering $<^{lex}_{\Delta} = \{(\overline{a}b, ab), (\overline{a}b, a\overline{b}), (\overline{a}\overline{b}, ab), (\overline{a}\overline{b}, a\overline{b})\}$.

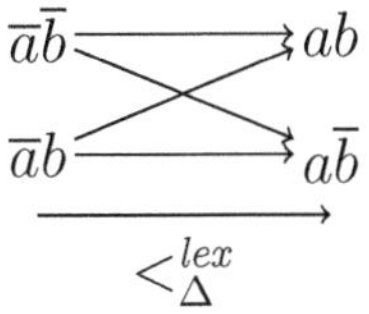

Therefore, $a \not\mathrel{|\!\sim}^{lex}_{\Delta} b$ and $a \not\mathrel{|\!\sim}^{lex}_{\Delta} \overline{b}$. This violates (DI). □

The following slightly adapted version of lexicographic inference does comply with (DI) and is a universal inductive inference operator.

Definition 3.24 (adapted lexicographic inference, $\mathrel{|\!\sim}^{alex}_{\Delta}$)**.** *For formulas* A, B*,* adapted lexicographic inference $\mathrel{|\!\sim}^{alex}_{\Delta}$ *is defined as*

$$A \mathrel{|\!\sim}^{alex}_{\Delta} B \quad \textit{iff} \quad \xi^\infty(\omega) \neq \emptyset \textit{ for all } \omega \in Mod_\Sigma(A) \textit{ or } A \mathrel{|\!\sim}^{lex}_{\Delta} B.$$

Proposition 3.25. *Adapted lexicographic inference satisfies (DI).*

Proof. Let Δ be a belief base with $EP(\Delta) = (\Delta^0, \ldots, \Delta^k, \Delta^\infty)$ and let $(B|A) \in \Delta$. If $\xi^\infty(\omega) \neq \emptyset$ for all $\omega \in Mod_\Sigma(A)$, then $A \mathrel{|\!\sim}^{alex}_{\Delta} B$ holds by Definition 3.24 of adapted lexicographic inference. Otherwise, there is at least one $\omega \in Mod_\Sigma(A)$ with $\xi^\infty(\omega) = \emptyset$. With Lemma 3.18 this implies that $(B|A) \in \Delta^i$ for some $i \in \{1, \ldots, k\}$. By the way $EP(\Delta)$ is constructed, there must be a world ω' that verifies $(B|A)$

without falsifying any of the worlds in $\bigcup_{j=i}^{k} \Delta^j \cup \Delta^\infty$. For this world ω' it holds that $|\xi^j(\omega')| = 0$ for all $j \in \{i, \ldots, k, \infty\}$. For any world ω'' modelling $A\overline{B}$ and thus falsifying $(B|A)$ it holds that $|\xi^i(\omega'')| \geq 1$ and therefore $\omega' <_{\Delta}^{lex} \omega''$. Because $\omega' \models AB$, it must be that $AB <_{\Delta}^{lex} A\overline{B}$. Therefore, $A \mathrel{|\!\sim}_{\Delta}^{lex} B$ and thus $A \mathrel{|\!\sim}_{\Delta}^{alex} B$. □

Proposition 3.26. *Let Δ be a belief base and $A, B \in \mathcal{L}_\Sigma$. If $A \mathrel{|\!\not\sim}_{\Delta}^{p} \bot$, then $A \mathrel{|\!\sim}_{\Delta}^{lex} B$ iff $A \mathrel{|\!\sim}_{\Delta}^{alex} B$.*

Proof. If $A \mathrel{|\!\not\sim}_{\Delta}^{p} \bot$, then $\kappa_{\Delta}^{z}(A) < \infty$ (see Lemma 3.17). This implies that there is a world $\omega \in Mod_\Sigma(A)$ that does not falsify a conditional in $\xi(\infty)$. Therefore, the first condition for $A \mathrel{|\!\sim}_{\Delta}^{alex} B$ in Definition 3.24 cannot be satisfied. This yields $A \mathrel{|\!\sim}_{\Delta}^{alex} B$ iff $A \mathrel{|\!\sim}_{\Delta}^{lex} B$. □

For any strongly consistent belief base Δ we have $A \mathrel{|\!\not\sim}_{\Delta}^{p} \bot$ for any A with $A \not\equiv \bot$. Therefore lexicographic inference and adapted lexicographic inference coincide for strongly consistent belief bases.

Example 3.27. *Consider the belief base $\Delta := \{(b|a), (\overline{b}|a), (b|\top)\}$ over $\Sigma := \{a, b\}$. We have $EP(\Delta) = (\Delta^0, \Delta^\infty)$ with $\Delta^0 = \{(b|\top)$ and $\Delta^\infty = \{(b|a), (\overline{b}|a)\}$. This induces the ordering $<_{\Delta}^{lex} = \{(\overline{a}b, \overline{a}\overline{b})$, $(\overline{a}b, ab), (\overline{a}b, a\overline{b}), (\overline{a}\overline{b}, ab), (\overline{a}\overline{b}, a\overline{b})\}$.*

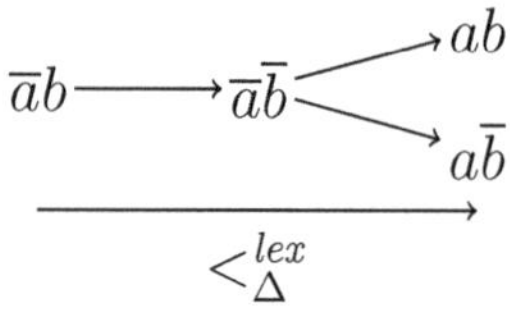

We have $\overline{a} \mathrel{|\!\sim}_{\Delta}^{alex} b$ because $\overline{a} \mathrel{|\!\sim}_{\Delta}^{lex} b$. We have $a \mathrel{|\!\sim}_{\Delta}^{lex} b$ and $a \mathrel{|\!\sim}_{\Delta}^{lex} \overline{b}$ because there is no model of a that does not falsify a conditional in Δ^∞.

Adapted lexicographic inference still satisfies system P and (RM), and contrary to lexicographic inference, adapted lexicographic inference also satisfies (Classic Preservation).

Proposition 3.28. *Adapted lexicographic inference satisfies system P and (RM).*

Proof. Let Δ be a belief base. Let $\mathcal{M}_{\Delta}^{alex} := \langle S, \mathrm{id}, <_{\Delta}^{lex} \rangle$ be a preferential model with $S := \{\omega \mid \xi^\infty(\omega) = \emptyset\}$. Note that $<_{\Delta}^{lex}$ is a modular ordering (cf. [LM92]) on S, therefore the inference relation $\mathrel{|\!\sim}_{\mathcal{M}_{\Delta}^{alex}}$ satisfies system P [KLM90] and (RM) [LM92].

For any $A, B \in \mathcal{L}_\Sigma$ we can show that $A \mathrel{|\!\sim}_{\mathcal{M}^{alex}_\Delta} B$ iff $A \mathrel{|\!\sim}^{alex}_\Delta B$ by distinguishing the two cases below. Showing that $\mathrel{|\!\sim}_{\mathcal{M}^{alex}_\Delta}$ coincides with $\mathrel{|\!\sim}^{alex}_\Delta$ proves that also $\mathrel{|\!\sim}^{alex}_\Delta$ satisfies system P and (RM).

Case 1: $\xi^\infty(\omega) \neq \emptyset$ for all $\omega \in Mod_\Sigma(A)$
In this case $[\![A]\!]_{\mathcal{M}^{alex}_\Delta} = \emptyset$. Therefore, $\min([\![A]\!]_{\mathcal{M}^{alex}_\Delta}, <^{lex}_\Delta) = \emptyset \subseteq [\![B]\!]_{\mathcal{M}^{alex}_\Delta}$ and thus $A \mathrel{|\!\sim}_{\mathcal{M}^{alex}_\Delta} B$. In this case it furthermore holds that $A \mathrel{|\!\sim}^{alex}_\Delta B$. Therefore, $A \mathrel{|\!\sim}_{\mathcal{M}^{alex}_\Delta} B$ iff $A \mathrel{|\!\sim}^{alex}_\Delta B$.

Case 2: There is an $\omega \in Mod_\Sigma(A)$ with $\xi^\infty(\omega) = \emptyset$
In this case $A \mathrel{|\!\sim}^{alex}_\Delta B$ iff $A \mathrel{|\!\sim}^{lex}_\Delta B$. To show that $A \mathrel{|\!\sim}_{\mathcal{M}^{alex}_\Delta} B$ iff $A \mathrel{|\!\sim}^{lex}_\Delta B$, we need to show that $\min([\![A]\!]_{\mathcal{M}^{alex}_\Delta}, <^{lex}_\Delta) \subseteq [\![B]\!]_{\mathcal{M}^{alex}_\Delta}$ iff $\min(Mod_\Sigma(AB), <^{lex}_\Delta) <^{lex}_\Delta \min(Mod_\Sigma(A\overline{B}), <^{lex}_\Delta)$. Observe that for any $\omega' \in S, \omega'' \in \Omega_\Sigma \setminus S$ we have $\omega' <^{lex}_\Delta \omega''$. Furthermore, $[\![A]\!]_{\mathcal{M}^{alex}_\Delta} \neq \emptyset$. Therefore, $\min([\![A]\!]_{\mathcal{M}^{alex}_\Delta}, <^{lex}_\Delta) = \min(Mod_\Sigma(A), <^{lex}_\Delta)$. This yields that

$$\begin{aligned} & \min([\![A]\!]_{\mathcal{M}^{alex}_\Delta}, <^{lex}_\Delta) \subseteq [\![B]\!]_{\mathcal{M}^{alex}_\Delta} \\ \text{iff } & \min(Mod_\Sigma(A), <^{lex}_\Delta) \subseteq Mod_\Sigma(B) \\ \text{iff } & \min(Mod_\Sigma(AB), <^{lex}_\Delta) <^{lex}_\Delta \min(Mod_\Sigma(A\overline{B}), <^{lex}_\Delta). \end{aligned}$$

□

Proposition 3.29. *Adapted lexicographic inference satisfies (Classic Preservation).*

Proof. Let $A \in \mathcal{L}_\Sigma$. It holds that $A \mathrel{|\!\not\sim}^{lex}_\Delta \bot$, and therefore $A \mathrel{|\!\sim}^{alex}_\Delta \bot$ iff for every $\omega \in Mod_\Sigma(A)$ we have $\xi^\infty(\omega) \neq \emptyset$, i.e., every model $\omega \in Mod_\Sigma(A)$ falsifies a conditional in Δ^∞. This is equivalent to $\kappa^{z+}_\Delta(A) = \infty$. By Lemma 3.17, $\kappa^{z+}_\Delta(A) = \infty$ is equivalent to $A \mathrel{|\!\sim}^{p}_\Delta \bot$. □

Adapted lexicographic inference coincides with lexicographic inference in many cases, and we saw that adapted lexicographic inference satisfies some of the key properties of lexicographic inference. Because of this, and because adapted lexicographic inference better matches the framework of inductive inference operators that is used through this thesis, we will use adapted lexicographic inference for comparison with other inductive inference operators later in Chapter 6.

3.7. Multipreference Closure

Multipreference-closure (short *MP-closure*) was introduced by Giordano and Gliozzi as an inference method for the description logic with typicality $\mathcal{ALC} + \mathbf{T}_\mathsf{R}$ in [GG18]. Then MP-closure was adapted for reasoning with conditionals based on propositional logic [GG21]. This MP-closure was shown to capture rational closure, and is captured by lexicographic inference [GG21]; it also captures *relevant closure* [Cas+14; GG21]. For description logics, MP-closure was shown to capture *sceptical closure* [GG20]. In this section we recall the definition of MP-closure as presented in [GG21]. This requires the definition of some other concepts first.

Definition 3.30 (exceptional formulas/conditionals [LM92]). *Let Δ be a belief base. A formula $A \in \mathcal{L}_\Sigma$ is* exceptional *for Δ if $\top \mathrel{|\!\!\sim}^p_\Delta \neg A$. A conditional $(B|A)$ is* exceptional *for Δ if A is exceptional for Δ. The set of conditionals in Δ that is exceptional for Δ is denoted as $E(\Delta)$.*

Definition 3.31 (rank of a formula/conditional [LM92], order of a belief base [GG21]). *Let Δ be belief base. We define the sequence of sets $C_0, C_1, \dots$ by $C_0 := \Delta$ and $C_i := E(C_{i-1})$ for $i > 0$. The least finite k with $C_k = C_{k+1}$ is called the* order *of Δ.*

The rank *of a formula A (with respect to Δ) is the smallest i such that A is not exceptional for C_i. If A is exceptional for all C_i it has rank ∞. The rank of a conditional is the rank of its antecedence.*

Note that a belief base Δ with order k does not contain conditionals with rank k; the rank of a conditional in Δ is at most $k - 1$.

Definition 3.32 (MP-seriousness ordering $\prec^{MP}_\Delta$ [GG21]). *Let Δ be a belief base with order k. For $X \subseteq \Delta$ let $(X_\infty, X_k, \dots, X_0)_X$ be a tuple of sets such that X_i is the set of conditionals in X with rank i. For any two tuples of sets $(X_n, \dots, X_1)$ and $(Y_n, \dots, Y_1)$ we define $\ll$ recursively by*

$$\begin{aligned} (X_1) \ll (Y_1) \quad & \textit{iff} \quad X_1 \subsetneq Y_1 \\ \textit{and } (X_k, \dots, X_1) \ll (Y_k, \dots, Y_1) \quad & \textit{iff} \quad X_k \subsetneq Y_k \textit{ or} \\ & \qquad X_k = Y_k \textit{ and } (X_{k-1} \ll Y_{k-1}). \end{aligned}$$

The MP-seriousness ordering *$\prec^{MP}_\Delta$ on subsets of Δ is defined by*

$$C \prec^{MP}_\Delta D \quad \textit{iff} \quad (C^\infty, C^k, \dots, C^0)_C \ll (D^\infty, D^k, \dots, D^0)_D.$$

Based on the MP-seriousness ordering, MP-bases are defined in [GG21]. MP-closure is then defined in terms of MP-bases.

Definition 3.33 (MP-basis [GG21]). *Let Δ be a belief base. Let $A \in \mathcal{L}_\Sigma$ be a formula with finite rank with respect to Δ. A set $D \subseteq \Delta$ is an* MP-basis *of A if*

- *A is consistent with $\widetilde{D} := \{B \to C \mid (C|B) \in D\}$, and*
- *D is maximal with respect to the MP-seriousness ordering among the subsets of Δ with this property.*

Definition 3.34 (MP-closure [GG21]). *Let Δ be a belief base. $A \mid\!\sim^{MP}_{\Delta} B$ is in the MP-closure of Δ if for all MP-bases D of A it holds that $\widetilde{D} \cup \{A\} \models B$.*

MP-closure is defined for every belief base Δ and therefore a universal inductive inference operator. This definition for MP-closure is similar to a characterization of lexicographic inference in [Leh95] using "bases"; but instead of the "seriousness ordering" $\prec$ used there, MP-closure uses the MP-ordering $\prec^{MP}_{\Delta}$ [GG21]. MP-closure satisfies system P but not (RM), it captures extended system Z (rational closure), and it is captured by lexicographic inference [GG21].

There is also a characterization of MP-closure with preferential models given in [GG21]. This characterization uses an ordering $<_{FIMS}$ on ranked models (the name of $<_{FIMS}$ is based on the term *fixed interpretations minimal semantics*).

Definition 3.35 (ranked model (adapted from [LM92])). *A* ranked model *is a preferential model $\mathcal{M} = \langle S, l, \prec \rangle$ with*

$$\textit{if } x \prec y \quad \textit{then } z \prec y \textit{ or } x \prec z \quad \textit{for any } x, y, z \in S. \qquad \text{(Modularity)}$$

Definition 3.36 (rank of a state/formula in a ranked model [Gio+15]). *Let $\mathcal{M} = \langle S, l, \prec \rangle$ be a finite preferential model. The* rank *of a state $s \in S$, denoted by $\mathbf{k}_{\mathcal{M}}(s)$, is the length of the longest chain of states $s_0 \prec \cdots \prec s$ from a minimal s_0 to s. The rank of a formula $A \in \mathcal{L}_\Sigma$ is $\mathbf{k}_{\mathcal{M}}(A) := \min\{\mathbf{k}_{\mathcal{M}}(s) \mid s \in S, l(s) \models A\}$.*

Definition 3.37 ($<_{FIMS}$, minimal ranked model [Gio+15; GG21]). *Let $\mathcal{M} = \langle S, l, \prec \rangle$ and $\mathcal{M}' = \langle S', l', \prec' \rangle$ be preferential models. The relation $<_{FIMS}$ is defined by $\mathcal{M} <_{FIMS} \mathcal{M}'$ if*

- *$S = S'$,*

- $l = l'$,
- $\mathbf{k}_{\mathcal{M}}(s) \leq \mathbf{k}_{\mathcal{M}'}(s)$ *for every* $s \in S$, *and*
- *there is an* $s \in S$ *such that* $\mathbf{k}_{\mathcal{M}}(s) < \mathbf{k}_{\mathcal{M}'}(s)$.

A ranked model $\mathcal{M}$ *is a* minimal ranked model *of a belief base* Δ *if* $\mathcal{M}$ *is minimal with respect to* $<_{FIMS}$ *among the models of* Δ.

Definition 3.38 (canonical model [Gio+15]). *A world* $\omega \in \Omega_\Sigma$ *is* compatible *with a belief base* Δ *if there is no* $A \in \mathcal{L}_\Sigma$ *with* $\omega \models A$ *and* $A \mathrel{|\!\sim}^{z+}_{\Delta} \bot$. *A* canonical model *of a belief base* Δ *is a preferential model* $\mathcal{M} = \langle S, l, \prec \rangle$ *of* Δ *such that for every world* $\omega \in \Omega_\Sigma$ *that is compatible with* Δ *there is a state* $s \in S$ *with* $l(s) \models \omega$.

Note that a world $\omega \in \Omega_\Sigma$ is compatible with a belief base Δ iff $\omega \mathrel{|\!\not\sim}^{z+}_{\Delta} \bot$.

Definition 3.39 (minimal canonical ranked model [GG21]). *A* minimal canonical ranked model *of a belief base* Δ *is a canonical ranked model of* Δ *that is minimal with respect to* $<_{FIMS}$ *among the canonical ranked models of* Δ. *The set of minimal canonical ranked models of* Δ *is denoted as* $Min_{RC}(\Delta)$.

Definition 3.40 (functor $\mathcal{F}_\Delta$ [GG21]). *Let* Δ *be a belief base. The functor* $\mathcal{F}_\Delta$ *is a mapping from minimal canonical ranked models of* Δ *to preferential models defined by*

$$\mathcal{F}_\Delta(\langle S, l, \prec \rangle) := \langle S, l, \prec_F \rangle$$

with $\prec_F$ *given by* $s \prec_F t$ *iff* $\xi(s) \prec^{MP}_{\Delta} \xi(t)$ *for* $s, t \in S$.

The functor $\mathcal{F}_\Delta$ *is extended to sets* P *of minimal canonical ranked models of* Δ *by* $\mathcal{F}_\Delta(P) := \{\mathcal{F}_\Delta(\mathcal{M}) \mid \mathcal{M} \in P\}$.

Definition 3.41 (MP-model [GG21]). *Let* Δ *be a belief base. An MP-model of* Δ *is any model in* $\mathcal{F}_\Delta(Min_{RC}(\Delta))$.

Proposition 3.42 (MP-closure representation theorem [GG21]). *Let* Δ *be a belief base. A conditional* $(B|A)$ *is accepted by every MP-model of* Δ *if and only if* $A \mathrel{|\!\sim}^{MP}_{\Delta} B$.

The MP-closure representation theorem uses sceptical inference over all MP-models of a belief base. However, all MP-models induce the same inference relation.

Proposition 3.43 ([GG21]). *Let $\mathcal{N}, \mathcal{N}'$ be two MP-models of a belief base Δ. Then $\mathcal{N}$ and $\mathcal{N}'$ are equivalent, i.e., for any $A, B \in \mathcal{L}_\Sigma$ we have $A \mid\!\sim_{\mathcal{N}} B$ iff $A \mid\!\sim_{\mathcal{N}'} B$.*

Therefore, the MP-closure of a belief base Δ is characterized by any MP-model of Δ.

3.8. c-Inference

c-Inference is an SCA-inductive inference operator that is based on c-representations, with c-representations being a special kind of ranking functions. c-Representations have been defined as follows.

Definition 3.44 (c-representation [Ker01; Ker04]). *A* c-representation *of a belief base $\Delta = \{(B_1|A_1), \dots, (B_n|A_n)\}$ over Σ is a ranking function $\kappa_{\vec{\eta}}$ constructed from integer impacts $\vec{\eta} = (\eta_1, \dots, \eta_n)$ with $\eta_i \in \mathbb{N}_0$, $i \in \{1, \dots, n\}$ assigned to each conditional $(B_i|A_i)$ such that $\kappa_{\vec{\eta}}$ accepts Δ and is given by:*

$$\kappa_{\vec{\eta}}(\omega) = \sum_{\substack{1 \leq i \leq n \\ \omega \models A_i \overline{B}_i}} \eta_i. \tag{3.6}$$

We will denote the set of all c-representations of Δ by $Mod^c_\Sigma(\Delta)$.

c-Representations were introduced as a much more general concept in [Ker01; Ker04]; Definition 3.44 of c-representations as ranking functions constructed from integer impacts is only one specific instance of the general concept by Kern-Isberner. A central result regarding (ranking function based) c-representations is that the condition that $\kappa_{\vec{\eta}}$ accepts Δ holds iff the impacts $\vec{\eta}$ satisfy a set of inequations involving the verification and falsification of the conditionals [Ker01]. We will come back to this later in Section 5.7.

For every strongly consistent belief base it is possible to construct a c-representation.

Lemma 3.45 ([Ker04]). *Every strongly consistent belief base has at least one c-representation.*

A belief base Δ that is not strongly consistent does not have any c-representations: by Definition 3.44, a c-representation of Δ is a finite ranking function modelling Δ, and if Δ is not strongly consistent, such a ranking function does not exist.

c-Inference is an inductive inference operator introduced by Beierle, Eichhorn, and Kern-Isberner [BEK16; Bei+18] that takes all c-representations of a belief base Δ into account.

Definition 3.46 (c-inference, $\mid\!\sim^{c}_{\Delta}$ [BEK16]). *Let Δ be a strongly consistent belief base and let A, B be formulas. B is a* c-inference *from A in the context of Δ, denoted by $A \mid\!\sim^{c}_{\Delta} B$, iff $A \mid\!\sim_{\kappa} B$ holds for all c-representations κ of Δ.*

c-Inference satisfies system P [Bei+21] but it does not satisfy (RM) [Kut21].

3.9. Syntax Splitting Postulates

In this section, we will recall and extend postulates for belief bases with a *syntax splitting*. The concept of syntax splittings was originally developed by Parikh [Par99] describing that a belief set contains independent information over different parts of the signature. Parikh proposed a postulate (P) for belief revisions stating that for a belief set with a syntax splitting the revision with a formula relevant to only one such part should only affect the information about that part of the signature. The notion of syntax splitting was later extended to other representations of beliefs such as ranking functions [KB17] and belief bases [KBB20]. Furthermore, Kern-Isberner, Beierle, and Brewka [KBB20] introduced the notion of inductive inference operators and formulated postulates for SCA-inductive inference operators that govern inference from belief bases with syntax splitting.

Definition 3.47 (syntax splitting for belief bases [KBB20]). *Let Δ be a belief base over a signature Σ. A partition $\{\Sigma_1, \dots, \Sigma_n\}$ of Σ is a* syntax splitting *for Δ if there is a partition $\{\Delta_1, \dots, \Delta_n\}$ of Δ such that $\Delta_i \subseteq (\mathcal{L}|\mathcal{L})_{\Sigma_i}$ for every $i = 1, \dots, n$.*

In this thesis, we focus on syntax splittings with two parts. Such a splitting $\{\Sigma_1, \Sigma_2\}$ of Σ with corresponding partition $\{\Delta_1, \Delta_2\}$ of Δ is denoted as [KBB20]

$$\Delta = \Delta_1 \bigcup_{\Sigma_1, \Sigma_2} \Delta_2.$$

Results for syntax splittings with more than two parts can be obtained by iteratively applying the postulates presented here.

Example 3.48. *Consider the signature $\Sigma := \{m, b, e, t, g\}$ for modelling aspects about vehicles with the intended meanings*

*m being a **m**otorized vehicle,*
*b being a **b**ike,*
*e having an **e**lectric motor,*
*t having **t**wo wheels, and*
*g requiring **g**asoline.*

The belief base

$$\Delta_{ve} := \{(m|e), (g|m), (\overline{g}|me), (t|b)\}$$

over Σ states that vehicles with an electric motor are usually motorized vehicles, motorized vehicles usually require gasoline, motorized vehicles with an electric motor usually do not require gasoline, and bikes usually have two wheels. This belief base has a syntax splitting

$$\Delta_{ve} = \Delta_1 \bigcup_{\Sigma_1, \Sigma_2} \Delta_2 \text{ with } \Sigma_1 = \{m, e, g\}, \Sigma_2 = \{b, t\} \text{ and}$$
$$\Delta_1 = \{(m|e), (g|m), (\overline{g}|me)\}, \Delta_2 = \{(t|b)\}.$$

In [KBB20], the authors introduced the postulates (Rel) and (Ind) to govern inference from belief bases with syntax splittings. For belief bases with syntax splitting, the postulate (Rel) requires that conditionals corresponding to one part of the syntax splitting do not have any influence on inferences that only use the other part of the syntax splitting, i.e., that only conditionals from the considered part of the syntax splitting are relevant.

(Rel) [KBB20] An SCA-inductive inference operator $C : \Delta \mapsto \mathrel{|\!\sim}_\Delta$ satisfies **(Rel)** if for $\Delta = \Delta_1 \bigcup_{\Sigma_1, \Sigma_2} \Delta_2$, for $i \in \{1, 2\}$, and for any $A, B \in \mathcal{L}_{\Sigma_i}$ we have that

$$A \mathrel{|\!\sim}_\Delta B \quad \text{iff} \quad A \mathrel{|\!\sim}_{\Delta_i} B.$$

The postulate (Ind) requires that inferences should not be affected by beliefs in formulas over other sub-signatures in the splitting. I.e., an inference using only atoms from one part of the syntax splitting should be drawn independently of beliefs about other parts of the splitting.

(Ind) [KBB20] An SCA-inductive inference operator $C : \Delta \mapsto \mid\!\sim_\Delta$ satisfies **(Ind)** if for $\Delta = \Delta_1 \bigcup_{\Sigma_1,\Sigma_2} \Delta_2$, for $i, j \in \{1,2\}, i \neq j$, and for any $A, B \in \mathcal{L}_{\Sigma_i}$, $D \in \mathcal{L}_{\Sigma_j}$ such that $D \not\mid\!\sim_\Delta \bot$, we have

$$A \mid\!\sim_\Delta B \quad \text{iff} \quad AD \mid\!\sim_\Delta B.$$

Differing from [KBB20] I added the requirement that $D \not\mid\!\sim_\Delta \bot$ to (Ind). Otherwise, (Ind) would have some clearly unintended consequences: For any formula $A \in \mathcal{L}_{\Sigma_1}$ and $D \in \mathcal{L}_{\Sigma_2}$ such that $D \mid\!\sim_\Delta \bot$ with (Ind) we have $AD \mid\!\sim_\Delta \bot$. Without the requirement that $D \not\mid\!\sim_\Delta \bot$, (Ind) would then require that $A \mid\!\sim_\Delta \bot$. Therefore, an inductive inference operator satisfying (Ind) without the requirement that $D \not\mid\!\sim_\Delta \bot$ would imply that $A \mid\!\sim_\Delta \bot$ for all $A \in \mathcal{L}_{\Sigma_1}$. For SCA-inductive inference operators that satisfy (Classic Preservation) $D \not\mid\!\sim_\Delta \bot$ is equivalent to the formula D being consistent.

The postulate (SynSplit) is the combination of (Rel) and (Ind):

(SynSplit) [KBB20] An SCA-inductive inference operator satisfies **(SynSplit)** if it satisfies (Rel) and (Ind).

The effect of the syntax splitting postulates is illustrated by the following example.

Example 3.49. *Consider the belief base* $\Delta_{ve} = \Delta_1 \bigcup_{\Sigma_1,\Sigma_2} \Delta_2$ *from Example 3.48. We have* $b \mid\!\sim_{\Delta_{ve}} t$ *for any inductive inference operator* $C : \Delta \mapsto \mid\!\sim_\Delta$ *because of (DI). The postulate (Rel) requires that* $b \mid\!\sim_{\Delta_2} t$ *holds because the formulas* b *and* t *contain only variables from* Σ_2*. The postulate (Ind) requires that* $be \mid\!\sim_{\Delta_{ve}} t$ *holds because* e *contains only variables from* Σ_1*.*

Note that in Example 3.49 we cannot deduce either $be \mid\!\sim^z_{\Delta_{ve}} t$ with system Z or $be \mid\!\sim^p_{\Delta_{ve}} t$ with p-entailment: the additional information e from the independent sub-signature Σ_1 prevents the deduction of t. This behaviour is not intuitive: Because the information about e is in no way connected to information on b or t, knowing e should not affect the inference $b \mid\!\sim_{\Delta_{ve}} t$. The postulate (Ind) does not allow this behaviour. This example shows that p-entailment and system Z do not fulfil (Ind). c-Inference on the other hand was shown to satisfy (SynSplit) [KBB20]. Lexicographic inference also satisfies (SynSplit)

[HKM22][1], and in Section 4.4 we will show that system W satisfies (SynSplit) as well.

Syntax splitting postulates are not only interesting because they are a sensible requirement for inferences from belief bases with syntax splitting. Exploiting syntax splittings could also be the key to computationally more efficient implementations of inference operators. Often the computational effort necessary to check if an inference is possible for a given inference operator grows significantly with the size of the signature or knowledge base that is considered; e.g., the number of worlds involved grows exponentially with the signature size. Inference operators satisfying (SynSplit) could be implemented in a way that considers only the relevant part of the signature and the belief base. By doing this, the the effort to check for an inference could be reduced greatly for instances where the syntax splitting postulates are applicable.

The postulates (Rel), (Ind), and (SynSplit) take only SCA-inductive inference operators into account. To fully evaluate universal inductive inference operators with respect to syntax splittings, we slightly extend these postulates to also cover inference from belief bases that are not strongly consistent. The resulting postulates (Rel$^+$), (Ind$^+$), and (SynSplit$^+$) are very similar to their counterparts for SCA-inductive inference operators, but also cover inference from weakly consistent belief bases.

(Rel$^+$) A universal inductive inference operator $C : \Delta \mapsto \mathrel{|\!\sim}_\Delta$ satisfies (Rel$^+$) if for a weakly consistent $\Delta = \Delta_1 \bigcup_{\Sigma_1,\Sigma_2} \Delta_2$, for $i = 1, 2$, and for any $A, B \in \mathcal{L}_{\Sigma_i}$ we have that

$$A \mathrel{|\!\sim}_\Delta B \quad \text{iff} \quad A \mathrel{|\!\sim}_{\Delta_i} B.$$

Note that for $B = \bot$, the postulate (Rel$^+$) requires that $A \mathrel{|\!\sim}_\Delta \bot$ iff $A \mathrel{|\!\sim}_{\Delta_i} \bot$, thus ensuring that the same formulas are considered feasible for $\mathrel{|\!\sim}_\Delta$ as for $\mathrel{|\!\sim}_{\Delta_i}$.

(Ind$^+$) A universal inductive inference operator $C : \Delta \mapsto \mathrel{|\!\sim}_\Delta$ satisfies (Ind$^+$) if for any weakly consistent $\Delta = \Delta_1 \bigcup_{\Sigma_1,\Sigma_2} \Delta_2$, and for

[1] Actually, in [HKM22] it was shown that lexicographic inference satisfies the more general property *conditional syntax splitting* (CSynSplit) (see Section 4.6) which implies (SynSplit).

$i, j \in \{1, 2\}, i \neq j$ and for any $A, B \in \mathcal{L}_{\Sigma_i}$, $D \in \mathcal{L}_{\Sigma_j}$ such that $D \not\mid\!\sim_\Delta \bot$, we have

$$A \mid\!\sim_\Delta B \quad \text{iff} \quad AD \mid\!\sim_\Delta B.$$

For $B = \bot$, the postulate (Ind$^+$) requires that $A \mid\!\sim_\Delta \bot$ iff $AD \mid\!\sim_\Delta \bot$ and thus ensures that A is considered feasible iff AD is considered feasible by $\mid\!\sim_\Delta$.

(SynSplit$^+$) is the combination of (Rel$^+$) and (Ind$^+$).

(SynSplit$^+$) A universal inductive inference operator $C : \Delta \mapsto \mid\!\sim_\Delta$ satisfies (SynSplit$^+$) if it satisfies both (Rel$^+$) and (Ind$^+$).

Obviously, (Rel$^+$) implies (Rel); (Ind$^+$) implies (Ind); and (SynSplit$^+$) implies (SynSplit).

While the postulates (Rel) and (Ind) provide the base for this direction of research, there are other notions of splitting like the more general *conditional syntax splitting* [Hey+23] (see Section 4.6) that continue this line of research. Syntax splittings are also investigated for other settings like the contraction of beliefs [HKB20; HBK21]; and further splitting notions like *semantic* and *constraint splitting* [BHK21a; Wil+23] have been introduced.

Chapter 4

Properties of System W

In this chapter we investigate the properties of Komo and Beierle's system W more closely. First, in Section 4.1, we evaluate system W with respect to postulates for inference relations like Semi-Monotony (SM), Rational Monotony (RM), and Weak Rational Monotony (WRM). In Section 4.2 we discuss how inference relations in general, and system W inference relations in particular, can be represented with SPOs and introduce the notion of *full SPOs on worlds* (*fSPO*).

One of the interesting things about system W is that it complies with syntax splittings quite well. We adapt the syntax splitting postulates for fSPO-representable inductive inference operators in Section 4.3, and use them to prove that system W satisfies syntax splitting in Section 4.4. We also discuss the effect of syntax splittings on the preferred structure on worlds that underlies system W in Section 4.5. Furthermore, in Section 4.6 we recall the postulates for conditional syntax splitting from [Hey+23], and adapt them to fSPO-representable inference operators. Using this postulates we show that system W also complies with conditional syntax splitting in Section 4.7.

The results regarding the properties of system W with respect to the postulates (SM), (RM), and (WRM) in Section 4.1, the syntax splitting postulates for fSPO-representable inductive inference operators in Section 4.3, and the proof that system W satisfies syntax splitting in Section 4.4 were first published in [HB22c]. Also the results on syntax splittings and the preferred structure on worlds in Section 4.5 origin from [HB22c]. Adapting the conditional syntax splitting postulates to fSPO-representable inductive inference opera-

(SM)	*Semi-Monotony* [Rei80; GP96]	$\Delta \subseteq \Delta'$, $A \mid\!\sim_{\Delta} B$ imply $A \mid\!\sim_{\Delta'} B$
(RM)	*Rational Monotony* [KLM90]	$A \mid\!\sim B$ and $A \not\mid\!\sim \overline{C}$ imply $AC \mid\!\sim B$
(WRM)	*Weak Rational Monotony* [Rot01]	$\top \mid\!\sim B$ and $\top \not\mid\!\sim \overline{A}$ imply $A \mid\!\sim B$
(DR)	*Disjunctive Rationality* [KLM90]	$A \not\mid\!\sim C$, $B \not\mid\!\sim C$ imply $A \vee B \not\mid\!\sim C$
(NR)	*Negation Rationality* [KLM90]	$AC \not\mid\!\sim B$ and $A\overline{C} \not\mid\!\sim B$ imply $A \not\mid\!\sim B$
(CPS)	*Contraposition* [KLM90]	$A \mid\!\sim B$ implies $\overline{B} \mid\!\sim \overline{A}$
(WCPS)	*Weak Contraposition* [FLM91]	$AB \mid\!\sim C$ and $A \not\mid\!\sim C$ imply $A\overline{C} \mid\!\sim \overline{B}$
(RC)	*Rational Contraposition* [BP96]	$A \mid\!\sim B$ and $\overline{B} \not\mid\!\sim A$ imply $\overline{B} \mid\!\sim \overline{A}$
(WD)	*Weak Determinancy* [BMP97]	$\top \mid\!\sim \overline{A}$ and $A \not\mid\!\sim B$ imply $A \mid\!\sim \overline{B}$
(CI)	*Conjunctive Insistence* [BMP97]	$A \mid\!\sim C$ and $B \mid\!\sim C$ imply $AB \mid\!\sim C$

Figure 4.1. Some more postulates for inference relations from literature.

tors and proving that system W satisfies conditional syntax splitting in Section 4.7 was my contribution to [Hey+23].

4.1. Evaluation with Respect to Selected Postulates

In Section 3.5 we already recalled that system W satisfies the postulates of system P. In the following we evaluate system W with respect to several other postulates for inference relations from literature, showing that system W satisfies *weak rational monotony* (WRM) but does not satisfy *rational monotony* (RM) or any of the other postulates listed in Figure 4.1.

First we observe that, like many other inductive inference operators, system W is not *semi-monotone*, i.e., it does not satisfy (SM).

Proposition 4.1. *System W does not fulfil semi-monotony (SM).*

Proof. Let $\Sigma := \{a, b\}$ and consider the belief bases $\Delta := \{(b|\top)\}$ and $\Delta' := \{(b|\top), (\overline{b}|a)\}$. We have $a \mid\!\sim^{\mathsf{w}}_{\Delta} b$ but $a \mid\!\sim^{\mathsf{w}}_{\Delta'} b$ does not hold. □

System W also does not satisfy rational monotony (RM). While (RM) is satisfied by some inductive inference operators like system Z and lexicographic inference, it is often perceived as too strict. It only allows inference relations that are induced by a single ranking function (or equivalently a total preorder on worlds) [LM92], and therefore prohibits inference relations that allow formulas which are incomparable with respect to plausibility. p-Entailment and c-inference also do not satisfy (RM).

Proposition 4.2. *System W does not fulfil rational monotony (RM).*

Proof. Let $\Sigma := \{a, b, c\}$. Consider the belief base $\Delta := \{(\overline{a}c \vee \overline{b}c|\top), (\overline{a} \vee \overline{b}|\top), (\overline{a}|\top), (\overline{a}\overline{b}|\top)\}$ and formulas $A := \neg(\overline{a}\overline{b}c)$, $B := \overline{a}\overline{b}\overline{c} \vee \overline{a}bc$, and $C := \neg(\overline{a}c)$. We have $A \mathrel{|\!\sim}^{\mathsf{w}}_{\Delta} B$ and $A \mathrel{|\!\not\sim}^{\mathsf{w}}_{\Delta} \overline{C}$ but not $AC \mathrel{|\!\sim}^{\mathsf{w}}_{\Delta} B$. □

However, system W does satisfy the weaker postulate *weak rational monotony* (WRM).

Proposition 4.3. *System W fulfils weak rational monotony (WRM).*

Proof. Let Σ be a signature and Δ be a strongly consistent belief base. Let $\mathrel{|\!\sim}^{\mathsf{w}}_{\Delta}$ be the system W inference relation induced by Δ and $<^{\mathsf{w}}_{\Delta}$ be the corresponding preferred structure on worlds. Let $A, B \in \mathcal{L}_{\Sigma}$ such that $\top \mathrel{|\!\sim}^{\mathsf{w}}_{\Delta} B$ and $\top \mathrel{|\!\not\sim}^{\mathsf{w}}_{\Delta} \overline{A}$.

Let $\Omega_{nf} \subseteq \Omega_{\Sigma}$ be the set of all worlds that falsify none of the conditionals in Δ. As Δ is strongly consistent, Ω_{nf} is not empty. The worlds in Ω_{nf} are lower than other worlds with respect to $<^{\mathsf{w}}_{\Delta}$: for every $\omega' \in \Omega_{nf}, \omega \in \Omega_{\Sigma} \setminus \Omega_{nf}$ we have $\omega' <^{\mathsf{w}}_{\Delta} \omega$. For worlds $\omega, \omega' \in \Omega_{nf}$ neither $\omega <^{\mathsf{w}}_{\Delta} \omega'$ nor $\omega' <^{\mathsf{w}}_{\Delta} \omega$ holds. Because $\top \mathrel{|\!\sim}^{\mathsf{w}}_{\Delta} B$, every world in Ω_{nf} models B, i.e. $\Omega_{nf} \subseteq Mod(B)$. Because $\top \mathrel{|\!\not\sim}^{\mathsf{w}}_{\Delta} \overline{A}$, there is at least one world $\omega^A \in \Omega_{nf}$ such that $\omega^A \models A$.

Let ω be a model of $A\overline{B}$. Because $\Omega_{nf} \subseteq Mod(B)$ (see above), we have that $\omega \notin \Omega_{nf}$. Because $\omega^A \in \Omega_{nf}$ and $\omega \notin \Omega_{nf}$ we know that $\omega^A <^{\mathsf{w}}_{\Delta} \omega$. Furthermore, we have $\omega^A \models AB$. Therefore, $A \mathrel{|\!\sim}^{\mathsf{w}}_{\Delta} B$. In summary, system W satisfies (WRM). □

The remaining postulates from Figure 4.1 were disproved by an automatic search for counterexamples. In [KB21b], an algorithm was proposed that, for a given inference relation and postulate, systematically searches for instances where the inference relation violates the postulate. Using this algorithm, a program that searches for instances where system W inference violates one of the postulates in question was implemented [Tei23]. This implementation is based on the library `InfOCF-Lib` for nonmonotonic reasoning with conditionals [Kut19] and the implementation of system W from [Kol21] as well as previous works that created or generated various sets of belief bases (e.g. [Mül19; HOB20; BK19; BH20a; BHK21b]). We can find counterexamples disproving all remaining postulates from Figure 4.1.

Proposition 4.4 ([Tei23]). *System W does not satisfy any of*

- *disjunctive rationality (DR),*
- *negation rationality (NR),*

- *contraposition (CPS),*
- *weak contraposition (WCPS),*
- *rational contraposition (RC),*
- *weak determinacy (WD), or*
- *conjunctive insistence (CI).*

Proof. We give a counterexample to each of the postulates. For this consider the belief base $\Delta := \{(b|a), (c|b), (c|a)\}$ over $\Sigma := \{a, b, c\}$. We have $EP(\Delta) = (\Delta^0, \Delta^\infty)$ with $\Delta^0 = \Delta$ and $\Delta^\infty = \emptyset$ and the preferred structure on worlds $<^{\mathsf{w}}_{\Delta} = \{(\overline{a}\overline{b}c, \overline{a}b\overline{c}), (abc, \overline{a}b\overline{c}), (\overline{a}\overline{b}\overline{c}, \overline{a}b\overline{c}), (\overline{a}bc, \overline{a}b\overline{c}), (\overline{a}\overline{b}c, a\overline{b}c), (abc, a\overline{b}c), (\overline{a}\overline{b}\overline{c}, a\overline{b}c), (\overline{a}bc, a\overline{b}c), (\overline{a}b\overline{c}, ab\overline{c}), (a\overline{b}c, a\overline{b}\overline{c}))\}$.

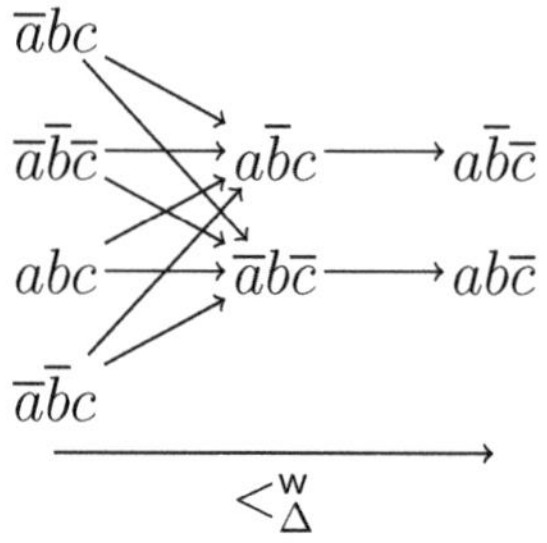

Now consider each of the postulates.

(DR) Let $A_1 := ab\overline{c} \vee a\overline{b}c$, $B_1 := a\overline{b}\overline{c} \vee \overline{a}b\overline{c}$, and $C_1 := a\overline{b}c \vee \overline{a}b\overline{c}$. We have $A_1 \not\mid\!\sim^{\mathsf{w}}_{\Delta} C_1$ because $\omega' = \overline{a}\overline{b}\overline{c} \models A_1\overline{C_1}$ and there is no model ω of A_1C_1 with $\omega <^{\mathsf{w}}_{\Delta} \omega'$. Similarly, check that $B_1 \not\mid\!\sim^{\mathsf{w}}_{\Delta} C_1$ and $A_1 \vee B_1 \mid\!\sim^{\mathsf{w}}_{\Delta} C_1$. This violates (DR).

(NR) Let $A_2 := ab\overline{c} \vee a\overline{b}c \vee a\overline{b}\overline{c} \vee \overline{a}b\overline{c}$, $B_2 := a\overline{b}c \vee \overline{a}b\overline{c}$, and $C_2 := ab\overline{c} \vee a\overline{b}c$. We have $A_2C_2 \not\mid\!\sim^{\mathsf{w}}_{\Delta} B_2$ and $A_2\overline{C_2} \not\mid\!\sim^{\mathsf{w}}_{\Delta} B_2$ but $A_2 \mid\!\sim^{\mathsf{w}}_{\Delta} B_2$.

(CPS) Let $A_3 := ab$ and $B_3 := bc \vee \overline{a}$. We have $A_3 \mid\!\sim^{\mathsf{w}}_{\Delta} B_3$ but $\overline{B_3} \not\mid\!\sim^{\mathsf{w}}_{\Delta} \overline{A_3}$.

(WCPS) Let $A_4 := a\overline{b} \vee a\overline{c}$, $B_4 := a\overline{b}$, and $C_4 := a\overline{b}c$. We have $A_4B_4 \mid\!\sim^{\mathsf{w}}_{\Delta} C_4$ and $A_4 \not\mid\!\sim^{\mathsf{w}}_{\Delta} C_4$ but $A_4\overline{C_4} \not\mid\!\sim^{\mathsf{w}}_{\Delta} \overline{B_4}$.

(RC) Let $A_5 := ab$ and $B_5 := bc \vee \overline{a}$. We have $A_5 \mid\!\sim^{\mathsf{w}}_{\Delta} B_5$ and $\overline{B_5} \not\mid\!\sim^{\mathsf{w}}_{\Delta} A_5$ but $\overline{B_5} \not\mid\!\sim^{\mathsf{w}}_{\Delta} \overline{A_5}$.

(WD) Let $A_6 := ab\overline{c} \vee a\overline{b}c$ and $B_6 := ab\overline{c}$. We have $\top \mid\!\sim^{\mathsf{w}}_{\Delta} \overline{A_6}$ and $A_6 \not\mid\!\sim^{\mathsf{w}}_{\Delta} B_6$ but $A_6 \not\mid\!\sim^{\mathsf{w}}_{\Delta} \overline{B_6}$.

(CI) Let $A_7 := ab$, $B_7 := ab\overline{c} \vee \overline{a}bc$, and $C_7 := bc$. We have $A_7 \mid\!\sim^{\mathsf{w}}_{\Delta} C_7$ and $B_7 \mid\!\sim^{\mathsf{w}}_{\Delta} C_7$ but $A_7B_7 \not\mid\!\sim^{\mathsf{w}}_{\Delta} C_7$.

□

Table 4.1 summarizes properties of system W and compares them to other inductive inference operators. System W behaves similar to c-inference with respect to system P, (RM), (WRM), and (SM), but in contrast to c-inference, it captures system Z, and thus also rational closure.

In this section we evaluated system W with respect to syntactic rules. The next section considers how inference operators can be represented semantically and introduces the class of SPO-repesentable inductive inference operators.

4.2. SPO-Representability

Ranking functions and preferential models are not the only structures that can model belief bases and induce an inference relation. Strict partial orders (SPO) on the possible worlds can also be used as models for conditionals and belief bases and induce inference relations. For now, we only consider *full* SPOs on worlds, which are SPOs on the set Ω_Σ of all models over the underlying signature. Later, in Chapter 5, we will also cover *limited* SPOs on subsets of Ω_Σ.

Definition 4.5 (full SPO on worlds, fSPO)**.** *A* full SPO (fSPO) on worlds *(over Σ) is an SPO $\prec$ on the set Ω_Σ. A full SPO on worlds $\prec$ is lifted to formulas by letting, for consistent $A, B \in \mathcal{L}_\Sigma$,*

$$A \prec B \quad \textit{iff} \quad \textit{for every } \omega' \in \textit{Mod}_\Sigma(B) \text{ there is an } \omega \in \textit{Mod}_\Sigma(A) \textit{ such that } \omega \prec \omega'. \tag{4.1}$$

A full SPO on worlds $\prec$ models *a conditional $(B|A)$, denoted as $\prec \models (B|A)$, iff either $A\overline{B}$ is inconsistent or both $AB, A\overline{B}$ are consistent and $AB \prec A\overline{B}$. We say $\prec$ models a belief base Δ if $\prec$ models every conditional in Δ; in this case $\prec$ is also called an* fSPO model *of Δ.*

Definition 4.5 matches the usual way to model conditionals with orderings over a set of possible worlds or states (see, e.g., preferential models [KLM90]). This definition is equivalent to saying that $\prec$ models a conditional $(B|A)$ iff for any $\omega' \in \textit{Mod}_\Sigma(A\overline{B})$ there is an $\omega \in \textit{Mod}_\Sigma(AB)$ with $\omega \prec \omega'$.

Definition 4.6. *The inference relation $\mathrel{|\!\sim}_\prec$ induced by a full SPO on worlds $\prec$ is defined by*

$$A \mathrel{|\!\sim}_\prec B \quad \textit{iff} \quad \prec \models (B|A). \tag{4.2}$$

	System P	(RM)	(WRM)	(SM)	(DR)	(NR)	(CPS)	(WCPS)	(RC)	(WD)	(CI)	Captures system Z
p-entailment	Yes	No	No	Yes	No	No	No	No	No	No	No	No
system Z	Yes	Yes	Yes	No	Yes	Yes	No	Yes	No	No	No	Yes
c-inference	Yes	No	Yes	No	No	No	No	No	No	No	No	No
system W	Yes	No	Yes	No	No	No	No	No	No	No	No	Yes
lexicographic inference	Yes	Yes	Yes	No	Yes	Yes	No	Yes	No	No	No	Yes

Table 4.1. Comparison of properties of inductive inference operators.
All mentioned inference operators have been established to be preferential inference operators in literature. Furthermore, it has been established that system Z and lexicographic inference satisfy (RM) [Pea90; Leh95] while p-entailment, c-inference, and system W do not (cf. [KLM90; BKB19] and Proposition 4.2). (WRM) is implied by (RM) and additionally satisfied by c-inference [Kut21, Prop. 134] and system W (Proposition 4.3). (RM) implies (DR) and (NR) [KLM90] as well as (WCPS) [FLM91]. An automated search for counterexamples yielded the belief base $\Delta_8 := \{(a|\top)\}$ and $A_8 := \top, B_8 := a$ as counterexample for (CPS) for each of the operators p-entailment, system Z, c-inference, and lexicographic inference. Similarly, we found $\Delta_9 := \{(b|a), (\overline{b}|a)\}$ with $A_9 := a, B_9 := b$ as a counterexample for (RC), $\Delta_{10} := \Delta_9$ with $A_{10} := \overline{b}, B_{10} := a\overline{b}$ as a counterexample for (WD), and $\Delta_{10} := \Delta_9$ with $A_{10} := a, B_{10} := \overline{a}b \vee a\overline{b}, C := b$ as a counterexample for (CI). The belief base $\Delta_{11} := \{(b|a), (c|b), (c|a), (a\overline{b}c \vee \overline{a}b\overline{c}|ab\overline{c} \vee a\overline{b}c \vee a\overline{b}\overline{c} \vee \overline{a}b\overline{c})\}$ with A_1, B_1, C_1 as in the proof of Proposition 4.4 is a counterexample of (DR) and Δ_{11} with A_2, B_2, C_2 as in the proof of Proposition 4.4 is a counterexample of (NR) for p-entailment and c-inference. The belief base $\Delta_{12} := \{(b|a), (c|b), (c|a), (a\overline{b}c|a\overline{b})\}$ with A_4, B_4, C_4 as in the proof of Proposition 4.4 is a counterexample of (WCPS) for p-entailment and c-inference.

Full SPO models are another way to characterize strong consistency of belief bases.

Lemma 4.7. *A belief base Δ has a full SPO model iff Δ is strongly consistent.*

Proof. We prove both directions of the "iff".

Direction $\Leftarrow$: If a belief base Δ is strongly consistent then there is a ranking function κ with $\kappa^{-1}(\infty) = \emptyset$ and $\kappa \models \Delta$. The full SPO on worlds $\prec$ induced by $\omega \prec \omega'$ iff $\kappa(\omega) < \kappa(\omega')$ is a full SPO model of Δ.

Direction $\Rightarrow$: If a belief base Δ has a full SPO model $\prec$ of Δ we can define a ranking function κ as follows. Let $\Omega^0 := \min(\Omega_\Sigma, \prec)$. Then let $\Omega^i := \min(\Omega_\Sigma \setminus (\Omega^0 \cup \cdots \cup \Omega^{i-1}))$ until $\Omega^{k+1} = \emptyset$. Define $\kappa(\omega) := i$ for $\omega \in \Omega^i$ for $i = 0, \ldots, k$. It holds that $\omega \prec \omega'$ entails $\kappa(\omega) < \kappa(\omega')$. We have that $\prec \models (B|A)$ implies $\kappa \models (B|A)$ for $(B|A) \in \Delta$. Therefore, $\kappa \models \Delta$ and Δ is strongly consistent. □

Based on (4.2) we can introduce a new class of inductive inference operators.

Definition 4.8 (fSPO-representable). *An inference relation $\mid\!\sim$ is* fSPO-representable *if there is a full SPO (fSPO) on worlds inducing $\mid\!\sim$. An inductive inference operator $C : \Delta \mapsto \mid\!\sim_\Delta$ is fSPO-representable if every inference relation $\mid\!\sim_\Delta$ in the image of C is fSPO-representable.*

Because the definition of an inductive inference operator already ensures that for a belief base Δ the induced inference relation $\mid\!\sim_\Delta$ complies with (DI) and (TV), we do not need to impose any additional restrictions on full SPOs in Definition 5.14.

Note that only SCA-inductive inference operators can be fSPO-representable. Because of (DI), universal inductive inference operators map belief bases that are not strongly consistent to inference relations that are not fSPO-representable. For example, if we have a consistent formula A and the belief base $\Delta := \{(\bot|A)\}$, by (DI) it must hold that $A \mid\!\sim_\Delta \bot$. However, because $A \wedge \top$ is consistent and $A \wedge \bot$ is inconsistent there is no fSPO $\prec$ such that $A \mid\!\sim_\prec \bot$ (see Definition 4.5).

An fSPO-representable inductive inference operator can alternatively be written as a mapping $C^{spo} : \Delta \mapsto \prec_\Delta$ that maps each belief base to a full SPO $\prec_\Delta$ on worlds. The induced inference relation $\mid\!\sim_\Delta$ is obtained from $\prec_\Delta$ as in (4.2). Then, (DI) amounts to $\prec_\Delta \models \Delta$ and

(TV) amounts to $\prec_\emptyset = \emptyset$. Every fSPO-representable inductive inference operator is also preferential and therefore satisfies system P. But not every preferential inference operator is also fSPO-representable.

As the preferred structure on worlds $<^{\mathsf{w}}_\Delta$ is a strict partial order, system W is an fSPO-based inductive inference operator $C^{\mathsf{w}} : \Delta \mapsto <^{\mathsf{w}}_\Delta$.

Proposition 4.9. *System W is an fSPO-representable inductive inference operator.*

Obviously, inductive inference operators where the inference relations are each induced by a single ranking function are fSPO-representable; e.g., this is the case for system Z.

In the next section, we will consider syntax splitting postulates for fSPO-representable inductive inference operators.

4.3. Syntax Splitting for fSPO-Representable Inductive Inference Operators

In this section we investigate syntax splitting postulates for fSPO-representable inductive inference operators. For inference operators where the inference relations are induced by ranking functions, the properties (Rel), (Ind), and (SynSplit) are lifted to properties (Rel^{ocf}), (Ind^{ocf}), and (SynSplit^{ocf}) of these ranking functions [KBB20]. In a similar way, (Rel), (Ind), and (SynSplit) are lifted to properties (Rel^{tpo}), (Ind^{tpo}), and (SynSplit^{tpo}) for inference relations induced by total preorders on worlds [KBB20]. Following this idea, we formulate syntax splitting postulates tailored to fSPO-representable inductive inference operators.

(Rel^{spo}) An fSPO-representable inductive inference operator $C^{spo} : \Delta \mapsto \prec_\Delta$ satisfies **(Rel^{spo})** if for $\Delta = \Delta_1 \bigcup_{\Sigma_1,\Sigma_2} \Delta_2$, for $i \in \{1,2\}$, and for consistent $A, B \in \mathcal{L}_{\Sigma_i}$ we have that

$$A \prec_\Delta B \quad \text{iff} \quad A \prec_{\Delta_i} B.$$

(Ind^{spo}) An fSPO-representable inductive inference operator $C^{spo} : \Delta \mapsto \prec_\Delta$ satisfies **(Ind^{spo})** if for any $\Delta = \Delta_1 \bigcup_{\Sigma_1,\Sigma_2} \Delta_2$, for $i, j \in \{1,2\}, i \neq j$, and for any consistent $A, B \in \mathcal{L}_{\Sigma_i}$, $D \in \mathcal{L}_{\Sigma_j}$ we have

$$A \prec_\Delta B \quad \text{iff} \quad AD \prec_\Delta BD.$$

(SynSplit^{spo}) An fSPO-representable inductive inference operator satisfies **(SynSplit^{spo})** if it satisfies (Rel^{spo}) and (Ind^{spo}).

For fSPO-representable inductive inference operators, the new postulates (Rel^{spo}) and (Ind^{spo}) are equivalent to the postulates (Rel) and (Ind).

Proposition 4.10. *An fSPO-representable inductive inference operator satisfies (Rel^{spo}) iff it satisfies (Rel).*

Proof. Let $\Delta = \Delta_1 \bigcup_{\Sigma_1,\Sigma_2} \Delta_2$. Let $i \in \{1,2\}$ and $A, B \in \mathcal{L}_{\Sigma_i}$.

Direction $\Rightarrow$: Assume that the inductive inference operator satisfies (Rel^{spo}). If $A\overline{B}$ is inconsistent, then both $A \mid\!\sim_\Delta B$ and $A \mid\!\sim_{\Delta_i} B$ hold, and (Rel) is satisfied. If $A\overline{B}$ is consistent and AB is inconsistent then both $A \not\mid\!\sim_\Delta B$ and $A \not\mid\!\sim_{\Delta_i} B$, and (Rel) is satisfied. For the remainder of the proof assume that both $AB, A\overline{B}$ are consistent. Because $AB, A\overline{B} \in \mathcal{L}_{\Sigma_i}$, we have

$$A \mid\!\sim_\Delta B \quad \text{iff} \quad AB \prec_\Delta A\overline{B} \quad \text{iff} \quad AB \prec_{\Delta_i} A\overline{B} \quad \text{iff} \quad A \mid\!\sim_{\Delta_i} B.$$

Direction $\Leftarrow$: Assume that the inductive inference operator satisfies (Rel), and let A, B be consistent. Because $A, A \vee B \in \mathcal{L}_{\Sigma_i}$, we have

$$A \prec_\Delta B \quad \text{iff} \quad A \vee B \mid\!\sim_\Delta A \quad \text{iff} \quad A \vee B \mid\!\sim_{\Delta_i} A \quad \text{iff} \quad A \prec_{\Delta_i} B.$$

□

Proposition 4.11. *An fSPO-representable inductive inference operator satisfies (Ind^{spo}) iff it satisfies (Ind).*

Proof. Let $\Delta = \Delta_1 \bigcup_{\Sigma_1,\Sigma_2} \Delta_2$. Let $i, j \in \{1,2\}, i \neq j$ and $A, B \in \mathcal{L}_{\Sigma_i}$, $D \in \mathcal{L}_{\Sigma_j}$.

Direction $\Rightarrow$: Assume that the inductive inference operator satisfies (Ind^{spo}) and that $D \not\mid\!\sim_\Delta \bot$. By Definitions 4.5 and 4.6 this implies that D is consistent. Observe that AB is consistent iff ABD is consistent and that $A\overline{B}$ is consistent iff $A\overline{B}D$ is consistent because D is consistent and D shares no atoms with A or B. If $A\overline{B}$ and thus also $A\overline{B}D$ are inconsistent, then both $A \mid\!\sim_\Delta B$ and $AD \mid\!\sim_\Delta B$ hold and (Ind) is satisfied. If $A\overline{B}$ is consistent but AB is inconsistent, then both $A \not\mid\!\sim_\Delta B$ and $A \not\mid\!\sim_{\Delta_i}$ B and (Ind) is satisfied. For the remainder of the proof assume that both AB and $A\overline{B}$ (and thus also ABD and $A\overline{B}D$) are consistent. Because $AB, A\overline{B} \in \mathcal{L}_{\Sigma_i}$, we have

$$A \mid\!\sim_\Delta B \quad \text{iff} \quad AB \prec_\Delta A\overline{B} \quad \text{iff} \quad ABD \prec_\Delta A\overline{B}D \quad \text{iff} \quad AD \mid\!\sim_\Delta B.$$

Direction $\Leftarrow$: Assume that the inductive inference operator satisfies (Ind) and let A, B, D be consistent. By Definition 4.5 this implies $D \not\mid\!\sim_\Delta \bot$. Because $A, A \vee B \in \mathcal{L}_{\Sigma_i}$ and $D \in \mathcal{L}_{\Sigma_j}$, we have

$$A \prec_\Delta B \quad \text{iff} \quad A \vee B \mid\!\sim_\Delta A \quad \text{iff} \quad (A \vee B)D \mid\!\sim_\Delta A \quad \text{iff} \quad AD \prec_\Delta BD.$$

□

Hence, an fSPO-based inductive inference operator C satisfies (SynSplit^{spo}) and thus both (Rel^{spo}) and (Ind^{spo}), if and only if it satisfies (SynSplit).

Having the postulates for fSPO-representable inference at hand enables easier and more succinct proofs for showing that an fSPO-representable inductive inference operator satisfies syntax splitting. In the following, we will exploit this for showing that system W fully complies with syntax splitting.

4.4. System W satisfies Syntax Splitting

In this section, we evaluate system W with respect to syntax splitting. As system W is an fSPO-representable inductive inference operator it is sufficient to check whether system W satisfies the postulates (Rel^{spo}), (Ind^{spo}), and (SynSplit^{spo}). For proving that system W fulfils these postulates, we will first show some lemmas on the properties of the preferred structure on worlds $<^{\mathsf{w}}_\Delta$ in the presence of a syntax splitting $\Delta = \Delta_1 \bigcup_{\Sigma_1,\Sigma_2} \Delta_2$.

Note that we consider the belief bases Δ_1, Δ_2 as belief bases over $\Sigma = \Sigma_1 \cup \Sigma_2$ in this section. Thus, in particular $<^{\mathsf{w}}_{\Delta_1}$ and $<^{\mathsf{w}}_{\Delta_2}$ are relations on Ω_Σ and the inference relations induced by Δ_1, Δ_2 are defined with respect to Σ, unless explicitly stated otherwise. This is justified because the inferences entailed by system W do not change if the signature is enlarged with additional elements that do not occur in the belief base.

Lemma 4.12. *Let Σ be a signature and $\Sigma' \subseteq \Sigma$. Let Δ be a strongly consistent belief base over Σ'. Let $<^{\mathsf{w}}_{\Delta}$ be the preferred structure on Ω_Σ with respect to Σ and let $<^{\mathsf{w}\prime}_{\Delta}$ be the preferred structure on $\Omega_{\Sigma'}$ with respect to Σ'.*

1. *Let $\omega^a, \omega^b \in \mathcal{L}_\Sigma$ and let $\omega^{a\prime} := \omega^a{}_{|\Sigma'}$ and $\omega^{b\prime} := \omega^b{}_{|\Sigma'}$. We have $\omega^a <^{\mathsf{w}}_{\Delta} \omega^b$ iff $\omega^{a\prime} <^{\mathsf{w}\prime}_{\Delta} \omega^{b\prime}$.*
2. *For consistent $A, B \in \mathcal{L}_{\Sigma'}$ we have $A <^{\mathsf{w}}_{\Delta} B$ iff $A <^{\mathsf{w}\prime}_{\Delta} B$.*

Proof. Let $\Sigma, \Sigma', \Delta, <^{\mathsf{w}}_{\Delta}, <^{\mathsf{w}\prime}_{\Delta}$ be as in the lemma.

Ad 1.: First, observe that the Z-partition of Δ is the same independent of the underlying signature. Let $\omega^a, \omega^b, \omega^{a\prime}, \omega^{b\prime}$ be as above. Because the conditionals in Δ only contain atoms from Σ' and $\omega^a, \omega^{a\prime}$ have the same variable assignment on Σ' , the worlds ω^a and $\omega^{a\prime}$ falsify the same conditionals in Δ. Analogously, ω^b and $\omega^{b\prime}$ falsify the same conditionals in Δ. Whether $\omega^x <^{\mathsf{w}}_{\Delta} \omega^y$ holds or not depends only on the conditionals in Δ falsified by ω^x and ω^y for $\omega^x \in \{\omega^a, \omega^{a\prime}\}$ and $\omega^y \in \{\omega^b, \omega^{b\prime}\}$. Hence, $\omega^a <^{\mathsf{w}}_{\Delta} \omega^b$ iff $\omega^{a\prime} <^{\mathsf{w}\prime}_{\Delta} \omega^{b\prime}$.

Ad 2.: We show both directions of the "iff".

Direction $\Rightarrow$: Let $A <^{\mathsf{w}}_{\Delta} B$ and let $\omega^{b\prime} \in Mod_{\Sigma'}(B)$. Let $\omega^b \in \Omega_\Sigma$ be a world with $\omega^b{}_{|\Sigma'} := \omega^{b\prime}$. Because $\omega^b \models B$ and $A <^{\mathsf{w}}_{\Delta} B$, there is a world $\omega^a \in Mod_\Sigma(A)$ with $\omega^a <^{\mathsf{w}}_{\Delta} \omega^b$. Let $\omega^{a\prime} := \omega^a{}_{|\Sigma'}$. We have $\omega^{a\prime} \models A$, and because of (1.) we have $\omega^{a\prime} <^{\mathsf{w}\prime}_{\Delta} \omega^{b\prime}$. Therefore, $A <^{\mathsf{w}\prime}_{\Delta} B$.

Direction $\Leftarrow$: Let $A <^{\mathsf{w}\prime}_{\Delta} B$ and let $\omega^b \in Mod_\Sigma(B)$. Let $\omega^{b\prime} := \omega^b{}_{|\Sigma'}$. Because $\omega^{b\prime} \models B$ and $A <^{\mathsf{w}\prime}_{\Delta} B$, there is a world $\omega^{a\prime} \in Mod_{\Sigma'}$ such that $\omega^{a\prime} <^{\mathsf{w}\prime}_{\Delta} \omega^{b\prime}$. Let $\omega^a \in \Omega_\Sigma$ be a world with $\omega^a{}_{|\Sigma'} = \omega^{a\prime}$. We have $\omega^a \models A$, and because of (1.) we have $\omega^a <^{\mathsf{w}}_{\Delta} \omega^b$. Therefore, $A <^{\mathsf{w}}_{\Delta} B$. □

A consequence of Lemma 4.12 is the following Lemma 4.13. For signatures $\Sigma' \subseteq \Sigma$ and a world $\omega \in \Omega_\Sigma$ it states that the position of ω in the preferred structure $<^{\mathsf{w}}_{\Delta}$ of worlds induced by a belief base Δ over Σ' only depends on the valuation of variables in Σ'.

Lemma 4.13. *Let Σ be a signature and $\Sigma' \subseteq \Sigma$. Let Δ be a strongly consistent belief base over Σ'. Let $\omega^a, \omega^b, \omega' \in \Omega_\Sigma$ with $\omega^a{}_{|\Sigma'} = \omega^b{}_{|\Sigma'}$. Then we have $\omega^a <^{\mathsf{w}}_{\Delta} \omega'$ iff $\omega^b <^{\mathsf{w}}_{\Delta} \omega'$ and $\omega' <^{\mathsf{w}}_{\Delta} \omega^a$ iff $\omega' <^{\mathsf{w}}_{\Delta} \omega^b$.*

Proof. Let $\omega^a, \omega^b, \omega'$ be as above and let $\omega^* := \omega^a{}_{|\Sigma'}$ and $\omega^{*\prime} := \omega'{}_{|\Sigma'}$. With Lemma 4.12 we have $\omega^a <^{\mathsf{w}}_{\Delta} \omega'$ iff $\omega^* <^{\mathsf{w}\prime}_{\Delta} \omega^{*\prime}$ iff $\omega^b <^{\mathsf{w}}_{\Delta} \omega'$. Analogously, $\omega' <^{\mathsf{w}}_{\Delta} \omega^a$ iff $\omega' <^{\mathsf{w}}_{\Delta} \omega^b$. □

The following Lemma 4.14 shows how a syntax splitting on a belief base carries over to the corresponding Z-partition. A similar observation about how syntax splittings of a belief base affect its Z-partition was made in [KBB20].

Lemma 4.14. *Let* $\Delta = \Delta_1 \bigcup_{\Sigma_1,\Sigma_2} \Delta_2$ *be a strongly consistent belief base with syntax splitting. Let* $OP(\Delta) = (\Delta^0, \ldots, \Delta^k)$ *be the Z-partition of* Δ *and for each* $i \in \{1,2\}$ *let* $OP(\Delta_i) = (\Delta_i^0, \ldots, \Delta_i^{l_i})$ *be the Z-partition of* Δ_i.

1. *For each* $i \in \{1,2\}$ *and* $j \in \{0,\ldots,l_i\}$ *we have* $\Delta_i^j = \Delta^j \cap \Delta_i$ *and thus especially* $\Delta_i^j \subseteq \Delta^j$.
2. *We have* $\max\{l_1, l_2\} = k$.
3. *For* $l_1 \leq l_2$, *we have* $\Delta^j = \begin{cases} \Delta_1^j \cup \Delta_2^j & \text{for } j = 1,\ldots,l_1 \\ \Delta_2^j & \text{for } j = l_1+1,\ldots,k. \end{cases}$

Proof. **Ad 1.:** Because we can swap the indices 1, 2 in the syntax splitting, we can assume $i = 1$ without loss of generality. We will show that $\Delta_1^0 = \Delta^0 \cap \Delta_1$ for $\Delta_1 \neq \emptyset$. This implies $\Delta_1^j = \Delta^j \cap \Delta_1$ for $j = 1,\ldots,l_1$ as the Z-partition is constructed by recursively selecting the conditionals tolerated by all other conditionals in the belief base.

Every conditional $r \in \Delta_1$ is tolerated by all conditionals in $(\mathcal{L}|\mathcal{L})_{\Sigma_2}$ that are not contradictory. Especially, r is tolerated by all conditionals in Δ_2. Therefore, r is tolerated by all conditionals in Δ iff it is tolerated by all conditional in Δ_1.

If $q \in \Delta_1^0$, then it is in Δ_1 and tolerated by every conditional in Δ_1. Hence, q is also in Δ and tolerated by every conditional in Δ (see above). Thus, $q \in \Delta^0 \cap \Delta_1$. If $p \in \Delta^0 \cap \Delta_1$, then p is in Δ_1 and p is tolerated by every conditional in Δ. Therefore, p is also tolerated by Δ_1. Thus, $p \in \Delta_1^0$. Together, we have $\Delta_1^0 = \Delta^0 \cap \Delta_1$.

Ad 2: As $\Delta_i \subseteq \Delta$ for $i = 1, 2$ we have $l_1, l_2 \leq k$. As Δ_k is not empty, it contains at least one conditional r. This r is either in Δ_1 or in Δ_2. Let $i \in \{1,2\}$ be such that $r \in \Delta_i$. Then there is some m such that $r \in \Delta_i^m$. With (1.) we have $\Delta_i^m \subseteq \Delta^m$. As r can only be in one set of the Z-partition of Δ we have $m = k$. Therefore, the Z-partition of Δ_i has at least k elements, i.e., $l_i = k$. In summary, $\max\{l_1, l_2\} = k$.

Ad 3: First, consider the case that $j \leq l_1$ and therefore also $j \leq l_2$. As $\Delta_i^j \subseteq \Delta^j$ for $i = 1, 2$ we get $\Delta^j \supseteq \Delta_1^j \cup \Delta_2^j$. Every $r \in \Delta^j$ is either in Δ_1 or in Δ_2. W.l.o.g. assume $r \in \Delta_1$. Then there is some m such that $r \in \Delta_1^m$. With (1.) we have $\Delta_1^m \subseteq \Delta^m$. As r can only be in one set of the Z-partition of Δ we have $m = j$. Therefore, $\Delta^j \subseteq \Delta_1^j \cup \Delta_2^j$ and thus $\Delta^j = \Delta_1^j \cup \Delta_2^j$.

Now consider $l_1 < j \leq k$. From (1.) we get $\Delta^j \supseteq \Delta_2^j$. Analogous to the first case, we know that every conditional $r \in \Delta^j$ is either in Δ_1^j or Δ_2^j. Because $j > l_1$ there is no Δ_1^j in the Z-partition of Δ_1, and thus we have $r \in \Delta_2^j$. Therefore, $\Delta^j \subseteq \Delta_2^j$ and thus, $\Delta^j = \Delta_2^j$. □

If we have $\omega <^{\mathsf{w}}_{\Delta} \omega'$, then there is some conditional r that is falsified by ω' but not by ω and thus causes the $\subsetneqq$ relation in (3.5) in Definition 3.19. If $\Delta = \Delta_1 \bigcup\limits_{\Sigma_1,\Sigma_2} \Delta_2$, this r is either in Δ_1 or in Δ_2. Lemma 4.15 states that the relation $\omega <^{\mathsf{w}}_{\Delta} \omega'$ can also be obtained using only Δ_1 or only Δ_2, respectively.

Lemma 4.15. *Let $\Delta = \Delta_1 \bigcup\limits_{\Sigma_1,\Sigma_2} \Delta_2$ be a strongly consistent belief base with syntax splitting and let $\omega, \omega' \in \Omega_\Sigma$. If $\omega <^{\mathsf{w}}_{\Delta} \omega'$, then $\omega <^{\mathsf{w}}_{\Delta_1} \omega'$ or $\omega <^{\mathsf{w}}_{\Delta_2} \omega'$.*

Proof. Let $OP(\Delta) = (\Delta^0, \ldots, \Delta^k)$ and let ξ, ξ^i be the functions mapping worlds to the set of falsified conditionals for Δ as in Definition 3.19. Let $\omega, \omega' \in \Omega_\Sigma$ be worlds with $\omega <^{\mathsf{w}}_{\Delta} \omega'$. By definition of $<^{\mathsf{w}}_{\Delta}$ there is an $m \in \{0, \ldots, k\}$ such that $\xi^i(\omega) = \xi^i(\omega')$ for every $i = m+1, \ldots, k$ and $\xi^m(\omega) \subsetneqq \xi^m(\omega')$. Therefore, there is an $r \in \Delta$ such that $r \in \xi^m(\omega')$ and $r \notin \xi^m(\omega)$. The conditional r is either in Δ_1 or Δ_2. Assume that $r \in \Delta_x$ with x being either 1 or 2. Let $OP(\Delta_x) = (\Delta_x^0, \ldots, \Delta_x^l)$ be the Z-partition of Δ_x. Let ξ_x, ξ_x^i for $i = 0, \ldots, k$ be the functions mapping worlds to the set of falsified conditionals for Δ_x. Because $\Delta_x^i = \Delta^i \cap \Delta_x$ (see Lemma 4.14) and $\xi^i(\omega) = \xi^i(\omega')$ for every $i = m+1, \ldots, k$ we have $\xi_x^i(\omega) = \xi_x^i(\omega')$ for every $i = m+1, \ldots, l$. And because $r \in \xi_x^m(\omega')$ and $r \notin \xi_x^m(\omega)$ we have $\xi_x^m(\omega) \subsetneqq \xi_x^m(\omega')$. Therefore, $\omega <^{\mathsf{w}}_{\Delta_x} \omega'$.

Hence, we have $\omega <^{\mathsf{w}}_{\Delta_1} \omega'$ or $\omega <^{\mathsf{w}}_{\Delta_2} \omega'$. □

Note, that both $\omega <^{\mathsf{w}}_{\Delta_1} \omega'$ and $\omega <^{\mathsf{w}}_{\Delta_2} \omega'$ can be true.

Lemma 4.16 considers the reverse direction of Lemma 4.15 and shows a situation where we can infer $\omega <^{\mathsf{w}}_{\Delta} \omega'$ from $\omega <^{\mathsf{w}}_{\Delta_1} \omega'$ for a belief base Δ with syntax splitting.

Lemma 4.16. *Let $\Delta = \Delta_1 \bigcup\limits_{\Sigma_1,\Sigma_2} \Delta_2$ be a strongly consistent belief base with syntax splitting, let $\omega, \omega' \in \Omega_\Sigma$, and let $i, j \in \{1, 2\}, i \neq j$. If $\omega <^{\mathsf{w}}_{\Delta_i} \omega'$ and $\omega_{|\Sigma_j} = \omega'_{|\Sigma_j}$, then $\omega <^{\mathsf{w}}_{\Delta} \omega'$.*

Proof. Because we can swap the indices 1, 2 in the syntax splitting, we can assume $i = 1$ and $j = 2$ without loss of generality. Let $\omega, \omega' \in \Omega_\Sigma$ with $\omega <^{\mathsf{w}}_{\Delta_1} \omega'$ and $\omega_{|\Sigma_2} = \omega'_{|\Sigma_2}$. Let $OP(\Delta) = (\Delta^0, \dots, \Delta^k)$ and let ξ, ξ^i be the functions mapping worlds to the set of falsified conditionals for Δ as in Definition 3.19. Let $OP(\Delta_1) = (\Delta_1^0, \dots, \Delta_1^l)$ be the Z-partition of Δ_1. Let ξ_x, ξ_x^i for $i = 0, \dots, k$ be the functions mapping worlds to the set of falsified conditionals for Δ_x. By definition of $<^{\mathsf{w}}_{\Delta_1}$ there is an $m \in \{0, \dots, l\}$ such that $\xi_1^i(\omega) = \xi_1^i(\omega')$ for every $i = m+1, \dots, l$ and $\xi_1^m(\omega) \subsetneqq \xi_1^m(\omega')$. With Lemma 4.14 we have, for every world ω^*, $x = 1, 2$, and $j = 0, \dots, l$, that $\xi_x^j(\omega^*) = \{r \in \Delta_x^j \mid \omega^* \text{ falsifies } r\} = \{r \in \Delta_x \cap \Delta^j \mid \omega^* \text{ falsifies } r\} = \xi^j(\omega^*) \cap \Delta_x$. This implies $\xi^i(\omega) \cap \Delta_1 = \xi_1^i(\omega) = \xi_1^i(\omega') = \xi^i(\omega') \cap \Delta_1$ for every $i = m+1, \dots, k$ and $\xi^m(\omega) \cap \Delta_1 = \xi_1^m(\omega) \subsetneqq \xi_1^m(\omega) = \xi^m(\omega') \cap \Delta_1$.

Because $\omega_{|\Sigma_2} = \omega'_{|\Sigma_2}$, we have $\xi^i(\omega) \cap \Delta_2 = \xi^i(\omega') \cap \Delta_2$ for every $i = 0, \dots, k$. Hence, we have $\xi^i(\omega) = \xi^i(\omega')$ for every $i = m+1, \dots, k$ and $\xi^m(\omega) \subsetneqq \xi^m(\omega')$ and therefore $\omega <^{\mathsf{w}}_{\Delta} \omega'$. □

The next Lemma 4.17 captures that the variable assignment for variables that do not occur in the belief base has no influence on the position of a world in the resulting preferred structure on worlds.

Lemma 4.17. *Let* $\Delta = \Delta_1 \bigcup_{\Sigma_1, \Sigma_2} \Delta_2$ *be a strongly consistent belief base with syntax splitting,* $i \in \{1, 2\}$, *and* $\omega^a, \omega^b, \omega' \in \Omega_\Sigma$ *with* $\omega^a{}_{|\Sigma_i} = \omega^b{}_{|\Sigma_i}$. *Then we have* $\omega^a <^{\mathsf{w}}_{\Delta_i} \omega'$ *iff* $\omega^b <^{\mathsf{w}}_{\Delta_i} \omega'$.

Proof. This follows immediately from Lemma 4.13. □

Using these lemmas above, we show that system W fulfils both (Rel^{spo}) and (Ind^{spo}).

Proposition 4.18. *System W fulfils* (Rel^{spo}).

Proof. Let $\Delta = \Delta_1 \bigcup_{\Sigma_1, \Sigma_2} \Delta_2$ be a strongly consistent belief base with syntax splitting, let $i \in \{1, 2\}$, and let $A, B \in \mathcal{L}_{\Sigma_i}$ be consistent formulas. We need to show that

$$A <^{\mathsf{w}}_{\Delta} B \quad \text{if and only if} \quad A <^{\mathsf{w}}_{\Delta_i} B. \tag{4.3}$$

Because we can swap the indices 1, 2 in the syntax splitting, we can assume $i = 1$ without loss of generality.

Direction $\Rightarrow$ of (4.3): Assume that $A <^{\mathsf{w}}_{\Delta} B$. We need to show that $A <^{\mathsf{w}}_{\Delta_1} B$. Let ω' be any world in $Mod_\Sigma(B)$. Now choose $\omega'_{min} \in \Omega_\Sigma$ such that

1. $\omega'_{min} \leq^{\mathsf{w}}_{\Delta} \omega'$,
2. $\omega'_{|\Sigma_1} = \omega'_{min|\Sigma_1}$, and
3. there is no $\omega'_* \in \Omega_\Sigma$ with $\omega'_* < \omega'_{min}$ that fulfils (1.) and (2.).

Such an ω'_{min} exists because ω' fulfils properties (1.) and (2.), $<^{\mathsf{w}}_{\Delta}$ is irreflexive and transitive, and there are only finitely many worlds in Ω_Σ.

Because of (2.) and because $\omega' \models B$ we have that $\omega'_{min} \models B$. Because $A <^{\mathsf{w}}_{\Delta} B$, there is a world ω such that $\omega \models A$ and $\omega <^{\mathsf{w}}_{\Delta} \omega'_{min}$. Lemma 4.15 yields that $\omega <^{\mathsf{w}}_{\Delta_1} \omega'_{min}$ or $\omega <^{\mathsf{w}}_{\Delta_2} \omega'_{min}$.

The case $\omega <^{\mathsf{w}}_{\Delta_2} \omega'_{min}$ is not possible: Assuming $\omega <^{\mathsf{w}}_{\Delta_2} \omega'_{min}$, it follows that for $\omega'_* := \omega'_{min|\Sigma_1}\omega_{|\Sigma_2}$ we have that $\omega'_* <^{\mathsf{w}}_{\Delta_2} \omega'_{min}$ with Lemma 4.17. With Lemma 4.16 it follows that $\omega'_{min2} <^{\mathsf{w}}_{\Delta} \omega'_{min}$. This contradicts (3.). Hence, $\omega <^{\mathsf{w}}_{\Delta_1} \omega'_{min}$. Because of (2.) and Lemma 4.17 it follows that $\omega <^{\mathsf{w}}_{\Delta_1} \omega'$. As we can find an ω such that $\omega <^{\mathsf{w}}_{\Delta_1} \omega'$ and $\omega \models A$ for every $\omega' \models B$ we have that $A <^{\mathsf{w}}_{\Delta_1} B$.

Direction $\Leftarrow$ of (4.3): Assume that $A <^{\mathsf{w}}_{\Delta_1} B$. We need to show that $A <^{\mathsf{w}}_{\Delta} B$. Let ω' be any world in $Mod_\Sigma(B)$. Because $A <^{\mathsf{w}}_{\Delta_1} B$, there is a world ω^* such that $\omega^* \models A$ and $\omega^* <^{\mathsf{w}}_{\Delta_1} \omega'$. Let $\omega := \omega^*_{|\Sigma_1}\omega'_{|\Sigma_2}$. Because $\omega^* \models A$ we have that $\omega \models A$. Furthermore, with Lemma 4.17 it follows that $\omega <^{\mathsf{w}}_{\Delta_1} \omega'$ and thus $\omega <^{\mathsf{w}}_{\Delta} \omega'$ with Lemma 4.16. As we can construct ω such that $\omega <^{\mathsf{w}}_{\Delta} \omega'$ and $\omega \models A$ for every $\omega' \models B$ we have that $A <^{\mathsf{w}}_{\Delta} B$. □

Proposition 4.19. *System W fulfils* (Ind^{spo}).

Proof. Let $\Delta = \Delta_1 \bigcup_{\Sigma_1,\Sigma_2} \Delta_2$ be a strongly consistent belief base with syntax splitting, let $i, j \in \{1, 2\}, i \neq j$, and let $A, B \in \mathcal{L}_{\Sigma_i}$ and $D \in \mathcal{L}_{\Sigma_j}$ be consistent formulas. We need to show that

$$A <^{\mathsf{w}}_{\Delta} B \text{ if and only if } AD <^{\mathsf{w}}_{\Delta} BD. \tag{4.4}$$

Because we can swap the indices 1, 2 in the syntax splitting, we can assume $i = 1$ and $j = 2$ without loss of generality.

Direction $\Rightarrow$ of (4.4): Assume that $A <^{\mathsf{w}}_{\Delta} B$. We need to show that $AD <^{\mathsf{w}}_{\Delta} BD$. Let ω' be any world in $Mod_\Sigma(BD)$. Now choose $\omega'_{min} \in \Omega$ such that

1. $\omega'_{min} \leq^{\mathsf{w}}_{\Delta} \omega'$,
2. $\omega'_{|\Sigma_1} = \omega'_{min|\Sigma_1}$, and
3. there is no $\omega'_* \in \Omega_\Sigma$ with $\omega'_* < \omega'_{min}$ that fulfils (1.) and (2.).

Such an ω'_{min} exists because ω' fulfils properties (1.) and (2.), $<^{\mathsf{w}}_{\Delta}$ is irreflexive and transitive, and there are only finitely many worlds in Ω_Σ. Because of (2.) and because $\omega' \models BD$ we have that $\omega'_{min} \models B$. Because $A <^{\mathsf{w}}_{\Delta} B$, there is a world ω^* such that $\omega^* \models A$ and $\omega^* <^{\mathsf{w}}_{\Delta} \omega'_{min}$. Lemma 4.15 yields that either $\omega^* <^{\mathsf{w}}_{\Delta_1} \omega'_{min}$ or $\omega^* <^{\mathsf{w}}_{\Delta_2} \omega'_{min}$.

The case $\omega^* <^{\mathsf{w}}_{\Delta_2} \omega'_{min}$ is not possible: Assuming $\omega^* <^{\mathsf{w}}_{\Delta_2} \omega'_{min}$, it follows that for $\omega'_* := \omega'_{min|\Sigma_1}\omega^*_{|\Sigma_2}$ we have that $\omega'_* <^{\mathsf{w}}_{\Delta_2} \omega'_{min}$ with Lemma 4.17. With Lemma 4.16 it follows that $\omega'_* <^{\mathsf{w}}_{\Delta} \omega'_{min}$. This contradicts (3.). Hence, $\omega^* <^{\mathsf{w}}_{\Delta_1} \omega'_{min}$. Let $\omega := \omega^*_{|\Sigma_1}\omega'_{|\Sigma_2}$. Because $\omega^* \models A$ we have that $\omega \models A$. Because $\omega' \models D$ we have that $\omega \models D$. Because of (2.) and Lemma 4.17 it follows that $\omega <^{\mathsf{w}}_{\Delta_1} \omega'$ and thus with Lemma 4.16 it follows that $\omega <^{\mathsf{w}}_{\Delta} \omega'$. As we can construct such an $\omega \in Mod_\Sigma(AD)$ for every $\omega' \in Mod_\Sigma(AB)$ we have that $AD <^{\mathsf{w}}_{\Delta} BD$.

Direction $\Leftarrow$ of (4.4): Assume that $AD <^{\mathsf{w}}_{\Delta} BD$. We need to show that $A <^{\mathsf{w}}_{\Delta} B$. Let ω' be any world in $Mod_\Sigma(B)$. Now choose $\omega'_{min} \in \Omega_\Sigma$ such that

1. $\omega'_{min} \models D$
2. $\omega'_{|\Sigma_1} = \omega'_{min|\Sigma_1}$, and
3. there is no $\omega'_* \in \Omega_\Sigma$ with $\omega'_* <^{\mathsf{w}}_{\Delta} \omega'_{min}$ that fulfils (1.) and (2.).

Such an ω'_{min} exists because D is consistent, $<^{\mathsf{w}}_{\Delta}$ is irreflexive and transitive, and there are only finitely many worlds in Ω_Σ. Because of (2.) and because $\omega' \models B$ we have that $\omega'_{min} \models B$. Because of (1.) we have that $\omega'_{min} \models D$. Because $AD <^{\mathsf{w}}_{\Delta} BD$, there is a world ω^* such that $\omega^* \models AD$ and $\omega^* <^{\mathsf{w}}_{\Delta} \omega'_{min}$. Lemma 4.15 yields that either $\omega^* <^{\mathsf{w}}_{\Delta_1} \omega'_{min}$ or $\omega^* <^{\mathsf{w}}_{\Delta_2} \omega'_{min}$.

The case $\omega^* <^{\mathsf{w}}_{\Delta_2} \omega'_{min}$ is not possible: Assuming $\omega^* <^{\mathsf{w}}_{\Delta_2} \omega'_{min}$, it follows that for $\omega'_* := \omega'_{min|\Sigma_1}\omega^*_{|\Sigma_2}$ we have that $\omega'_* <^{\mathsf{w}}_{\Delta_2} \omega'_{min}$ with Lemma 4.17. With Lemma 4.16 it follows that $\omega'_* <^{\mathsf{w}}_{\Delta} \omega'_{min}$. This contradicts (3.). Hence, $\omega^* <^{\mathsf{w}}_{\Delta_1} \omega'_{min}$. Let $\omega := \omega^*_{|\Sigma_1}\omega'_{|\Sigma_2}$. Because $\omega^* \models A$ we have that $\omega \models A$. Because of (2.) and Lemma 4.17 it follows that $\omega <^{\mathsf{w}}_{\Delta_1} \omega'$ and thus with Lemma 4.16 $\omega <^{\mathsf{w}}_{\Delta} \omega'$. As we can construct such an $\omega \in Mod_\Sigma(A)$ for every $\omega' \in Mod_\Sigma(B)$ we have that $A <^{\mathsf{w}}_{\Delta} B$. □

The satisfaction of the postulates (Ind^{spo}) and (Rel^{spo}) for fSPO-representable inductive inference operators immediately implies that system W also fulfils the general syntax splitting postulates.

Proposition 4.20. *System W fulfils (Rel).*

Proof. This follows from Proposition 4.18 and Proposition 4.10. □

Proposition 4.21. *System W fulfils (Ind).*

Proof. This follows from Proposition 4.19 and Proposition 4.11. □

Combining Propositions 4.20 and 4.21 yields that system W fulfils (SynSplit).

Proposition 4.22. *System W fulfils (SynSplit).*

Thus, by employing the syntax splitting postulates for fSPO-representable inference operators, we have established a proof that system W fulfils (SynSplit). This makes system W one of the few known inference operators besides c-inference and lexicographic inference that satisfies syntax splitting.

The next section further investigates the effect of a syntax splitting of a belief base on the induced preferred structure on worlds.

4.5. Effect of Syntax Splittings on the Preferred Structure on Worlds

Let us assume that we have a belief base $\Delta = \Delta_1 \bigcup_{\Sigma_1,\Sigma_2} \Delta_2$ with syntax splitting. In the previous Section 4.4 we studied the effect of the syntax splitting on the inference relation induced from Δ by system W. To answer a query "does A entail B" for $A, B \in (\mathcal{L}|\mathcal{L})_{\Sigma_1}$ (or $A, B \in (\mathcal{L}|\mathcal{L})_{\Sigma_2}$) we can employ (SynSplit) and consider only Δ_1 (or Δ_2, respectively).

However, if A, B contain variables from both Σ_1 and Σ_2, or if we want to determine the preferred structure over Δ, (SynSplit) is not applicable. To use syntax splittings also in this situation, we show how a syntax splitting affects the preferred structure on worlds over the whole belief base.

For relating two worlds in $<^{\mathsf{w}}_{\Delta}$, the conditionals falsified by these worlds in each part of the Z-partition are central. The following notion of the *highest differentiating layer* captures the most specific set Δ^i in the Z-partition where the two worlds falsify different conditionals.

Definition 4.23 ($hdl(\omega, \omega', \Delta)$). *Let Δ be a strongly consistent belief base, let $OP(\Delta) = (\Delta^0, \dots, \Delta^k)$ and let ξ, ξ^i be defined as in Definition 3.19. We define* the number of the highest layer differentiating *between $\omega, \omega' \in \Omega_\Sigma$ as*

$$hdl(\omega, \omega', \Delta) := \max\{i \in \mathbb{N} \mid \xi^i(\omega) \neq \xi^i(\omega')\},$$

i.e., $i = hdl(\omega, \omega', \Delta)$ is the highest number with $\xi^i(\omega) \neq \xi^i(\omega')$ and $\xi^j(\omega) = \xi^j(\omega')$ for $j > i$. If ω, ω' falsify the same conditionals in Δ, we define $hdl(\omega, \omega', \Delta) = -1$.

Example 4.24. *Consider the belief base Δ_{ve} from Example 3.48. We have $OP(\Delta_{ve}) = (\Delta^0, \Delta^1)$ with $\Delta^0 = \{(g|m), (t|b)\}$ and $\Delta^1 = \{(m|e), (\overline{g}|me)\}$. For $\omega := mbetg$ and $\omega' := mbet\overline{g}$ we have $hdl(\omega, \omega', \Delta_{ve}) = 1$ because ω falsifies $(\overline{g}|me)$ from Δ^1 and ω' does not. The falsification behaviour of ω, ω' regarding Δ^0 is irrelevant here.*

For $\omega'' := \overline{m}\overline{b}e\overline{t}g$ and $\omega''' := \overline{m}be\overline{t}g$ we have $hdl(\omega'', \omega''', \Delta_{ve}) = 0$ because $\xi^1(\omega'') = \xi^1(\omega''') = \{(m|e)\}$ and $\xi^0(\omega'') = \emptyset$ does not equal $\xi^0(\omega''') = \{(t|b)\}$.

For ω'' and $\omega'''' := \overline{m}\overline{b}e\overline{t}\overline{g}$ we have $hdl(\omega'', \omega'''' \Delta_{ve}) = -1$ because $\xi(\omega'') = \xi(\omega'''') = \{(m|e)\}$.

The following proposition states that to decide whether $\omega <^{\mathsf{w}}_{\Delta} \omega'$ holds for a pair of worlds ω, ω' and a belief based Δ with syntax splitting, it is sufficient to determine the preferred structure on worlds separately for each part of the syntax splitting. Then, the number $hdl(\omega, \omega', \Delta)$ indicates how the preferred structures induced by each part of the belief base should be combined. In some cases it is only necessary to consider one of the parts in the syntax splitting, making answering the query even easier.

Proposition 4.25. *Let $\Delta = \Delta_1 \bigcup_{\Sigma_1, \Sigma_2} \Delta_2$ be a strongly consistent belief base with syntax splitting and $\omega, \omega' \in \Omega_\Sigma$. Then $\omega <^{\mathsf{w}}_{\Delta} \omega'$ iff either*

- *$hdl(\omega, \omega', \Delta_1) > hdl(\omega, \omega', \Delta_2)$ and $\omega_{|\Sigma_1} <^{\mathsf{w}}_{\Delta_1} \omega'_{|\Sigma_1}$ or*
- *$hdl(\omega, \omega', \Delta_1) < hdl(\omega, \omega', \Delta_2)$ and $\omega_{|\Sigma_2} <^{\mathsf{w}}_{\Delta_2} \omega'_{|\Sigma_2}$ or*
- *$hdl(\omega, \omega', \Delta_1) = hdl(\omega, \omega', \Delta_2)$ and $\omega_{|\Sigma_1} <^{\mathsf{w}}_{\Delta_1} \omega'_{|\Sigma_1}$ and $\omega_{|\Sigma_2} <^{\mathsf{w}}_{\Delta_2} \omega'_{|\Sigma_2}$.*

Proof. Let $\Delta = \Delta_1 \bigcup_{\Sigma_1, \Sigma_2} \Delta_2$ and let $\omega, \omega' \in \Omega_\Sigma$. We will prove both directions of the "iff" separately.

Direction $\Rightarrow$: Assume $\omega <^{\mathsf{w}}_{\Delta} \omega'$. We can distinguish three cases for the numbers $k = hdl(\omega, \omega', \Delta_1)$ and $l = hdl(\omega, \omega', \Delta_2)$.

Case 1: $hdl(\omega, \omega', \Delta_1) > hdl(\omega, \omega', \Delta_2)$ In this case, we have $\xi_1^k(\omega) \neq \xi_1^k(\omega')$ and $\xi_2^k(\omega) = \xi_2^k(\omega')$. Additionally, we have $\xi_1^i(\omega) = \xi_1^i(\omega')$ and $\xi_2^i(\omega) = \xi_2^i(\omega')$ for $i > k$. With Lemma 4.14 it follows that $\xi^i(\omega) = \xi^i(\omega')$ for $i > k$ and $\xi^k(\omega) \neq \xi^k(\omega')$. As $\omega <^{\mathsf{w}}_{\Delta} \omega'$ we know that $\xi^k(\omega) \subsetneqq \xi^k(\omega')$ and therefore $\xi_1^k(\omega) \subsetneqq \xi_1^k(\omega')$ because of $\xi_2^k(\omega) = \xi_2^k(\omega')$ and Lemma 4.14. As the falsification of conditionals in Δ_1 over Σ_1 does not depend on the assignments of truth values for Σ_2, we have that $\xi_1^k(\omega_{|\Sigma_1}) \subsetneqq \xi_1^k(\omega'_{|\Sigma_1})$ and therefore $\omega_{|\Sigma_1} <^{\mathsf{w}}_{\Delta_1} \omega'_{|\Sigma_1}$.

Case 2: $hdl(\omega, \omega', \Delta_1) < hdl(\omega, \omega', \Delta_2)$ Analogous to Case 1 we conclude $\omega_{|\Sigma_2} <^{\mathsf{w}}_{\Delta_2} \omega'_{|\Sigma_2}$.

Case 3: $hdl(\omega, \omega', \Delta_1) = hdl(\omega, \omega', \Delta_2)$ In this case, we have $\xi_1^k(\omega) \neq \xi_1^k(\omega')$ and $\xi_2^k(\omega) \neq \xi_2^k(\omega')$. Additionally, we have $\xi_1^i(\omega) = \xi_1^i(\omega')$ and $\xi_2^i(\omega) = \xi_2^i(\omega')$ for $i > k$. With Lemma 4.14 it follows that $\xi^i(\omega) = \xi^i(\omega')$ for $i > k$ and $\xi^k(\omega) \neq \xi^k(\omega')$. As $\omega <^{\mathsf{w}}_{\Delta} \omega'$ we know that $\xi^k(\omega) \subsetneqq \xi^k(\omega')$. Therefore, we have $\xi_1^k(\omega) \subsetneqq \xi_1^k(\omega')$ and $\xi_2^k(\omega) \subsetneqq \xi_2^k(\omega')$. As the falsification of conditionals in Δ_1 over Σ_1 does not depend on the assignments of truth values for Σ_2, we have that $\xi_1^k(\omega_{|\Sigma_1}) \subsetneqq \xi_1^k(\omega'_{|\Sigma_1})$ and $\xi_2^k(\omega_{|\Sigma_2}) \subsetneqq \xi_2^k(\omega'_{|\Sigma_2})$. Hence, $\omega_{|\Sigma_1} <^{\mathsf{w}}_{\Delta_1} \omega'_{|\Sigma_1}$ and $\omega_{|\Sigma_2} <^{\mathsf{w}}_{\Delta_2} \omega'_{|\Sigma_2}$.

Direction $\Leftarrow$: Assume one of the three items in the proposition is true.

Case 1: $hdl(\omega, \omega', \Delta_1) > hdl(\omega, \omega', \Delta_2)$ and $\omega_{|\Sigma_1} <^{\mathsf{w}}_{\Delta_1} \omega'_{|\Sigma_1}$. We have $\xi_1^k(\omega) \neq \xi_1^k(\omega')$ and $\xi_2^k(\omega) = \xi_2^k(\omega')$. Additionally, we have $\xi_1^i(\omega) = \xi_1^i(\omega')$ and $\xi_2^i(\omega) = \xi_2^i(\omega')$ for $i > k$. Because of $\omega_{|\Sigma_1} <^{\mathsf{w}}_{\Delta_1} \omega'_{|\Sigma_1}$, we have $\xi_1^k(\omega) \subsetneqq \xi_1^k(\omega')$. With Lemma 4.14 it follows that $\xi^i(\omega) = \xi^i(\omega')$ for $i > k$ and $\xi^k(\omega) \subsetneqq \xi^k(\omega')$. Therefore $\omega <^{\mathsf{w}}_{\Delta} \omega'$.

Case 2: $hdl(\omega, \omega', \Delta_1) < hdl(\omega, \omega', \Delta_2)$ and $\omega_{|\Sigma_2} <^{\mathsf{w}}_{\Delta_2} \omega'_{|\Sigma_2}$. Analogous to Case 1 we have $\omega <^{\mathsf{w}}_{\Delta} \omega'$.

Case 3: $hdl(\omega, \omega', \Delta_1) = hdl(\omega, \omega', \Delta_2)$ and $\omega_{1|\Sigma_1} <^{\mathsf{w}}_{\Delta_1} \omega_{2|\Sigma_1}$ and $\omega_{|\Sigma_2} <^{\mathsf{w}}_{\Delta_2} \omega'_{|\Sigma_2}$. We have $\xi_1^i(\omega) = \xi_1^i(\omega')$ and $\xi_2^i(\omega) = \xi_2^i(\omega')$ for $i > k$. Because of $\omega_{|\Sigma_1} <^{\mathsf{w}}_{\Delta_1} \omega'_{|\Sigma_1}$, we have $\xi_1^k(\omega) \subsetneqq \xi_1^k(\omega')$. Because of $\omega_{|\Sigma_2} <^{\mathsf{w}}_{\Delta_2} \omega'_{|\Sigma_2}$, we have $\xi_2^k(\omega) \subsetneqq \xi_2^k(\omega')$. With Lemma 4.14 it follows that $\xi^i(\omega) = \xi^i(\omega')$ for $i > k$ and $\xi^k(\omega) \subsetneqq \xi^k(\omega')$. Therefore, $\omega <^{\mathsf{w}}_{\Delta} \omega'$. □

Proposition 4.25 can be used to decide whether $\omega <^{\mathsf{w}}_{\Delta} \omega'$ holds in presence of a syntax splitting $\Delta = \Delta_1 \bigcup_{\Sigma_1, \Sigma_2} \Delta_2$ considering Δ_1 and Δ_2

separately.

Example 4.26. *Consider again the belief base* $\Delta_{ve} = \Delta_1 \bigcup_{\Sigma_1,\Sigma_2} \Delta_2$ *from Example 3.48. For checking whether* $\omega <^{\mathsf{w}}_{\Delta_{ve}} \omega'$ *holds for* $\omega := mbet\overline{g}$ *and* $\omega' := mbetg$*, we first determine* $h_1 = hdl(\omega, \omega', \Delta_1) = 1$ *and* $h_2 = hdl(\omega, \omega', \Delta_2) = 0$*. As* $h_1 > h_2$ *we have that* $\omega <^{\mathsf{w}}_{\Delta_{ve}} \omega'$ *iff* $\omega_{|\Sigma_1} <^{\mathsf{w}}_{\Delta_1} \omega'_{|\Sigma_1}$*.*

Applications of this approach include the computation of $<^{\mathsf{w}}_{\Delta}$ or parts of this relation. Deciding whether $\omega <^{\mathsf{w}}_{\Delta} \omega'$ holds also coincides with deciding whether Δ entails the base conditional [Ker01] $(\omega|\omega \vee \omega')$ with system W. More generally, deciding whether a conditional $(B|A)$ is entailed by a certain belief base Δ requires only comparing models of the antecedent A in $<^{\mathsf{w}}_{\Delta}$. If A has only few models, it is not necessary to calculate the complete preferred structure $<^{\mathsf{w}}_{\Delta}$ but only the small part of it on $Mod_{\Sigma}(A)$ to decide whether $(B|A)$ holds. Here, Proposition 4.25 might be used as well for reducing the computational effort.

4.6. Conditional Syntax Splitting

As seen in Section 3.9, respecting syntax splittings is an interesting property for inductive inference operators. However, depending on the application, syntax splittings into completely separate sub-bases might be rare. In some cases a belief base may nearly split into two parts that are only connected by a few atoms. Inspired by the conditional independence in probability theory, we can consider the parts of the belief base independent from each other *conditional* on the common atoms: under the condition that the values of these common atoms are known, the parts of the belief base can be considered as being independent.

This idea was formalized as *conditional syntax splitting* and first presented, together with corresponding postulates for inference operators, by Heyninck, Kern-Isberner, and Meyer [HKM22]; work on this was later expanded in [Hey+23].

Definition 4.27 (conditional syntax splitting [Hey+23])**.** *We say a belief base* Δ *can be* split into sub-bases Δ_1, Δ_2 conditional on a sub-signature Σ_3*, if there are sub-signatures* Σ_1, Σ_2 *such that* Σ_1, Σ_2, *and* Σ_3 *are pairwise disjoint,* $\Delta_i = \Delta \cap (\mathcal{L}|\mathcal{L})_{\Sigma_i \cup \Sigma_3}$ *for* $i = 1, 2$, *and* $\Sigma = \Sigma_1 \cup \Sigma_2 \cup \Sigma_3$. *This is denoted as*

$$\Delta = \Delta_1 \bigcup_{\Sigma_1,\Sigma_2} \Delta_2 \mid \Sigma_3.$$

A belief base $\Delta = \Delta_1 \bigcup_{\Sigma_1,\Sigma_2} \Delta_2 \mid \Sigma_3$ can be split into Δ_1, Δ_2 conditional on Σ_3, if every conditional in Δ_1 only uses atoms from $\Sigma_1 \cup \Sigma_3$ and every conditional in Δ_2 only uses atoms from $\Sigma_2 \cup \Sigma_3$. That means that the atoms in Σ_3 are the only link between Δ_1 and Δ_2. This thesis only covers conditional syntax splittings in two parts. Defining conditional splittings in arbitrary many parts and developing corresponding syntax splitting postulates for this kind of splittings is left for future research.

However, the above notion of conditional syntax splittings fails to completely separate the reasoning over Σ_1 and Σ_2. Verifying the conditionals in Δ_1 might require a certain valuation of Σ_3 which in turn causes falsification of conditionals in Δ_2. This is, for example, a problem for the construction of the Z-partition that is used by many inductive inference operators: the Z-partition on one sub-base may be affected by the other sub-base. An example and more detailed explanation of this can be found in [Hey+23]. To avoid this effect, the notion of *safe* conditional syntax splittings was introduced.

Definition 4.28 (safe conditional syntax splitting [Hey+23]). *A belief base* Δ *can be* safely split into sub-bases Δ_1, Δ_2 conditional on a sub-alphabet Σ_3, *if* $\Delta = \Delta_1 \bigcup_{\Sigma_1,\Sigma_2} \Delta_2 \mid \Sigma_3$ *and if, for* $i, j \in \{1, 2\}$ *with* $i \neq j$ *and for every* $\omega^3 \in \Omega_{\Sigma_i \cup \Sigma_3}$, *there is an* $\omega^j \in \Omega_{\Sigma^j}$ *such that* $\omega^j \omega^3 \not\models \bigvee_{(F|E) \in \Delta^j} E\overline{F}$. *This is denoted as*

$$\Delta = \Delta_1 \overset{s}{\bigcup_{\Sigma_1,\Sigma_2}} \Delta_2 \mid \Sigma_3.$$

Safe conditonal splittings are conditional splittings that additionally require that a valuation of Σ_3 may not imply the falsification of a conditional in Δ_1 or Δ_2. Thus, any information about $\Sigma_1 \cup \Sigma_3$ is compatible with conditionals in Δ_2 and any information about $\Sigma_2 \cup \Sigma_3$ is compatible with conditionals in Δ_1. This avoids the effect described above that verification of the conditional in one sub-base requires falsifying conditionals in the other sub-base. Safe conditional splittings ensure that tolerance of a conditional with respect to one sub-base of the syntax splitting is independent of the other sub-base.

Example 4.29. *Consider the signature* $\Sigma := \{m, b, e, t, g\}$ *from Example 3.48 and the belief base*

$$\Delta'_{ve} := \{(m|e), (g|m), (\overline{g}|me), (t|b), (\overline{m}|b)\}$$

over Σ. *The belief base* Δ'_{ve} *is* Δ_{ve} *extended by a conditional stating that bikes usually do not have motors. This belief base does not have a syntax splitting. However, it has the conditional syntax splitting*

$$\Delta'_{ve} = \Delta_1 \bigcup^{\mathsf{s}}_{\Sigma_1,\Sigma_2} \Delta_2 \mid \Sigma_3 \text{ with } \Sigma_1 = \{e, g\}, \Sigma_2 = \{b, t\}, \Sigma_3 = \{m\} \text{ and}$$
$$\begin{aligned} \Delta_1 &= \{(m|e), (g|m), (\overline{g}|me)\}, \\ \Delta_2 &= \{(t|b), (\overline{m}|b)\}. \end{aligned} \tag{4.5}$$

Let $\dot{m}\dot{b}\dot{t}$ *be a complete conjunction over* $\Sigma_3 \cup \Sigma_2$. *We can check that both for* $\dot{m}\dot{b}\dot{t} \models m$ *and for* $\dot{m}\dot{b}\dot{t} \models \overline{m}$ *the conjunction* $\overline{e}g\dot{m}\dot{b}\dot{t}$ *does not falsify any conditional in* Δ_1. *Let now* $\dot{m}\dot{e}\dot{g}$ *be a complete conjunction over* $\Sigma_3 \cup \Sigma_1$. *We can check that* $\overline{b}\,\overline{t}\dot{m}\dot{b}\dot{t}$ *does not falsify any conditional in* Δ_2. *Therefore, the conditional splitting in* (4.5) *is safe.*

Note that only belief bases that are at least weakly consistent can have safe conditional syntax splittings. For belief bases that are not weakly consistent we cannot find extensions $\omega^1\omega^3$ and $\omega^2\omega^3$ of any ω^3 without violating at least one conditional in Δ.

Proposition 4.30 ([Hey+23]). *Let* Δ *be a belief base with the safe conditional syntax splitting* $\Delta = \Delta_1 \bigcup^{\mathsf{s}}_{\Sigma_1,\Sigma_2} \Delta_2 \mid \Sigma_3$. *Then for* $i = 1, 2$ *it holds that* Δ_i *tolerates a conditional* $(B|A) \in \Delta_i$ *iff* Δ *tolerates* $(B|A)$.

Similarly to the postulates (Rel) and (Ind) based on syntax splittings, postulates for inductive inference operators can be formulated based on the notion of safe conditional syntax splittings. Assuming that a belief base has a safe conditional syntax splitting, the postulates (CRel) and (CInd) formalize independence between the sub-bases [Hey+23]. In these postulates, fixing a valuation of the atoms in Σ_3, as required for conditional independence, is realized by adding a complete conjunction over Σ_3 to the antecedents of the considered inferences.

(CRel) [Hey+23] An SCA-inductive inference operator $C : \Delta \mapsto \mathrel{|\!\sim}_\Delta$ satisfies **(CRel)** if for $\Delta = \Delta_1 \overset{s}{\underset{\Sigma_1,\Sigma_2}{\bigcup}} \Delta_2 \mid \Sigma_3$, for $i \in \{1,2\}$, for $A, B \in \mathcal{L}_{\Sigma_i}$ and for a complete conjunction $E \in \mathcal{L}_{\Sigma_3}$ we have that

$$AE \mathrel{|\!\sim}_\Delta B \quad \text{iff} \quad AE \mathrel{|\!\sim}_{\Delta_i} B.$$

(CInd) [Hey+23] An SCA-inductive inference operator $C : \Delta \mapsto \mathrel{|\!\sim}_\Delta$ satisfies **(CInd)** if for $\Delta = \Delta_1 \overset{s}{\underset{\Sigma_1,\Sigma_2}{\bigcup}} \Delta_2 \mid \Sigma_3$, for $i, j \in \{1,2\}, i \neq j$, for any $A, B \in \mathcal{L}_{\Sigma_i}$, $D \in \mathcal{L}_{\Sigma_j}$, and a complete conjunction $E \in \mathcal{L}_{\Sigma_3}$ such that $DE \mathrel{|\!\not\sim}_\Delta \bot$ we have

$$AE \mathrel{|\!\sim}_\Delta B \quad \text{iff} \quad ADE \mathrel{|\!\sim}_\Delta B.$$

The requirement that $DE \mathrel{|\!\not\sim}_\Delta \bot$ was added here analogous to the requirement that $D \mathrel{|\!\not\sim}_\Delta \bot$ in (Ind). Otherwise, (CInd) would require that $A \mathrel{|\!\sim}_\Delta \bot$ for every formula A (cf. Section 3.9).

The postulate (CSynSplit) is the combination of (CRel) and (CInd):

(CSynSplit) [Hey+23] An SCA-inductive inference operator satisfies **(CSynSplit)** if it satisfies (CRel) and (CInd).

Observe that each of the conditional splitting postulates (CRel), (CInd), and (CSynSplit) is a generalization of its corresponding splitting postulate (Rel), (Ind), or (CSynSplit), respectively. Every belief base with syntax splitting $\Delta = \Delta_1 \underset{\Sigma_1,\Sigma_2}{\bigcup} \Delta_2$ also has the conditional syntax splitting $\Delta = \Delta_1 \underset{\Sigma_1,\Sigma_2}{\bigcup} \Delta_2 \mid \Sigma_3$ with $\Sigma_3 = \emptyset$. If Δ is weakly consistent, this conditional syntax splitting is safe.

Proposition 4.31. *Let $\Delta = \Delta_1 \underset{\Sigma_1,\Sigma_2}{\bigcup} \Delta_2$ be a weakly consistent belief base with syntax splitting. Then $\Delta = \Delta_1 \overset{s}{\underset{\Sigma_1,\Sigma_2}{\bigcup}} \Delta_2 \mid \Sigma_3$ with $\Sigma_3 = \emptyset$ is a safe conditional syntax splitting for Δ.*

Proof. Because $\Delta = \Delta_1 \underset{\Sigma_1,\Sigma_2}{\bigcup} \Delta_2$ is a syntax splitting for Δ, we have that $\Delta = \Delta_1 \underset{\Sigma_1,\Sigma_2}{\bigcup} \Delta_2 \mid \Sigma_3$ is a conditional syntax splitting for Δ. Because Δ is weakly consistent, there is a world $\omega^* \in \Omega_\Sigma$ that does not falsify any conditional in Δ (see Lemma 2.2). Therefore, for $i, j \in \{1, 2\}$ such that $i \neq j$ we have that $\omega_j^* := \omega_{|\Sigma_j}$ does not falsify any conditional in Δ_j. Because of the syntax splitting, for every $\omega^3 \in \Omega_{\Sigma_i \cup \Sigma_3}$ we have that $\omega^j \omega^3$ does not falsify any conditional in Δ_j, i.e., $\omega^j \omega^3 \not\models \bigvee_{(F|E) \in \Delta^j} E\overline{F}$. Hence, $\Delta = \Delta_1 \overset{s}{\underset{\Sigma_1, \Sigma_2}{\bigcup}} \Delta_2 \mid \Sigma_3$ is a safe conditional syntax splitting. □

Therefore, (CRel) implies (Rel), the postulate (CInd) implies (Ind), and thus (CSynSplit) implies (SynSplit), as stated formally in the following lemma.

Lemma 4.32. *Let $C : \Delta \mapsto \mid\!\sim_\Delta$ be an SCA-inductive inference operator.*

1. *If C satisfies (CRel) then it satisfies (Rel).*
2. *If C satisfies (CInd) then it satisfies (Ind).*
3. *If C satisfies (CSynSplit) then it satisfies (SynSplit).*

Proof. Let $\Delta = \Delta_1 \underset{\Sigma_1, \Sigma_2}{\bigcup} \Delta_2$ be a weakly consistent belief base with syntax splitting. Proposition 4.31 yields that $\Delta = \Delta_1 \overset{s}{\underset{\Sigma_1, \Sigma_2}{\bigcup}} \Delta_2 \mid \Sigma_3$ with $\Sigma_3 = \emptyset$ is a safe conditional syntax splitting for Δ. The only complete conjunction over $\Sigma_3 = \emptyset$ is $\top$.

Ad (1): For any $i \in \{1, 2\}$ and $A, B \in \mathcal{L}_{\Sigma_i}$, with (CRel) we have that $AE \mid\!\sim_\Delta B$ iff $AE \mid\!\sim_{\Delta_i} B$. For the only complete conjunction $E = \top$, this implies $A \mid\!\sim_\Delta B$ iff $A \mid\!\sim_{\Delta_i} B$. Therefore, (Rel) holds.

Ad (2): For any $i, j \in \{1, 2\}$ such that $i \neq j$ and $A, B \in \mathcal{L}_{\Sigma_i}$ $D \in \Sigma_j$, with (CInd) we have that $AE \mid\!\sim_\Delta B$ iff $ADE \mid\!\sim_\Delta B$. For the only complete conjunction $E = \top$, this implies $A \mid\!\sim_\Delta B$ iff $AD \mid\!\sim_\Delta B$. Therefore, (Ind) holds.

Ad (3): This follows from (1) and (2) because (CSynSplit) is the conjunction of (CRel) and (CInd), and (SynSplit) is the conjunction of (Rel) and (Ind). □

Conditional syntax splitting is closely related to the drowning problem (see Section 3.4): an inference operator suffering from the drowning problem violates (CInd). In this sense "violating (CInd)" can be seen as a formal definition of the drowning problem that does not depend on a single example [Hey+23].

Similarly to (Rel^{spo}) and (Ind^{spo}) we can formulate versions of the conditional splitting postulates for fSPO-representable inductive inference operators.

($\mathbf{CRel}^{spo}$) An fSPO-representable inductive inference operator $C^{spo}: \Delta \mapsto \prec_\Delta$ satisfies **($\mathbf{CRel}^{spo}$)** if for $\Delta = \Delta_1 \bigcup_{\Sigma_1,\Sigma_2} \Delta_2 \mid \Sigma_3$, for $i \in \{1,2\}$, for $A, B \in \mathcal{L}_{\Sigma_i}$, and for a complete conjunction $E \in \mathcal{L}_{\Sigma_3}$ such that AE, BE are consistent we have that

$$AE \prec_\Delta BE \quad \text{iff} \quad AE \prec_{\Delta_i} BE.$$

($\mathbf{CInd}^{spo}$) An fSPO-representable inductive inference operator $C^{spo}: \Delta \mapsto \prec_\Delta$ satisfies **($\mathbf{CInd}^{spo}$)** if for $\Delta = \Delta_1 \bigcup_{\Sigma_1,\Sigma_2} \Delta_2 \mid \Sigma_3$, for $i, j \in \{1,2\}, i \neq j$, for $A, B \in \mathcal{L}_{\Sigma_i}$, $D \in \mathcal{L}_{\Sigma_j}$, and for a complete conjunction $E \in \mathcal{L}_{\Sigma_3}$ such that AE, BE, DE are consistent we have

$$AE \prec_\Delta BE \quad \text{iff} \quad ADE \prec_\Delta BDE.$$

($\mathbf{CSynSplit}^{spo}$) An fSPO-representable inductive inference operator satisfies **($\mathbf{CSynSplit}^{spo}$)** if it satisfies (CRel^{spo}) and (CInd^{spo}).

For fSPO-representable inference operators, the conditional syntax splitting postulates are equivalent to their general versions.

Proposition 4.33. *An fSPO-representable inductive inference operator satisfies ($CRel^{spo}$) iff it satisfies (CRel).*

Proof. Let $\Delta = \Delta_1 \overset{s}{\bigcup_{\Sigma_1,\Sigma_2}} \Delta_2 \mid \Sigma_3$ be a strongly consistent belief base. For $i \in \{1,2\}$ let $A, B \in \mathcal{L}_{\Sigma_i}$ and let E be a complete conjunction over Σ_3.

Direction $\Rightarrow$: Assume that the inductive inference operator satisfies (CRel^{spo}). If $A\overline{B}E$ is inconsistent, then $AE \mid\!\sim_\Delta B$ and $AE \mid\!\sim_{\Delta_i} B$ and (CRel) holds. If $A\overline{B}E$ is consistent and ABE is inconsistent, then $AE \not\mid\!\sim_\Delta B$ and $AE \not\mid\!\sim_{\Delta_i} B$ and (CRel) holds. If both $A\overline{B}E$ and ABE are consistent, we have, because $AB, A\overline{B} \in \mathcal{L}_{\Sigma_i}$,

$$AE \mid\!\sim_\Delta B \quad \text{iff} \quad ABE \prec_\Delta A\overline{B}E \quad \text{iff} \quad ABE \prec_{\Delta_i} A\overline{B}E \quad \text{iff} \quad AE \mid\!\sim_{\Delta_i} B.$$

Direction $\Leftarrow$: Assume that the inductive inference operator satisfies (CRel), and let AE, BE be consistent. Because $A, A \vee B \in \mathcal{L}_{\Sigma_i}$, we have

$$AE \prec_\Delta BE \quad \text{iff} \quad (A \vee B)E \mid\!\sim_\Delta A \quad \text{iff} \quad (A \vee B)E \mid\!\sim_{\Delta_i} A \quad \text{iff} \quad AE \prec_{\Delta_i} BE.$$

□

Proposition 4.34. *An fSPO-representable inductive inference operator satisfies (CInd^{spo}) iff it satisfies (CInd).*

Proof. Let $\Delta = \Delta_1 \overset{\mathsf{s}}{\bigcup}_{\Sigma_1,\Sigma_2} \Delta_2 \mid \Sigma_3$ be a strongly consistent belief base. For $i, j \in \{1, 2\}, i \neq j$ let $A, B \in \mathcal{L}_{\Sigma_i}$, $D \in \mathcal{L}_{\Sigma_j}$, and let E be a complete conjunction over Σ_3 such that $DE \not\mid\!\sim_\Delta \bot$. By Definitions 4.5 and 4.6 this implies that DE is consistent.

Direction $\Rightarrow$: Assume that the inductive inference operator satisfies (CInd^{spo}). Observe that ABE is consistent iff $ABDE$ is consistent and that $A\overline{B}E$ is consistent iff $A\overline{B}DE$ is consistent, because DE is consistent, E is a complete conjunction over Σ_3, and D does not share any atoms with A or B outside of Σ_3. If $A\overline{B}E$ and thus $A\overline{B}DE$ are inconsistent, then $AE \mid\!\sim_\Delta B$ and $ADE \mid\!\sim_{\Delta_i} B$ hold, and (CInd) is satisfied. If $A\overline{B}E$ is consistent and ABE inconsistent, then $AE \not\mid\!\sim_\Delta B$ and $ADE \not\mid\!\sim_{\Delta_i} B$, and (CInd) is satisfied. For the remainder of the proof assume that ABE and $A\overline{B}E$ (and thus also $ABDE$ and $A\overline{B}DE$) are consistent. Because $AB, A\overline{B} \in \mathcal{L}_{\Sigma_i}$, we have

$$AE \mid\!\sim_\Delta B \quad \text{iff} \quad ABE \prec_\Delta A\overline{B}E \quad \text{iff} \quad ABDE \prec_\Delta A\overline{B}DE \quad \text{iff} \quad ADE \mid\!\sim_\Delta B.$$

Direction $\Leftarrow$: Assume that the inductive inference operator satisfies (CInd) and let AE, BE be consistent. Because $A, A\vee B \in \mathcal{L}_{\Sigma_i}$ and $D \in \mathcal{L}_{\Sigma_j}$, we have

$$AE \prec_\Delta BE \quad \text{iff} \quad (A \vee B)E \mid\!\sim_\Delta A \quad \text{iff} \quad (A \vee B)DE \mid\!\sim_\Delta A \quad \text{iff} \quad ADE \prec_\Delta BDE.$$

□

Thus, an fSPO-representable inductive inference operator satisfies (CSynSplit^{spo}) iff it satisfies (CSynSplit).

We will use the postulates (CRel^{spo}), (CInd^{spo}), and (CSynSplit^{spo}) to show that system W complies with conditional syntax splitting.

4.7. System W satisfies Conditional Syntax Splitting

In this section, we show that system W satisfies the conditional syntax splitting postulates. Because system W is an fSPO-representable inductive inference operator we can do this by showing that system W satisfies (CRel^{spo}), (CInd^{spo}), and thus (CSynSplit^{spo}). First, we prove four lemmas on the properties of the preferred structure on worlds $<^{\mathsf{w}}_{\Delta}$ induced by a belief base with a conditional syntax splitting $\Delta = \Delta_1 \bigcup^{\mathsf{s}}_{\Sigma_1,\Sigma_2} \Delta_2 \mid \Sigma_3$. Then we use these lemmas to show that system W satisfies (CSynSplit^{spo}).

As in Section 4.4 we consider the belief bases Δ_1, Δ_2 as belief bases over $\Sigma = \Sigma_1 \cup \Sigma_2$ in this section. In particular, $<^{\mathsf{w}}_{\Delta_1}$ and $<^{\mathsf{w}}_{\Delta_2}$ are relations on Ω_Σ and the inference relations induced by Δ_1, Δ_2 are defined with respect to Σ.

The following Lemma 4.35 shows the effect of a conditional syntax splitting of a belief base on its corresponding Z-partition.

Lemma 4.35. *Let $\Delta = \Delta_1 \bigcup^{\mathsf{s}}_{\Sigma_1,\Sigma_2} \Delta_2 \mid \Sigma_3$ be a strongly consistent belief base with safe conditional syntax splitting. Let $OP(\Delta) = (\Delta^0, \dots, \Delta^k)$ be the Z-partition of Δ and for $i \in \{1,2\}$, let $OP(\Delta_i) = (\Delta_i^0, \dots, \Delta_i^{l_i})$ be the Z-partition of Δ_i.*

1. *For $i \in \{1,2\}$ and $j \in \{0,\dots,l_i\}$, it holds that $\Delta_i^j = \Delta^j \cap \Delta_i$ and thus especially $\Delta_i^j \subseteq \Delta^j$.*
2. $\max\{l_1, l_2\} = k$
3. *If $l_1 \leq l_2$, we have* $\Delta^j = \begin{cases} \Delta_1^j \cup \Delta_2^j & \text{for } j = 1,\dots,l_1 \\ \Delta_2^j & \text{for } j = l_1+1,\dots,k \end{cases}$

Proof. **Ad 1.:** Because we can swap the indices 1, 2 in the conditional syntax splitting, we can assume that $i = 1$ and $j = 2$ without loss of generality. We will show that $\Delta_1^0 = \Delta^0 \cap \Delta_1$ for $\Delta_1 \neq \emptyset$. This implies $\Delta_1^j = \Delta^j \cap \Delta_1$ for $j = 1,\dots,l_1$ as the Z-partition can be constructed by recursively selecting the conditionals tolerated by all other conditionals in the belief base.

A conditional $r \in \Delta_1$ is tolerated by all conditionals in Δ iff it is tolerated by all conditional in Δ_1 (see Proposition 4.30). If $q \in \Delta_1^0$, then it is in Δ_1 and tolerated by every conditional in Δ_1. Hence, q is also in Δ and tolerated by every conditional in Δ (see above). Thus,

$q \in \Delta^0 \cap \Delta_1$. If $p \in \Delta^0 \cap \Delta_1$, then it is in Δ_1 and it is tolerated by every conditional in Δ. Therefore, q is also tolerated by Δ_1. Thus, $q \in \Delta_1^0$. Together, we have $\Delta_1^0 = \Delta^0 \cap \Delta_1$.

Ad 2: As $\Delta_i \subseteq \Delta$ for $i = 1, 2$ we have $l_1, l_2 \leq k$. As Δ_k is not empty, it contains at least one conditional r. This r is either in Δ_1 or in Δ_2. Let $i \in \{1, 2\}$ be such that $r \in \Delta_i$. Then there is some m such that $r \in \Delta_i^m$. With (1.) we have $\Delta_i^m \subseteq \Delta^m$. As r can only be in one set of the Z-partition of Δ we have $m = k$. Therefore, the Z-partition of Δ_i has at least k elements, and thus $l_i = k$.

Ad 3: First, consider the case that $j \leq l_1$ and therefore also $j \leq l_2$. As $\Delta_i^j \subseteq \Delta^j$ for $i = 1, 2$ we get $\Delta^j \supseteq \Delta_1^j \cup \Delta_2^j$. Every $r \in \Delta^j$ is either in Δ_1 or in Δ_2. W.l.o.g. assume $r \in \Delta_1$. Then there is some m such that $r \in \Delta_1^m$. With (1.) we have $\Delta_1^m \subseteq \Delta^m$. As r can only be in one set of the Z-partition of Δ we have $m = j$. Therefore, $\Delta^j \subseteq \Delta_1^j \cup \Delta_2^j$ and thus $\Delta^j = \Delta_1^j \cup \Delta_2^j$.

Now consider $l_1 < j \leq k$. From (1.) we get $\Delta^j \supseteq \Delta_2^j$. Analogous to the first case, we know that every conditional $r \in \Delta^j$ is either in Δ_1^j or Δ_2^j. Because $j > l_1$ there is no Δ_1^j in the Z-partition of Δ_1, and thus we have $r \in \Delta_2^j$. Therefore, $\Delta^j \subseteq \Delta_2^j$ and thus $\Delta^j = \Delta_2^j$. □

If we have $\omega <^{\mathsf{w}}_{\Delta} \omega'$, then there is some conditional r that falsifies ω' but not ω and thus causes the $\subsetneqq$ relation in (3.5) in Definition 3.19. For $\Delta = \Delta_1 \overset{\mathsf{s}}{\underset{\Sigma_1,\Sigma_2}{\bigcup}} \Delta_2 \mid \Sigma_3$, this r is either in Δ_1 or in Δ_2 (or both). Lemma 4.36 states that the relation $\omega <^{\mathsf{w}}_{\Delta} \omega'$ can then also be obtained using only Δ_1 or only Δ_2.

Lemma 4.36. *Let $\Delta = \Delta_1 \overset{\mathsf{s}}{\underset{\Sigma_1,\Sigma_2}{\bigcup}} \Delta_2 \mid \Sigma_3$ be a strongly consistent belief base and let $\omega, \omega' \in \Omega_\Sigma$. If $\omega <^{\mathsf{w}}_{\Delta} \omega'$, then $\omega <^{\mathsf{w}}_{\Delta_1} \omega'$ or $\omega <^{\mathsf{w}}_{\Delta_2} \omega'$.*

Proof. Let $\Delta = \Delta_1 \overset{\mathsf{s}}{\underset{\Sigma_1,\Sigma_2}{\bigcup}} \Delta_2 \mid \Sigma_3$. Let $OP(\Delta) = (\Delta^0, \ldots, \Delta^k)$ be the Z-partition of Δ and let ξ, ξ^i be the functions mapping worlds to the sets of falsified conditionals as in Definition 3.19. Let $\omega, \omega' \in \Omega_\Sigma$ be worlds with $\omega <^{\mathsf{w}}_{\Delta} \omega'$. By definition of $<^{\mathsf{w}}_{\Delta}$ there is an $m \in \{0, \ldots, k\}$ such that $\xi^i(\omega) = \xi^i(\omega')$ for every $i = m+1, \ldots, k$ and $\xi^m(\omega) \subsetneqq \xi^m(\omega')$. Therefore, there is an $r \in \Delta$ such that $r \in \xi^m(\omega')$ and $r \notin \xi^m(\omega)$. The conditional r must be in Δ_1 or Δ_2. Assume that $r \in \Delta_x$ with x being either 1 or 2. Let $OP(\Delta_x) = (\Delta_x^0, \ldots, \Delta_x^l)$ be the Z-partition of Δ_x

and let ξ_x, ξ_x^i for $i = 0, \dots, k$ be the functions mapping worlds to the set of falsified conditionals for Δ_x. Because $\Delta_x^i \subseteq \Delta^i$ (see Lemma 4.35) and $\xi^i(\omega) = \xi^i(\omega')$ for every $i = m+1, \dots, k$ we have $\xi_x^i(\omega) = \xi_x^i(\omega')$ for every $i = m+1, \dots, l$. And because $r \in \xi_x^m(\omega')$ and $r \notin \xi_x^m(\omega)$ we have $\xi_x^m(\omega) \subsetneqq \xi_x^m(\omega')$. Therefore, $\omega <^{\mathsf{w}}_{\Delta_x} \omega'$.

Hence, we have $\omega <^{\mathsf{w}}_{\Delta_1} \omega'$ or $\omega <^{\mathsf{w}}_{\Delta_2} \omega'$. □

Note, that both $\omega <^{\mathsf{w}}_{\Delta_1} \omega'$ and $\omega <^{\mathsf{w}}_{\Delta_2} \omega'$ might be true.

The next Lemma 4.37 considers the reverse direction of Lemma 4.36 and shows a situation where we can infer $\omega <^{\mathsf{w}}_{\Delta} \omega'$ from $\omega <^{\mathsf{w}}_{\Delta_1} \omega'$ for a belief base $\Delta = \Delta_1 \overset{\mathsf{s}}{\underset{\Sigma_1,\Sigma_2}{\bigcup}} \Delta_2 \mid \Sigma_3$.

Lemma 4.37. *Let* $\Delta = \Delta_1 \overset{\mathsf{s}}{\underset{\Sigma_1,\Sigma_2}{\bigcup}} \Delta_2 \mid \Sigma_3$ *be a strongly consistent belief base, let* $\omega, \omega' \in \Omega_\Sigma$, *and let* $i, j \in \{1, 2\}, i \neq j$. *If* $\omega <^{\mathsf{w}}_{\Delta_i} \omega'$ *and* $\omega_{|\Sigma_j \cup \Sigma_3} = \omega'_{|\Sigma_j \cup \Sigma_3}$, *then* $\omega <^{\mathsf{w}}_{\Delta} \omega'$.

Proof. Because we can swap the indices 1, 2 in the conditional syntax splitting, we can assume $i = 1$ and $j = 2$ without loss of generality. Let $\omega, \omega' \in \Omega_\Sigma$ with $\omega <^{\mathsf{w}}_{\Delta_1} \omega'$ and $\omega_{|\Sigma_2 \cup \Sigma_3} = \omega'_{|\Sigma_2 \cup \Sigma_3}$. Let $OP(\Delta) = (\Delta^0, \dots, \Delta^k)$ be the Z-partition of Δ and let ξ, ξ^i be the functions mapping worlds to the sets of falsified conditionals as in Definition 3.19. Let $OP(\Delta_1) = (\Delta_1^0, \dots, \Delta_1^l)$ be the Z-partition of Δ_1. For $x \in \{1, 2\}$ and for $i \in \{0, \dots, k\}$ let ξ_x, ξ_x^i be the functions mapping worlds to the sets of falsified conditionals for Δ_x. By definition of $<^{\mathsf{w}}_{\Delta_1}$ there is an $m \in \{0, \dots, l\}$ such that $\xi_1^i(\omega) = \xi_1^i(\omega')$ for every $i = m+1, \dots, l$ and $\xi_1^m(\omega) \subsetneqq \xi_1^m(\omega')$. For every world ω^*, $x = 1, 2$ and $j = 0, \dots, l$ with Lemma 4.35 we have that $\xi_x^j(\omega^*) = \{r \in \Delta_x^j \mid \omega \text{ falsifies } r\} = \{r \in \Delta_x \cap \Delta^j \mid \omega^* \text{ falsifies } r\} = \xi^j(\omega^*) \cap \Delta_x$. This implies $\xi^i(\omega) \cap \Delta_1 = \xi_1^i(\omega) = \xi_1^i(\omega') = \xi^i(\omega') \cap \Delta_1$ for every $i = m+1, \dots, k$ and $\xi^m(\omega) \cap \Delta_1 = \xi_1^m(\omega) \subsetneqq \xi_1^m(\omega) = \xi^m(\omega') \cap \Delta_1$. Because $\omega_{|\Sigma_2 \cup \Sigma_3} = \omega'_{|\Sigma_2 \cup \Sigma_3}$, we have $\xi^i(\omega) \cap \Delta_2 = \xi^i(\omega') \cap \Delta_2$ for every $i = 0, \dots, k$. Hence, we have $\xi^i(\omega) = \xi^i(\omega')$ for every $i = m+1, \dots, k$ and $\xi^m(\omega) \subsetneqq \xi^m(\omega')$; and therefore $\omega <^{\mathsf{w}}_{\Delta} \omega'$. □

The next Lemma 4.38 states that the variable assignment for variables that do not occur in the belief base has no influence on the position of a world in the preferred structure on worlds induced by this belief base.

Lemma 4.38. *Let* $\Delta = \Delta_1 \bigcup_{\Sigma_1,\Sigma_2} \Delta_2 \mid \Sigma_3$ *be a strongly consistent belief base with conditional syntax splitting, let* $i \in \{1,2\}$, *and let* $\omega^a, \omega^b, \omega' \in \Omega_\Sigma$ *with* $\omega^a{}_{|\Sigma_i \cup \Sigma_3} = \omega^b{}_{|\Sigma_i \cup \Sigma_3}$. *Then we have* $\omega^a <^{\mathsf{w}}_{\Delta_i} \omega'$ *iff* $\omega^b <^{\mathsf{w}}_{\Delta_i} \omega'$ *and we have* $\omega' <^{\mathsf{w}}_{\Delta_i} \omega^a$ *iff* $\omega' <^{\mathsf{w}}_{\Delta_i} \omega^b$.

Proof. This is an immediate consequence of Lemma 4.13. □

Using these lemmas, we show that system W fulfils both (CRel^{spo}) and (CInd^{spo}).

Proposition 4.39. *System W fulfils (CRel^{spo}).*

Proof. Let $\Delta = \Delta_1 \bigcup^{\mathsf{s}}_{\Sigma_1,\Sigma_2} \Delta_2 \mid \Sigma_3$ be a strongly consistent belief base with a safe conditional syntax splitting, let $i \in \{1,2\}$, let $A, B \in \mathcal{L}_{\Sigma_i}$ be propositional formulas, and let $E \in \mathcal{L}_{\Sigma_3}$ be a complete disjunction such that AE, BE are consistent. We need to show that

$$AE <^{\mathsf{w}}_{\Delta} BE \text{ if and only if } AE <^{\mathsf{w}}_{\Delta_i} BE. \tag{4.6}$$

Because we can swap the indices 1, 2 in the conditional syntax splitting, we can assume $i = 1$ without loss of generality.

Direction ⇒ of (4.6): Assume that $AE <^{\mathsf{w}}_{\Delta} BE$. We need to show that $AE <^{\mathsf{w}}_{\Delta_1} BE$. Let ω' be any world in $Mod_\Sigma(BE)$. Now choose $\omega'_{min} \in \Omega_\Sigma$ such that

1. $\omega'_{min} \preceq^{\mathsf{w}}_{\Delta} \omega'$,
2. $\omega'_{|\Sigma_1 \cup \Sigma_3} = \omega'_{min|\Sigma_1 \cup \Sigma_3}$, and
3. there is no $\omega'_* \in \Omega_\Sigma$ with $\omega'_* < \omega'_{min}$ that fulfils (1.) and (2.).

Such an ω'_{min} exists because ω' fulfils properties (1.) and (2.), $<^{\mathsf{w}}_{\Delta}$ is irreflexive and transitive, and there are only finitely many worlds in Ω_Σ.

Because of (2.) and because $\omega' \models BE$ we have that $\omega'_{min} \models BE$. Because $AE <^{\mathsf{w}}_{\Delta} BE$, there is a world ω such that $\omega \models AE$ and $\omega <^{\mathsf{w}}_{\Delta} \omega'_{min}$. Lemma 4.36 yields that $\omega <^{\mathsf{w}}_{\Delta_1} \omega'_{min}$ or $\omega <^{\mathsf{w}}_{\Delta_2} \omega'_{min}$. The case $\omega <^{\mathsf{w}}_{\Delta_2} \omega'_{min}$ is not possible: Assuming $\omega <^{\mathsf{w}}_{\Delta_2} \omega'_{min}$, it follows that for $\omega'_* := \omega'_{min|\Sigma_1} \omega_{|\Sigma_2 \cup \Sigma_3}$ we have $\omega_{min2} <^{\mathsf{w}}_{\Delta_2} \omega'_{min}$ with Lemma 4.38. Because $\omega \models E$ and $\omega'_{min} \models E$ we have that $\omega_{|\Sigma_3} = \omega'_{min|\Sigma_3}$ and therefore $\omega'_{*|\Sigma_1 \cup \Sigma_3} = \omega'_{min|\Sigma_1 \cup \Sigma_3}$. With Lemma 4.37 it follows that $\omega'_* <^{\mathsf{w}}_{\Delta} \omega'_{min}$. This contradicts (3.). Hence, $\omega <^{\mathsf{w}}_{\Delta_1} \omega'_{min}$. Because of (2.) and Lemma 4.38 it follows that $\omega <^{\mathsf{w}}_{\Delta_1} \omega'$. As we can find an ω

such that $\omega <^{\mathsf{w}}_{\Delta_1} \omega'$ and $\omega \models AE$ for every $\omega' \models BE$ we have that $AE <^{\mathsf{w}}_{\Delta_1} BE$.

Direction $\Leftarrow$ of (4.6): Assume that $AE <^{\mathsf{w}}_{\Delta_1} BE$. We need to show that $AE <^{\mathsf{w}}_{\Delta} BE$. Let ω' be any world in $Mod_\Sigma(BE)$. Because $AE <^{\mathsf{w}}_{\Delta_1} BE$, there is a world ω^* such that $\omega^* \models AE$ and $\omega^* <^{\mathsf{w}}_{\Delta_1} \omega'$. Let $\omega := \omega^*_{|\Sigma_1 \cup \Sigma_3} \omega'_{|\Sigma_2}$. Because $\omega^* \models AE$ we have that $\omega \models AE$. Because $\omega^* \models E$ and $\omega' \models E$ we have that $\omega^*_{|\Sigma_3} = \omega'_{|\Sigma_3}$ and therefore $\omega_{|\Sigma_2 \cup \Sigma_3} = \omega'_{|\Sigma_2 \cup \Sigma_3}$. Furthermore, with Lemma 4.38 it follows that $\omega <^{\mathsf{w}}_{\Delta_1} \omega'$ and thus $\omega <^{\mathsf{w}}_{\Delta} \omega'$ with Lemma 4.37. As we can construct an ω such that $\omega <^{\mathsf{w}}_{\Delta} \omega'$ and $\omega \models AE$ for every $\omega' \models BE$ we have that $AE <^{\mathsf{w}}_{\Delta} BE$. □

Proposition 4.40. *System W fulfils* ($CInd^{spo}$).

Proof. Let $\Delta = \Delta_1 \bigcup^{s}_{\Sigma_1,\Sigma_2} \Delta_2 \mid \Sigma_3$ be a strongly consistent belief base with a safe conditional syntax splitting and let $i, j \in \{1, 2\}, i \neq j$. Let $A, B \in \mathcal{L}_{\Sigma_i}$ and $D \in \mathcal{L}_{\Sigma_j}$, and let $E \in \mathcal{L}_{\Sigma_3}$ be a complete conjunction such that AE, BE, DE are consistent. We need to show that

$$AE <^{\mathsf{w}}_{\Delta} BE \text{ if and only if } ADE <^{\mathsf{w}}_{\Delta} BDE. \tag{4.7}$$

Because we can swap the indices 1, 2 in the conditional syntax splitting, we can assume $i = 1$ and $j = 2$ without loss of generality.

Direction $\Rightarrow$ of (4.7): Assume that $AE <^{\mathsf{w}}_{\Delta} BE$. We need to show that $ADE <^{\mathsf{w}}_{\Delta} BDE$. Let ω' be any world in $Mod_\Sigma(BDE)$. Now choose $\omega'_{min} \in \Omega_\Sigma$ such that

1. $\omega'_{min} \preceq^{\mathsf{w}}_{\Delta} \omega'$,
2. $\omega'_{|\Sigma_1 \cup \Sigma_3} = \omega'_{min|\Sigma_1 \cup \Sigma_3}$, and
3. there is no $\omega'_* \in \Omega_\Sigma$ with $\omega'_* < \omega'_{min}$ that fulfils (1.) and (2.).

Such an ω'_{min} exists because ω' fulfils properties (1.) and (2.), $<^{\mathsf{w}}_{\Delta}$ is irreflexive and transitive, and there are only finitely many worlds in Ω_Σ. Because of (2.) and because $\omega' \models BDE$ we have that $\omega'_{min} \models BE$. Because $AE <^{\mathsf{w}}_{\Delta} BE$, there is a world ω^* such that $\omega^* \models AE$ and $\omega^* <^{\mathsf{w}}_{\Delta} \omega'_{min}$. Lemma 4.36 yields that either $\omega^* <^{\mathsf{w}}_{\Delta_1} \omega'_{min}$ or $\omega^* <^{\mathsf{w}}_{\Delta_2} \omega'_{min}$. The case $\omega^* <^{\mathsf{w}}_{\Delta_2} \omega'_{min}$ is not possible: Assuming $\omega^* <^{\mathsf{w}}_{\Delta_2} \omega'_{min}$, it follows that for $\omega'_* := \omega'_{min|\Sigma_1} \omega^*_{|\Sigma_2 \cup \Sigma_3}$ we have that $\omega'_* <^{\mathsf{w}}_{\Delta_2} \omega'_{min}$ with Lemma 4.38. With Lemma 4.37 it follows that $\omega'_{min2} <^{\mathsf{w}}_{\Delta} \omega'_{min}$. This contradicts (3.). Hence, $\omega^* <^{\mathsf{w}}_{\Delta_1} \omega'_{min}$. Let $\omega := \omega^*_{|\Sigma_1 \cup \Sigma_3} \omega'_{|\Sigma_2}$. Because $\omega^* \models AE$ we have that $\omega \models AE$. Because $\omega' \models D$ we have that $\omega \models D$.

Because $\omega^* \models E$ and $\omega' \models E$ we have that $\omega^*_{|\Sigma_3} = \omega'_{|\Sigma_3}$ and therefore $\omega_{|\Sigma_2 \cup \Sigma_3} = \omega'_{|\Sigma_2 \cup \Sigma_3}$. Because of (2.) and Lemma 4.38 it follows that $\omega <^{\mathsf{w}}_{\Delta_1} \omega'$ and thus with Lemma 4.37 it follows that $\omega <^{\mathsf{w}}_{\Delta} \omega'$. As we can construct an ω for every ω' we have that $ADE <^{\mathsf{w}}_{\Delta} BDE$.

Direction $\Leftarrow$ of (4.7): Assume that $ADE <^{\mathsf{w}}_{\Delta} BDE$. We need to show that $AE <^{\mathsf{w}}_{\Delta} BE$. Let ω' be any world in $Mod_{\Sigma}(BE)$. Now choose $\omega'_{min} \in \Omega_{\Sigma}$ such that

1. $\omega'_{min} \models D$
2. $\omega'_{|\Sigma_1 \cup \Sigma_3} = \omega'_{min|\Sigma_1 \cup \Sigma_3}$, and
3. there is no $\omega'_* \in \Omega_{\Sigma}$ with $\omega_* <^{\mathsf{w}}_{\Delta} \omega'_{min}$ that fulfils (1.) and (2.).

Such an ω'_{min} exists because D is consistent, $<^{\mathsf{w}}_{\Delta}$ is irreflexive and transitive, and there are only finitely many worlds in Ω_{Σ}. Because of (2.) and because $\omega' \models BE$ we have that $\omega'_{min} \models BE$. Because of (1.) we have that $\omega'_{min} \models D$. Because $ADE <^{\mathsf{w}}_{\Delta} BDE$, there is a world ω^* such that $\omega^* \models ADE$ and $\omega^* <^{\mathsf{w}}_{\Delta} \omega'_{min}$. Lemma 4.36 yields that either $\omega^* <^{\mathsf{w}}_{\Delta_1} \omega'_{min}$ or $\omega^* <^{\mathsf{w}}_{\Delta_2} \omega'_{min}$. The case $\omega^* <^{\mathsf{w}}_{\Delta_2} \omega'_{min}$ is not possible: Assuming $\omega^* <^{\mathsf{w}}_{\Delta_2} \omega'_{min}$, it follows that for $\omega'_* := \omega'_{min|\Sigma_1} \omega^*_{|\Sigma_2 \cup \Sigma_3}$ we have that $\omega'_* <^{\mathsf{w}}_{\Delta_2} \omega'_{min}$ with Lemma 4.38. With Lemma 4.37 it follows that $\omega'_* <^{\mathsf{w}}_{\Delta} \omega'_{min}$. This contradicts (3.). Hence, $\omega^* <^{\mathsf{w}}_{\Delta_1} \omega'_{min}$. Let $\omega := \omega^*_{|\Sigma_1 \cup \Sigma_3} \omega'_{|\Sigma_2}$. Because $\omega^* \models AE$ we have that $\omega \models AE$. Because $\omega^* \models E$ and $\omega' \models E$ we have that $\omega^*_{|\Sigma_3} = \omega'_{|\Sigma_3}$ and therefore $\omega_{|\Sigma_2 \cup \Sigma_3} = \omega'_{|\Sigma_2 \cup \Sigma_3}$. Because of (2.) and Lemma 4.38 it follows that $\omega <^{\mathsf{w}}_{\Delta_1} \omega'$ and thus with Lemma 4.37 $\omega <^{\mathsf{w}}_{\Delta} \omega'$. As we can construct such an ω for every ω' we have that $A <^{\mathsf{w}}_{\Delta} B$. □

Combining the results from Proposition 4.39 and Proposition 4.40 with the Propositions 4.33 and 4.34 yields the following Proposition.

Proposition 4.41. *System W fulfils (CRel) and (CInd), and thus (CSynSplit).*

This makes system W, besides lexicographic inference ([Leh95], see Section 3.6), the up to now only inductive inference operator that has been proven to satisfy both syntax splitting and also conditional syntax splitting [Hey+23].

To summarize, in this chapter we investigate various properties of system W. We found proofs or counterexamples for system W regarding a set of common postulates for inference relations and pointed out that system W belongs to a class of inference operators that can be represented by full SPOs on worlds. Furthermore, we showed that system W complies with syntax splittings and even the more general conditional syntax splittings.

Chapter 5

Dealing with Infeasible Worlds

System W and c-inference are defined as SCA-inductive inference operators; i.e., they are only defined for inference from strongly consistent belief bases but not for belief bases that are only weakly consistent. In this chapter we fill this gap by extending system W and c-inference to weakly consistent belief bases. To distinguish the different definitions, we call the new inference operators *extended* system W and *extended* c-inference.

Towards this goal, we first discuss the role of infeasible worlds for modelling belief bases that are only weakly consistent in Section 5.1. Then, in Section 5.2 we introduce extended system W and evaluate it with respect to the postulates that we already applied to system W in Section 4.1. In Section 5.3 we introduce *limited* SPOs on worlds (*lSPO*), which are SPOs over a subset of Ω_Σ. Limited SPOs on worlds are a generalization of full SPOs on worlds and are semantic structures that can represent the extended system W inference relations. We adapt the syntax splitting postulates for SPO-representable inference operators in Section 5.4 and use them to show that, similar to system W, extended system W also satisfies syntax splitting in Section 5.5.

In Section 5.6, we introduce extended c-representations as semantic models that are able to deal with infeasible worlds, and based on that we define extended c-inference. We show how extended c-representations (Section 5.7) and extended c-inference (Section 5.8) can be characterized by constraint satisfaction problems. Furthermore, we show that extended c-inference, just as c-inference, complies with syntax splitting in Section 5.9.

Extended system W was first introduced and shown to satisfy syntax splitting in [Hal+23a], while 1SPO-representablity was first covered (with a different name and notation) in [Hal+23b]. Extended c-representations and extended c-inference, as well as the corresponding characterizations via CSPs origin from [HBK23b]. The result that extended c-inference complies with syntax splitting is also published in [HBK24].

5.1. Modelling Not Strongly Consistent Belief Bases with Infeasible Worlds

If a ranking function κ models a belief base Δ that is not strongly consistent, by Definition 2.1 of strong consistency, κ must assign rank ∞ to at least one world, i.e., consider at least one world infeasible. But not only ranking functions, also preferential inference relations that satisfy (DI) with respect to Δ must consider some worlds to be infeasible. More specifically, with Lemma 3.17 we see that for a world ω it holds that $\omega \mathrel{|\!\sim}^{p}_{\Delta} \bot$ iff $\kappa^{z+}_{\Delta}(\omega) = \infty$. Thus, by Definition 3.16 of κ^{z+}_{Δ}, we have that $\omega \mathrel{|\!\sim}^{p}_{\Delta} \bot$ if and only if ω falsifies at least one conditional in the set Δ^{∞} from the extended Z-partition of Δ. Note that by Proposition 3.15, Δ^{∞} is empty only if Δ is strongly consistent.

Lemma 5.1. *Let Δ be a belief base with $EP(\Delta) = (\Delta^0, \ldots, \Delta^k, \Delta^{\infty})$. For any world $\omega \in \Omega_{\Sigma}$ it holds that $\omega \mathrel{|\!\sim}^{p}_{\Delta} \bot$ iff ω falsifies a conditional in Δ^{∞}.*

For every preferential inductive inference operator $C : \Delta \mapsto \mathrel{|\!\sim}_{\Delta}$ it holds that $\omega \mathrel{|\!\sim}^{p}_{\Delta} \bot$ implies $\omega \mathrel{|\!\sim}_{\Delta} \bot$. Therefore, inference relations induced by a preferential inference operator must consider worlds that falsify a conditional in Δ^{∞} infeasible, i.e., $\omega \mathrel{|\!\sim}_{\Delta} \bot$. A semantic model inducing $\mathrel{|\!\sim}_{\Delta}$ should reflect this in some way. For example, ranking functions use rank ∞ to mark worlds as infeasible (cf. Subsection 2.1.2) and preferential models just do not assign infeasible worlds to any state. Observe that an inference operator C might yield inference relations that consider more worlds to be infeasible than required by p-entailment; in this case C would not satisfy (Classic Preservation).

5.2. Extended System W

In the definition of system W ([KB20], cf. Definition 3.20) the preferred structure on worlds is a strict partial order on the set of all worlds Ω_{Σ}.

To accommodate infeasible worlds that are necessary to model belief bases which are not strongly consistent, in the following we allow the preferred structure on worlds to order only a subset $\Omega^{feas} \subseteq \Omega_\Sigma$ of feasible worlds. The worlds in $\Omega_\Sigma \setminus \Omega^{feas}$ are the infeasible worlds. All infeasible worlds are considered (equally) impossible. Modifying the definition of preferred structures on worlds accordingly leads to the following notion of an *extended* preferred structure on worlds. This definition makes the set Ω^{feas} explicit by defining the extended preferred structure on worlds as a tuple of Ω^{feas} and the plausibility ordering $<^{\mathsf{w}+}$ on it.

Definition 5.2 (extended preferred structure on worlds, $<^{\mathsf{w}+}_\Delta$). *Let Δ be a belief base over Σ with the extended Z-partition $EP(\Delta) = (\Delta^0, \dots, \Delta^k, \Delta^\infty)$. Analogously to Definition 3.19, for $j = 0, \dots, k, \infty$ let the functions ξ^j and ξ map each world ω to the set of conditionals in Δ^j or Δ, respectively, that are falsified by ω. Let*

$$\Omega^{feas}_\Delta := \Omega_\Sigma \setminus \{\omega \mid \xi^\infty(\omega) \neq \emptyset\}$$

be the set of feasible worlds *(with respect to Δ). The* extended preferred structure on worlds *for Δ is the tuple $(\Omega^{feas}_\Delta, <^{\mathsf{w}+}_\Delta)$ consisting of Ω^{feas}_Δ and the relation $<^{\mathsf{w}+}_\Delta \subseteq \Omega^{feas}_\Delta \times \Omega^{feas}_\Delta$ defined by, for any $\omega, \omega' \in \Omega^{feas}_\Delta$,*

$$\begin{aligned} \omega <^{\mathsf{w}+}_\Delta \omega' \quad \textit{iff} \quad & \textit{there exists an } m \in \{0, \dots, k\} \textit{ such that} \\ & \xi^i(\omega) = \xi^i(\omega') \quad \textit{for each } i \in \{m+1, \dots, k\} \textit{ and} \\ & \xi^m(\omega) \subsetneqq \xi^m(\omega'). \end{aligned}$$

The extended preferred structure on worlds considers those worlds to be infeasible that violate a conditional in the set Δ^∞ in the extended Z-partition of Δ. These are exactly the worlds for which $\kappa^z_\Delta(\omega) = \infty$ holds (see Definition 3.16), and exactly the worlds for which $\omega \mid\!\sim^p_\Delta \bot$ with p-entailment (see Lemma 3.17). The feasible worlds are ordered according to which conditionals they falsify and where the falsified conditionals are placed in the extended Z-partition $EP(\Delta)$. We have that $\omega <^{\mathsf{w}+}_\Delta \omega'$ if and only if ω falsifies strictly fewer conditionals than ω' in the part with the highest index m where the conditionals falsified by ω and ω' differ. The ordering $<^{\mathsf{w}+}_\Delta$ is an SPO on Ω^{feas}_Δ.

The extended preferred structure on worlds is defined with inference from weakly consistent belief bases in mind. But note that

Definition 5.2 does not exclude the edge case of belief bases which are not weakly consistent, i.e., technically every belief base Δ induces an extended preferred structure on worlds $<^{\mathsf{w}+}_{\Delta}$. For such belief bases Δ that are not weakly consistent the set Ω^{feas}_{Δ} and thus $<^{\mathsf{w}+}_{\Delta}$ are empty. In a similar way, most of the other definitions and results in this chapter focus on weakly consistent belief bases but technically also cover the edge case of belief bases that are not weakly consistent.

For strongly consistent belief bases the extended preferred structure on worlds coincides with the preferred structure on worlds.

Lemma 5.3. *Let* $(\Omega^{feas}_{\Delta}, <^{\mathsf{w}+}_{\Delta})$ *be the extended preferred structure on worlds for a strongly consistent belief base* Δ. *Then we have* $\Omega^{feas}_{\Delta} = \Omega_{\Sigma}$ *and* $<^{\mathsf{w}+}_{\Delta} = <^{\mathsf{w}}_{\Delta}$.

Based on the extended preferred structured on worlds we can define *extended* system W as a universal inductive inference operator.

Definition 5.4 (extended system W, $\mid\!\sim^{\mathsf{w}+}_{\Delta}$). *Let* Δ *be a belief base with extended preferred structure on worlds* $(\Omega^{feas}_{\Delta}, <^{\mathsf{w}+}_{\Delta})$ *and* $A, B \in \mathcal{L}_{\Sigma}$. *Then* B *is an* extended system W inference *from* A, *denoted* $A \mid\!\sim^{\mathsf{w}+}_{\Delta} B$, *if for every* $\omega' \in Mod_{\Sigma}(A\overline{B}) \cap \Omega^{feas}_{\Delta}$ *there is an* $\omega \in Mod_{\Sigma}(AB) \cap \Omega^{feas}_{\Delta}$ *such that* $\omega <^{\mathsf{w}+}_{\Delta} \omega'$.

Differing from the Definition 3.20 for system W, for the inference $A \mid\!\sim^{\mathsf{w}+}_{\Delta} B$ the definition for extended system W compares only the feasible models of AB and $A\overline{B}$. The formulation in Definition 5.4 ensures that everything can be entailed from a formula A without feasible models, i.e., if $Mod_{\Sigma}(A) \cap \Omega^{feas}_{\Delta} = \emptyset$ then $A \mid\!\sim^{\mathsf{w}+}_{\Delta} B$ for any formula B.

For strongly consistent belief bases extended system W and system W coincide.

Proposition 5.5. *Let* Δ *be a strongly consistent belief base and* $A, B \in \mathcal{L}_{\Sigma}$. *We have* $A \mid\!\sim^{\mathsf{w}}_{\Delta} B$ *iff* $A \mid\!\sim^{\mathsf{w}+}_{\Delta} B$.

Proof. Let Δ be a strongly consistent belief base and $A, B \in \mathcal{L}_{\Sigma}$. By Lemma 5.3 we have $\Omega^{feas}_{\Delta} = \Omega_{\Sigma}$ and $<^{\mathsf{w}+}_{\Delta} = <^{\mathsf{w}}_{\Delta}$. In this case Definition 5.4 becomes equivalent to Definition 3.20. □

In Section 4.1, system W was evaluated with respect to some postulates. Here we show that the same postulates hold for extended system W.

First, note that extended system W's inference relations are induced by an SPO on a set of worlds; therefore extended system W is a preferential inductive inference operator.

Furthermore, extended system W, just like system W, satisfies weak rational monotony.

Proposition 5.6. *Extended system W satisfies weak rational monotony (WRM), i.e., for a belief base Δ and any $A, B \in \mathcal{L}_\Sigma$ it holds that $\top \mid\!\sim^{\mathsf{w+}}_\Delta B$ and $\top \not\mid\!\sim^{\mathsf{w+}}_\Delta \overline{A}$ imply $A \mid\!\sim^{\mathsf{w+}}_\Delta B$.*

Proof. Let Δ be a belief base over Σ.

If Δ is not weakly consistent, we have $\mid\!\sim^{\mathsf{w+}}_\Delta = \mathcal{L}_\Sigma \times \mathcal{L}_\Sigma$ and therefore trivially there is no formula A such that $\top \not\mid\!\sim^{\mathsf{w+}}_\Delta \overline{A}$. The precondition $\top \not\mid\!\sim^{\mathsf{w+}}_\Delta \overline{A}$ of (WRM) is never satisfied and therefore (WRM) holds for all $A, B \in \mathcal{L}_\Sigma$.

Otherwise, let $A, B \in \mathcal{L}_\Sigma$ such that $\top \mid\!\sim^{\mathsf{w+}}_\Delta B$ and $\top \not\mid\!\sim^{\mathsf{w+}}_\Delta \overline{A}$. Let $\Omega_{nf} \subseteq \Omega_\Sigma$ be the set of all worlds that falsify none of the conditionals in Δ. As Δ is weakly consistent, by Ω_{nf} is not empty (see Lemma 2.2). The worlds in Ω_{nf} are ordered lower than other worlds with respect to $<^{\mathsf{w+}}_\Delta$: for every $\omega' \in \Omega_{nf}, \omega \in \Omega_\Sigma \setminus \Omega_{nf}$ we have $\omega' <^{\mathsf{w+}}_\Delta \omega$. For worlds $\omega, \omega' \in \Omega_{nf}$ neither $\omega <^{\mathsf{w+}}_\Delta \omega'$ nor $\omega' <^{\mathsf{w+}}_\Delta \omega$ holds. Because $\top \mid\!\sim^{\mathsf{w+}}_\Delta B$, every world in Ω_{nf} models B, i.e. $\Omega_{nf} \subseteq Mod_\Sigma(B)$. Because $\top \not\mid\!\sim^{\mathsf{w+}}_\Delta \overline{A}$, there is at least one feasible world $\omega^A \in \Omega_{nf}$ such that $\omega \models A$.

Let ω be a feasible model of $A\overline{B}$. Because $\Omega_{nf} \subseteq Mod_\Sigma(B)$ (see above) we have that $\omega \notin \Omega_{nf}$. Because $\omega^A \in \Omega_{nf}$ and $\omega \notin \Omega_{nf}$ we know that $\omega^A <^{\mathsf{w+}}_\Delta \omega$. Furthermore, we have $\omega^A \models AB$. Therefore, $A \mid\!\sim^{\mathsf{w+}}_\Delta B$. In summary, extended system W fulfils (WRM). □

All other postulates beside (WRM) that were considered in Section 4.1 are not satisfied by system W. Because system W and extended system W coincide for strongly consistent belief bases, these postulates are also violated by extended system W: a strongly consistent belief base for which system W violates one of these postulates is also an example of extended system W violating the postulate.

Proposition 5.7. *Extended system W does not satisfy any of*

- *semi-monotony (SM),*
- *rational monotony (RM),*
- *disjunctive rationality (DR),*
- *negation rationality (NR),*

- *contraposition (CPS),*
- *weak contraposition (WCPS),*
- *rational contraposition (RC),*
- *weak determinacy (WD), or*
- *conjunctive insistence (CI).*

Finally, we observe that extended system W satisfies (Classic Preservation).

Proposition 5.8. *Extended system W satisfies (Classic Preservation).*

Proof. Let $A \in \mathcal{L}_\Sigma$. Because $A \wedge \bot$ has no models, it holds that $A \mathrel{|\!\sim}^{\mathsf{w}+}_{\Delta} \bot$ iff A has no feasible models in Ω^{feas}_{Δ}. This is the case iff every model $\omega \in Mod_\Sigma(A)$ falsifies a conditional in Δ^∞ which is equivalent to $\kappa^{z+}_{\Delta}(A) = \infty$. By Lemma 3.17 this is equivalent to $A \mathrel{|\!\sim}^{p}_{\Delta} \bot$. □

In this section we considered extended system W and the extended preferred structure on worlds. The next section considers more generally how SPOs on subsets of Ω_Σ can be used to represent inference relations.

5.3. Representing Extended System W with SPOs on Worlds

In Section 4.2 we introduced full SPOs on worlds (fSPO) as models for conditionals and belief bases and showed that system W is fSPO-representable. However, full SPOs on worlds can only model strongly consistent belief bases. Related to that, we saw that only SCA-inductive inference operators are fSPO-representable. To model weakly consistent belief bases with strict partial orders we need a more general definition for SPOs on worlds that allows representing SPOs on only a selected set of feasible worlds. In Definition 5.2 of the extended preferred structure on worlds we saw how this can be accomplished by explicitly stating a set of feasible worlds together with an SPO on them. We generalize this approach and define SPOs on worlds as models for conditionals and conditional belief bases independently of extended system W.

Definition 5.9 (limited SPO on worlds, lSPO,$(\Omega^{feas}, \prec)$). *A* limited SPO (lSPO) on worlds *(over Σ) is a tuple $(\Omega^{feas}, \prec)$ consisting of a set $\Omega^{feas} \subseteq \Omega_\Sigma$ of* feasible *worlds and an SPO $\prec$ on Ω^{feas}.*

A limited SPO on worlds $(\Omega^{feas}, \prec)$ *is lifted to formulas by defining that a formula* A *is* feasible *if at least one model of* A *is feasible and by letting, for feasible* $A, B \in \mathcal{L}_\Sigma$,

$$A \prec B \quad \textit{iff} \quad \textit{for every } \omega' \in Mod_\Sigma(B) \cap \Omega^{feas} \\ \textit{there is an } \omega \in Mod_\Sigma(A) \cap \Omega^{feas} \textit{ such that } \omega \prec \omega'.$$

A limited SPO on worlds $(\Omega^{feas}, \prec)$ models *a conditional* $(B|A)$, *denoted as*

$$(\Omega^{feas}, \prec) \models (B|A), \textit{ if either } A\overline{B} \textit{ is infeasible} \\ \textit{or } AB \textit{ and } A\overline{B} \textit{ are both feasible and } AB \prec A\overline{B}.$$

We say $(\Omega^{feas}, \prec)$ *models a belief base* Δ *if it models every conditional in* Δ, *in this case* $(\Omega^{feas}, \prec)$ *is also called an* lSPO model *of* Δ.

A limited SPO $(\Omega^{feas}, \prec)$ orders only the subset Ω^{feas} of all worlds in Ω_Σ. This allows modelling weakly consistent belief bases. Especially, limited SPOs on worlds can also model conditionals of the form $(\bot|\overline{A})$ by choosing $\Omega^{feas} \subseteq Mod_\Sigma(A)$.

A limited SPO on worlds modelling a conditional is equivalently described by the following condition.

Lemma 5.10. *Let* $(\Omega^{feas}, \prec)$ *be a limited SPO on worlds and* $(B|A)$ *be a conditional. We have* $(\Omega^{feas}, \prec) \models (B|A)$ *iff*

$$\textit{for any } \omega' \in Mod_\Sigma(A\overline{B}) \cap \Omega^{feas} \\ \textit{there is an } \omega \in Mod_\Sigma(AB) \cap \Omega^{feas} \textit{ with } \omega \prec \omega'. \tag{5.1}$$

Proof. If $A\overline{B}$ is infeasible, then $(\Omega^{feas}, \prec) \models (B|A)$ by definition and the condition (5.1) holds trivially because there are no $\omega' \in Mod_\Sigma(A\overline{B}) \cap \Omega^{feas}$.

Otherwise, $(\Omega^{feas}, \prec) \models (B|A)$ iff $AB \prec A\overline{B}$ which is equivalent to (5.1). □

Just as full SPOs on worlds, also limited SPOs on worlds induce inference relations.

Definition 5.11. *The inference relation* $\mid\!\sim_{(\Omega^{feas}, \prec)}$ *induced by a limited SPO on worlds* $(\Omega^{feas}, \prec)$ *is defined by*

$$A \mid\!\sim_{(\Omega^{feas}, \prec)} B \quad \textit{iff} \quad (\Omega^{feas}, \prec) \models (B|A). \tag{5.2}$$

Example 5.12. *Let* $\Delta := \{(a|b), (c|a), (\overline{a}|b)\}$ *be a belief base over signature* $\Sigma := \{a, b, c\}$. *Let* $(\Omega^{feas}, \prec)$ *be a limited SPO on worlds with* $\Omega^{feas} := \{a\overline{b}c, a\overline{b}\overline{c}, \overline{a}\overline{b}c, \overline{a}\overline{b}\overline{c}\}$ *and* $\prec := \{(a\overline{b}c, a\overline{b}\overline{c}), (\overline{a}\overline{b}c, a\overline{b}\overline{c}), (\overline{a}\overline{b}\overline{c}, a\overline{b}\overline{c})\}$.

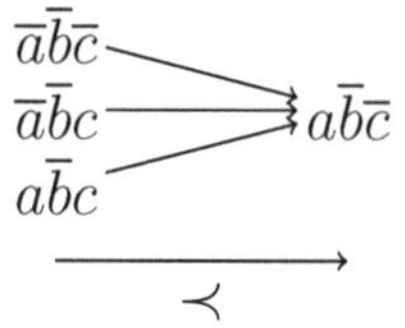

Then $(\Omega^{feas}, \prec) \models \Delta$ *and we have, for example,* $b \mid\!\sim_{(\Omega^{feas}, \prec)} \perp$ *and* $\overline{c} \mid\!\sim_{(\Omega^{feas}, \prec)} \overline{a}$.

Observe that every full SPO $\prec$ on worlds corresponds to the limited SPO on worlds $(\Omega_\Sigma, \prec)$ in the sense that $\prec$ and $(\Omega_\Sigma, \prec)$ induce the same inference relation and model the same conditionals and belief bases. Therefore, every full SPO $\prec$ on worlds can be seen as limited SPO $(\Omega_\Sigma, \prec)$, and a limited SPO worlds of the form $(\Omega_\Sigma, \prec)$ can be seen as a full SPO $\prec$ on worlds.

Technically, every belief base Δ has an lSPO "model" because $(\Omega^{feas}, \prec)$ with $\Omega^{feas} = \prec = \emptyset$ is not ruled out by Definition 5.9 of limited SPOs on worlds and $(\Omega^{feas}, \prec) \models \Delta$. However, having no feasible worlds at all, the limited SPO on worlds $(\emptyset, \emptyset)$ is not a very useful interpretation of a belief base. Therefore, the following Lemma 5.13 states that every weakly consistent belief base has an lSPO model that considers at least some worlds feasible.

Lemma 5.13. *A belief base is weakly consistent iff it has an lSPO model* $(\Omega^{feas}, \prec)$ *with* $\Omega^{feas} \neq \emptyset$.

Proof. Let Δ be a belief base. We show both directions of the "iff".

Direction $\Rightarrow$*:* Let Δ be weakly consistent. Then there is a ranking function κ modelling Δ. Because κ is a ranking function, there is a world ω with $\kappa(\omega) = 0$. Let $\Omega^{feas} = \{\omega \mid \kappa(\omega) < \infty\}$ and for $\omega, \omega' \in \Omega^{feas}$ let $\omega \prec \omega'$ iff $\kappa(\omega) < \kappa(\omega')$. Obviously, $\omega \in \Omega^{feas}$ and therefore $\Omega^{feas} \neq \emptyset$. Furthermore, if $\kappa \models (B|A)$ then $(\Omega^{feas}, \prec) \models (B|A)$ and therefore $(\Omega^{feas}, \prec)$ is a model of Δ.

Direction $\Leftarrow$*:* Let Δ be a belief base with an lSPO model $(\Omega^{feas}, \prec)$ such that $\Omega^{feas} \neq \emptyset$. We can define a ranking function κ as follows. Let $\Omega^0 := \min(\Omega^{feas}, \prec)$, and for $i > 0$ let $\Omega^i := \min(\Omega^{feas} \setminus (\Omega^0 \cup \dots \cup \Omega^{i-1}), \prec)$. Let k be the least i such that $\Omega^{i+1} = \emptyset$. Define $\kappa(\omega) := i$ for $\omega \in \Omega^i$ for $i = 0, \dots, k$ and $\kappa(\omega) := \infty$ for $\omega \in \Omega_\Sigma \setminus \Omega^{feas}$. Because

$\Omega^{feas} \neq \emptyset$ there is at least one world with rank 0. We have that $\prec \models (B|A)$ implies $\kappa \models (B|A)$. Therefore, $\kappa \models \Delta$ and Δ is weakly consistent. □

The notion of limited SPOs on worlds enables us to introduce a new class of inductive inference operators that is a generalization of the fSPO-representable inductive inference operators.

Definition 5.14 (lSPO-representable inductive inference operator). *An inference relation* $\mid\!\sim$ *is* lSPO-representable *if there is an lSPO on worlds inducing* $\mid\!\sim$. *An* lSPO-representable inductive inference operator *is an inductive inference operator* $C : \Delta \mapsto \mid\!\sim_\Delta$ *such that every* $\mid\!\sim_\Delta$ *in the image of* C *is an lSPO-representable inference relation.*

An lSPO-representable inductive inference operator can alternatively be written as a mapping $C^{spo} : \Delta \mapsto (\Omega^{feas}_\Delta, \prec_\Delta)$ that maps each belief base to an limited SPO on worlds $(\Omega^{feas}_\Delta, \prec_\Delta)$. The induced inference relation $\mid\!\sim_\Delta$ is obtained from $(\Omega^{feas}_\Delta, \prec_\Delta)$ as in (5.2). Then (DI) is equivalent to $(\Omega^{feas}_\Delta, \prec_\Delta) \models \Delta$ and (TV) is equivalent to $\Omega^{feas}_\emptyset = \Omega_\Sigma$ and $\prec_\emptyset = \emptyset$.

Using the observation that for every full SPO on worlds there is a corresponding limited SPO on worlds, it is clear that every fSPO-representable inference relation is an lSPO-representable inference relation and that every fSPO-representable inductive inference operator is an lSPO-representable inductive inference operator.

For every limited SPO on worlds, there is an equivalent preferential model on the respective subset of worlds inducing the same inference relation.

Proposition 5.15. *Let* $(\Omega^{feas}, \prec)$ *be a limited SPO on worlds. The preferential model* $\mathcal{M} := \langle \Omega^{feas}, \mathrm{id}, \prec \rangle$ *induces the inference relation* $\mid\!\sim_{(\Omega^{feas}, \prec)}$.

Proof. Let $A, B \in \mathcal{L}_\Sigma$. We have $A \mid\!\sim_\mathcal{M} B$ iff $\min([\![A]\!]_\mathcal{M}, \prec) \subseteq [\![B]\!]_\mathcal{M}$, the latter being equivalent to $\min(Mod_\Sigma(A) \cap \Omega^{feas}, \prec) \subseteq Mod_\Sigma(B) \cap \Omega^{feas}$. For $Mod_\Sigma(A) \cap \Omega^{feas} = \emptyset$, we have both $A \mid\!\sim_{(\Omega^{feas}, \prec)} B$ and $A \mid\!\sim_\mathcal{M} B$; the proposition holds. For the remainder of the proof assume $Mod_\Sigma(A) \cap \Omega^{feas} = \emptyset$.

If $A \mid\!\sim_{(\Omega^{feas}, \prec)} B$, then for every $\omega' \in Mod_\Sigma(A\overline{B}) \cap \Omega^{feas}$ there is an $\omega \in Mod_\Sigma(AB) \cap \Omega^{feas}$ such that $\omega \prec \omega'$. Therefore, a minimal feasible model of A cannot be a feasible model of $\overline{B}$ and is hence a model of B. Thus, $A \mid\!\sim_{\mathcal{M}} B$.

If $A \mid\!\sim_{\mathcal{M}} B$, then any $\omega' \in Mod_{\Sigma}(A\overline{B}) \cap \Omega^{feas}$ is not minimal in $Mod_{\Sigma}(A) \cap \Omega^{feas}$. Using the smoothness condition, there must be a minimal $\omega \in Mod_{\Sigma}(A) \cap \Omega^{feas}$ with $\omega \prec \omega'$. The world ω is a feasible model of A and B. Therefore $A \mid\!\sim_{(\Omega^{feas},\prec)} B$. □

Therefore, every lSPO-representable inference relation is a preferential inference relation and every lSPO-representable inductive inference operator is a preferential inductive inference operator. This implies that every lSPO-representable inductive inference operator C captures p-entailment, i.e., for a belief base Δ, and formulas A, B we have that $A \mid\!\sim^{p}_{\Delta} B$ implies $A \mid\!\sim^{C}_{\Delta} B$. Because not every preferential inference relation is induced by a limited SPO on worlds, the inference relations induced by limited SPOs on worlds form a proper subclass of all preferential inference relations.

Lemma 5.16. *There are preferential inference relations that are not lSPO-representable.*

Proof. Consider the inference relation $\mid\!\sim_{\mathcal{M}}$ induced by the preferential model $\mathcal{M} = \langle S, l, < \rangle$ with $S := \{1, 2, 3, 4\}$, $< := \{(3, 1), (4, 2)\}$, and $l: \ 1 \mapsto ab, 2 \mapsto ab, 3 \mapsto a\overline{b}, 4 \mapsto \overline{a}b$.

Towards a contradiction, assume that $\mid\!\sim_{\mathcal{M}}$ is induced by a limited SPO on worlds $(\Omega^{feas}, \prec)$. We observe that $\omega \mid\!\sim_{\mathcal{M}} \bot$ holds exactly for the world $\omega := \overline{a}\overline{b}$, therefore we have $\Omega^{feas} = \{ab, a\overline{b}, \overline{a}b\}$. By checking that $a\overline{b} \vee \overline{a}b \not\mid\!\sim_{\mathcal{M}} a\overline{b}$ and $a\overline{b} \vee \overline{a}b \not\mid\!\sim_{\mathcal{M}} \overline{a}b$ we can see that $a\overline{b}$ and $\overline{a}b$ must be incomparable in $\prec$. Similarly, we can conclude that $a\overline{b}$ and ab as well as $\overline{a}b$ and ab must be incomparable in $\prec$. Therefore, $\prec$ must be the empty SPO over Ω^{feas}. But $\mid\!\sim_{\mathcal{M}}$ allows for the non-trivial inference $\top \mid\!\sim_{\mathcal{M}} a\overline{b} \vee \overline{a}b$ which contradicts that $\mid\!\sim_{\mathcal{M}}$ is induced by $(\Omega^{feas}, \emptyset)$. □

In fact, the class of inference relations that are induced by *injective models* [Fre93] is equivalent to the class of lSPO-representable inference relations; an injective model being a preferential model $\mathcal{M} = \langle S, l, \prec \rangle$ where the function l is injective.

Proposition 5.17. *An inference relation* $\mid\!\sim$ *is lSPO-representable iff there is an injective model* $\mathcal{M} = \langle S, l, \prec \rangle$ *inducing* $\mid\!\sim$, *i.e.*, $\mid\!\sim \, = \, \mid\!\sim_{\mathcal{M}}$.

Proof. We show both directions of the "iff".

Direction $\Rightarrow$: Assume that $\mid\!\sim$ is lSPO-representable, i.e., there is a limited SPO on worlds $(\Omega^{feas}, \prec)$ such that $\mid\!\sim \; = \; \mid\!\sim_{(\Omega^{feas},\prec)}$. According to Proposition 5.15, $\mathcal{M} := \langle \Omega^{feas}, \mathrm{id}, \prec \rangle$ also induces $\mid\!\sim$, and because id is injective, $\mathcal{M}$ is an injective model.

Direction $\Leftarrow$: Assume that there is an injective model $\mathcal{M} = \langle S, l, \prec \rangle$ inducing $\mid\!\sim$. As l is injective, we can obtain an equivalent model $\mathcal{M}' := \langle S, \mathrm{id}, \prec' \rangle$ by replacing every state $s \in S$ by $l(s)$ and defining $\prec'$ by $\omega \prec' \omega'$ iff $l^{-1}(\omega) \prec l^{-1}(\omega')$. We have that $S' \subseteq \Omega_\Sigma$, meaning that $(S', \prec')$ is a limited SPO on worlds inducing $\mid\!\sim$ (cf. Proposition 5.15). □

To conclude this section, we observe that extended system W is an lSPO-representable inductive inference operator.

Proposition 5.18. *Extended system W is an lSPO-representable inductive inference operator.*

Proof. For every belief base Δ, the extended preferred structure on worlds $(\Omega^{feas}_\Delta, <^{\mathsf{w}+}_\Delta)$ is a limited SPO on worlds inducing the inference relation $\mid\!\sim^{\mathsf{w}+}_\Delta$. □

Combining Propositions 5.15 and 5.18 shows how preferential models for the inference relations induced by extended system W can be obtained.

5.4. Syntax Splitting for Universal lSPO-representable Inductive Inference Operators

In Section 4.3 we introduced (Rel^{spo}) and (Ind^{spo}) as equivalent versions of the syntax splitting postulates (Rel) and (Ind) for fSPO-representable inductive inference operators. Using these postulates we then showed that system W satisfies (SynSplit). Similarly, we can give equivalent versions of (Rel$^+$) and (Ind$^+$) for universal lSPO-representable inductive inference operators.

(Rel^{spo+}) A universal lSPO-representable inductive inference operator $C^{spo} : \Delta \mapsto (\Omega^{feas}_\Delta, \prec_\Delta)$ satisfies (Rel^{spo+}) if for a weakly consistent $\Delta = \Delta_1 \bigcup_{\Sigma_1,\Sigma_2} \Delta_2$, for $i \in \{1,2\}$, and for any $A, B, F \in \mathcal{L}_{\Sigma_i}$

such that A, B are feasible for $(\Omega_{\Delta}^{feas}, \prec_{\Delta})$ it holds that

$$Mod_{\Sigma}(F) \cap \Omega_{\Delta}^{feas} \neq \emptyset \quad \text{iff} \quad Mod_{\Sigma}(F) \cap \Omega_{\Delta_i}^{feas} \neq \emptyset \quad \text{and}$$
$$A \prec_{\Delta} B \quad \text{iff} \quad A \prec_{\Delta_i} B.$$

(Ind^{spo+}) A universal lSPO-representable inductive inference operator $C^{spo} : \Delta \mapsto (\Omega_{\Delta}^{feas}, \prec_{\Delta})$ satisfies (Ind^{spo+}) if for a weakly consistent $\Delta = \Delta_1 \bigcup_{\Sigma_1,\Sigma_2} \Delta_2$, for $i, j \in \{1, 2\}, i \neq j$, and for any $A, B, F \in \mathcal{L}_{\Sigma_i}$, $D \in \mathcal{L}_{\Sigma_j}$ such that A, B, D are feasible for $(\Omega_{\Delta}^{feas}, \prec_{\Delta})$, it holds that

$$Mod_{\Sigma}(F) \cap \Omega_{\Delta}^{feas} \neq \emptyset \quad \text{iff} \quad Mod_{\Sigma}(FD) \cap \Omega_{\Delta}^{feas} \neq \emptyset \quad \text{and}$$
$$A \prec_{\Delta} B \quad \text{iff} \quad AD \prec_{\Delta} BD.$$

(SynSplit^{spo+}) A universal SPO-representable inference operator satisfies (SynSplit^{spo+}) if it satisfies both (Rel^{spo+}) and (Ind^{spo+}).

Compared to (Rel^{spo}) and (Ind^{spo}), the postulates (Rel^{spo+}) and (Ind^{spo+}) include additional statements governing the feasibility of formulas. The first "iff" in (Rel^{spo+}) states that F is feasible with respect to $(\Omega_{\Delta}^{feas}, \prec_{\Delta})$ if and only if it is feasible with respect to $(\Omega_{\Delta_i}^{feas}, \prec_{\Delta_i})$. Similarly, the first "iff" in (Ind^{spo+}) states that F is feasible with respect to $(\Omega_{\Delta}^{feas}, \prec_{\Delta})$ if and only if FD is feasible with respect to $(\Omega_{\Delta}^{feas}, \prec_{\Delta})$. The second "iff" in each (Rel^{spo+}) and (Ind^{spo+}) express conditions on the order of feasible formulas induced by $(\Omega_{\Delta}^{feas}, \prec_{\Delta})$.

In the following proofs, for a universal lSPO-representable inductive inference operator $C^{spo} : \Delta \mapsto (\Omega_{\Delta}^{feas}, \prec_{\Delta})$, let $\mid\!\sim_{\Delta}$ denote the inference relation induced by $(\Omega_{\Delta}^{feas}, \prec_{\Delta})$.

Proposition 5.19. *Let C^{spo} be a universal lSPO-representable inductive inference operator. C^{spo} satisfies (Rel^{spo+}) iff it satisfies (Rel^{+}).*

Proof. Let $\Delta = \Delta_1 \bigcup_{\Sigma_1,\Sigma_2} \Delta_2$ be weakly consistent, and let $i \in \{1, 2\}$.

Direction $\Rightarrow$: Assume that C^{spo} satisfies (Rel^{spo+}) and let $A, B \in \mathcal{L}_{\Sigma_i}$. If $A\overline{B}$ is not feasible for $(\Omega_{\Delta}^{feas}, \prec_{\Delta})$, i.e., $Mod_{\Sigma}(A\overline{B}) \cap \Omega_{\Delta}^{feas} = \emptyset$ then $Mod_{\Sigma}(A\overline{B}) \cap \Omega_{\Delta_i}^{feas} = \emptyset$ by (Rel^{spo+}). In this case both $A \mid\!\sim_{\Delta} B$ and $A \mid\!\sim_{\Delta_i} B$ holds, and (Rel^{+}) is satisfied.

Assume that $A\overline{B}$ is feasible for $(\Omega_{\Delta}^{feas}, \prec_{\Delta})$, and therefore $A\overline{B}$ is also feasible for $(\Omega^{feas}_{\Delta_i}, \prec_{\Delta_i})$. Then, with (Rel^{spo+}) we have

$$\begin{aligned} A \mid\!\sim_\Delta B &\text{ iff } AB \text{ is feasible w.r.t. } (\Omega^{feas}_{\Delta}, \prec_\Delta) \text{ and } AB \prec_\Delta A\overline{B} \\ &\text{ iff } AB \text{ is feasible w.r.t. } (\Omega^{feas}_{\Delta_i}, \prec_{\Delta_i}) \text{ and } AB \prec_{\Delta_i} A\overline{B} \\ &\text{ iff } A \mid\!\sim_{\Delta_i} B. \end{aligned}$$

In summary, (Rel$^+$) holds.

Direction $\Leftarrow$: Assume that C^{spo} satisfies (Rel$^+$) and let $A, B, F \in \mathcal{L}_{\Sigma_i}$ such that A, B are feasible for $(\Omega^{feas}_{\Delta}, \prec_{\Delta_i})$. We have that

$$\begin{aligned} Mod_\Sigma(F) \cap \Omega^{feas}_\Delta \neq \emptyset \quad &\text{iff} \quad F \not\mid\!\sim_\Delta \bot \\ &\text{iff} \quad F \not\mid\!\sim_{\Delta_i} \bot \\ &\text{iff} \quad Mod_\Sigma(F) \cap \Omega^{feas}_{\Delta_i} \neq \emptyset. \end{aligned}$$

Using this argumentation, we can see that A, B are also feasible for $(\Omega^{feas}_{\Delta_i}, \prec_{\Delta_i})$. Furthermore, we have that

$$\begin{aligned} A \prec_\Delta B \quad &\text{iff} \quad A \vee B \mid\!\sim_\Delta A \\ &\text{iff} \quad A \vee B \mid\!\sim_{\Delta_i} A \\ &\text{iff} \quad A \prec_{\Delta_i} B. \end{aligned}$$

In summary, (Rel^{spo+}) holds. □

Proposition 5.20. *Let C^{spo} be a universal lSPO-representable inductive inference operator. C^{spo} satisfies (Ind^{spo+}) iff it satisfies (Ind$^+$).*

Proof. Let $\Delta = \Delta_1 \bigcup_{\Sigma_1,\Sigma_2} \Delta_2$ be weakly consistent, and let $i, j \in \{1,2\}, i \neq j$.

Direction $\Rightarrow$: Assume that C^{spo} satisfies (Ind^{spo+}) and let $A, B \in \mathcal{L}_{\Sigma_i}, D \in \mathcal{L}_{\Sigma_j}$ such that $D \not\mid\!\sim_\Delta \bot$. This implis that D is feasible for $(\Omega^{feas}_\Delta, \prec_\Delta)$. If $A\overline{B}$ is not feasible for $(\Omega^{feas}_\Delta, \prec_\Delta)$, i.e., $Mod_\Sigma(A\overline{B}) \cap \Omega^{feas}_\Delta = \emptyset$ then $Mod_{\Sigma_i}(A\overline{B}D) \cap \Omega^{feas}_{\Delta_i} = \emptyset$ by (Ind^{spo+}). In this case both $A \mid\!\sim_\Delta B$ and $AD \mid\!\sim_{\Delta_i} B$ holds, and (Ind$^+$) is satisfied.

Assume that $A\overline{B}$ and thus also $A\overline{B}D$ are feasible for $(\Omega^{feas}_\Delta, \prec_\Delta)$. Then, with (Ind^{spo+}) we have

$$\begin{aligned} A \mid\!\sim_\Delta B &\text{ iff } AB \text{ is feasible w.r.t. } (\Omega^{feas}_{\Delta}, \prec_\Delta) \text{ and } AB \prec_\Delta A\overline{B} \\ &\text{ iff } ABD \text{ is feasible w.r.t. } (\Omega^{feas}_{\Delta}, \prec_\Delta) \text{ and } ABD \prec_\Delta A\overline{B}D \\ &\text{ iff } AD \mid\!\sim_\Delta B. \end{aligned}$$

In summary, (Ind^+) holds.

Direction $\Leftarrow$: Assume that C^{spo} satisfies (Ind^+) and let $A, B, F \in \mathcal{L}_{\Sigma_i}, D \in \Sigma_j$ such that A, B, D are feasible for $(\Omega_\Delta^{feas}, \prec_\Delta)$. This implies that $D \not\mathrel{|\!\sim}_\Delta \bot$. We have that

$$\begin{aligned} Mod_\Sigma(F) \cap \Omega_\Delta^{feas} \neq \emptyset \quad & \text{iff} \quad F \not\mathrel{|\!\sim}_\Delta \bot \\ & \text{iff} \quad FD \not\mathrel{|\!\sim}_{\Delta_i} \bot \\ & \text{iff} \quad Mod_\Sigma(FD) \cap \Omega_\Delta^{feas} \neq \emptyset. \end{aligned}$$

Furthermore, we have that

$$\begin{aligned} A \prec_\Delta B \quad & \text{iff} \quad A \vee B \mathrel{|\!\sim}_\Delta A \\ & \text{iff} \quad (A \vee B)D \mathrel{|\!\sim}_\Delta AD \\ & \text{iff} \quad AD \prec_\Delta BD. \end{aligned}$$

In summary, (Ind^{spo+}) holds. □

Combining Propositions 5.19 and 5.20 yields that a universal lSPO-representable inductive inference operator satisfies (SynSplit^{spo+}) iff it satisfies (SynSplit^+). Using these results we will show that extended system W satisfies (SynSplit^+) in the next section.

5.5. Extended System W satisfies Syntax Splitting

In this section we show that extended system W satisfies (SynSplit^+). Using the fact that extended system W is lSPO-representable, we do this by showing that extended system W satisfies (Rel^{spo+}) and (Ind^{spo+}).

For proving that extended system W complies with (Rel^{spo+}) and (Ind^{spo+}) we adapt the lemmas in Section 4.4 to describe the extended preferred structures on worlds induced by belief bases with syntax splitting. First we show that system W inference does not change if the signature is enlarged with additional elements that do not occur in the belief base.

Lemma 5.21. *Let Σ be a signature and $\Sigma' \subseteq \Sigma$. Let Δ be a weakly consistent belief base over Σ'. Let $(\Omega^{feas}, <_\Delta^{\mathsf{w}+})$ be the extended preferred structure on Ω_Σ w.r.t. signature Σ and let $(\Omega_\Delta^{feas'}, <_\Delta^{\mathsf{w}+'})$ be the extended preferred structure on $\Omega_{\Sigma'}$ w.r.t. signature Σ'.*

1. *Let* $\omega^a, \omega^b \in \Omega_\Sigma$ *and let* $\omega^{a\prime} := \omega^a{}_{|\Sigma'}$ *and* $\omega^{b\prime} := \omega^b{}_{|\Sigma'}$. *We have*

   (a) $\omega^a \in \Omega^{feas}_\Delta$ *iff* $\omega^{a\prime} \in \Omega^{feas\prime}_\Delta$ *and*
   (b) *if* $\omega^a, \omega^b \in \Omega^{feas}_\Delta$ *then* $\omega^a <^{\mathsf{w}+}_\Delta \omega^b$ *iff* $\omega^{a\prime} <^{\mathsf{w}+\prime}_\Delta \omega^{b\prime}$.

2. *For* $A, B \in \mathcal{L}_{\Sigma'}$ *we have*

   (a) *A is feasible for* $(\Omega^{feas}, <^{\mathsf{w}+}_\Delta)$ *iff A is feasible for* $(\Omega^{feas\prime}_\Delta, <^{\mathsf{w}+\prime}_\Delta)$ *and*
   (b) *if* A, B *are feasible for* $(\Omega^{feas}, <^{\mathsf{w}+}_\Delta)$ *then* $A <^{\mathsf{w}+}_\Delta B$ *iff* $A <^{\mathsf{w}+\prime}_\Delta B$.

Proof. Let $\Sigma, \Sigma', \Delta, <^{\mathsf{w}+}_\Delta, <^{\mathsf{w}+\prime}_\Delta$ be as in the lemma.

Ad 1.: First, observe that the extended Z-partition of Δ is the same independent of the underlying signature. Let $\omega^a, \omega^b, \omega^{a\prime}, \omega^{b\prime}$ be as above. Because the conditionals in Δ only contain atoms from Σ' and $\omega^a, \omega^{a\prime}$ have the same variable assignment on Σ' , the worlds ω^a and $\omega^{a\prime}$ falsify the same conditionals in Δ. Similarly, ω^b and $\omega^{b\prime}$ falsify the same conditionals in Δ. Whether ω^x is feasible and whether $\omega^x <^{\mathsf{w}+}_\Delta \omega^y$ holds or not depends only on the conditionals in Δ falsified by ω^x and ω^y for $\omega^x \in \{\omega^a, \omega^{a\prime}\}$ and $\omega^y \in \{\omega^b, \omega^{b\prime}\}$. Hence, ω^a is feasible iff $\omega^{a\prime}$ is feasible and $\omega^a <^{\mathsf{w}+}_\Delta \omega^b$ iff $\omega^{a\prime} <^{\mathsf{w}+\prime}_\Delta \omega^{b\prime}$.

Ad 2. (a): We show both directions of the "iff".
Direction $\Rightarrow$*:* Let A be feasible for $(\Omega^{feas}, <^{\mathsf{w}+}_\Delta)$. Therefore, there is a feasible model $\omega \in \Omega^{feas}_\Delta \cap Mod_\Sigma(A)$. Then $\omega' := \omega_{|\Sigma'}$ is also model of A and with (1. a) we have that $\omega' \in \Omega^{feas\prime}_\Delta$. Hence, A is feasible for $(\Omega^{feas\prime}_\Delta, <^{\mathsf{w}+\prime}_\Delta)$.
Direction $\Leftarrow$*:* Let A be feasible for $(\Omega^{feas\prime}_\Delta, <^{\mathsf{w}+\prime}_\Delta)$, i.e., there is a feasible model $\omega' \in \Omega^{feas\prime}_\Delta \cap Mod_{\Sigma'}(A)$. Let $\omega \in \Omega_\Sigma$ be any world such that $\omega_{|\Sigma'} = \omega'$. Then ω is also a model of A and with (1. a) we have that $\omega' \in \Omega^{feas}_\Delta$. Hence, A is feasible for $(\Omega^{feas}, <^{\mathsf{w}+}_\Delta)$.

Ad 2. (b): Let A, B be feasible for $(\Omega^{feas}, <^{\mathsf{w}+}_\Delta)$. With (2. a) we have that A, B are also feasible for $(\Omega^{feas\prime}_\Delta, <^{\mathsf{w}+\prime}_\Delta)$. We show both directions of the "iff".
Direction $\Rightarrow$*:* Let $A <^{\mathsf{w}+}_\Delta B$ and let $\omega^{b\prime} \in Mod_{\Sigma'}(B)$. Let $\omega^b \in \Omega_\Sigma$ be a world with $\omega^b{}_{|\Sigma'} = \omega^{b\prime}$. Because $\omega^b \models B$ and $A <^{\mathsf{w}+}_\Delta B$, there is a world $\omega^a \in Mod_\Sigma(A)$ with $\omega^a <^{\mathsf{w}}_\Delta \omega^b$. Let $\omega^{a\prime} := \omega^a{}_{|\Sigma'}$. We have $\omega^{a\prime} \models A$, and because of (1.) we have $\omega^{a\prime} <^{\mathsf{w}+\prime}_\Delta \omega^{b\prime}$. Therefore, $A <^{\mathsf{w}+\prime}_\Delta B$.

Direction $\Leftarrow$: Let $A <^{\mathsf{w}+'}_{\Delta} B$ and let $\omega^b \in Mod_{\Sigma}(B)$. Let $\omega^{b'} := \omega^b{}_{|\Sigma'}$. Because $\omega^{b'} \models B$ and $A <^{\mathsf{w}+'}_{\Delta} B$, there is a world $\omega^{a'} \in Mod_{\Sigma'}$ such that $\omega^{a'} <^{\mathsf{w}+'}_{\Delta} \omega^{b'}$. Let $\omega^a \in \Omega_{\Sigma}$ be a world with $\omega^a{}_{|\Sigma'} = \omega^{a'}$. We have $\omega^a \models A$, and because of (1.) we have $\omega^a <^{\mathsf{w}+}_{\Delta} \omega^b$. Therefore, $A <^{\mathsf{w}+}_{\Delta} B$. ☐

Lemma 5.21 implies the following Lemma 5.22: For signatures $\Sigma' \subseteq \Sigma$ and a world $\omega \in \Omega_{\Sigma}$ Lemma 5.22 states that the position of ω in the extended preferred structure $<^{\mathsf{w}+}_{\Delta}$ of worlds induced by a belief base Δ over Σ' only depends on the valuation of variables in Σ'.

Lemma 5.22. *Let Σ be a signature and $\Sigma' \subseteq \Sigma$. Let Δ be a weakly consistent belief base over Σ'. Let $\omega^a, \omega^b, \omega' \in \Omega_{\Sigma}$ with $\omega^a{}_{|\Sigma'} = \omega^b{}_{|\Sigma'}$. Then we have*

1. $\omega^a \in \Omega^{feas}_{\Delta}$ *iff* $\omega^b \in \Omega^{feas}_{\Delta}$ *and*
2. *if* $\omega^a, \omega^b \in \Omega^{feas}_{\Delta}$ *then* $\omega^a <^{\mathsf{w}+}_{\Delta} \omega'$ *iff* $\omega^b <^{\mathsf{w}+}_{\Delta} \omega'$ *and* $\omega' <^{\mathsf{w}+}_{\Delta} \omega^a$ *iff* $\omega' <^{\mathsf{w}+}_{\Delta} \omega^b$.

Proof. Let $\omega^a, \omega^b, \omega'$ be as above and let $\omega^* := \omega^a{}_{|\Sigma'}$ and $\omega^{*\prime} := \omega'{}_{|\Sigma'}$. With Lemma 5.21 (1. a) we have $\omega^a \in \Omega^{feas}_{\Delta}$ iff $\omega^* \in \Omega^{feas'}_{\Delta}$ iff $\omega^b \in \Omega^{feas}_{\Delta}$. With Lemma 5.21 (1. b) we have $\omega^a <^{\mathsf{w}+}_{\Delta} \omega'$ iff $\omega^* <^{\mathsf{w}+'}_{\Delta} \omega^{*\prime}$ iff $\omega^b <^{\mathsf{w}+}_{\Delta} \omega'$. Analogously, $\omega' <^{\mathsf{w}+}_{\Delta} \omega^a$ iff $\omega' <^{\mathsf{w}+}_{\Delta} \omega^b$. ☐

The following Lemma 5.23 shows how a syntax splitting on a belief base carries over to the corresponding extended Z-partition.

Lemma 5.23. *Let $\Delta = \Delta_1 \bigcup_{\Sigma_1,\Sigma_2} \Delta_2$ be a weakly consistent belief base with syntax splitting. Let $EP(\Delta) = (\Delta^0, \dots, \Delta^k, \Delta^\infty)$ be the extended Z-partition of Δ, and for each $i \in \{1,2\}$ let $EP(\Delta_i) = (\Delta_i^0, \dots, \Delta_i^l, \Delta_i^\infty)$ be the extended Z-partition of Δ_i.*

1. *For each $i \in \{1,2\}$ and $j \in \{0, \dots, l_i, \infty\}$ we have $\Delta_i^j = \Delta^j \cap \Delta_i$ and thus especially $\Delta_i^j \subseteq \Delta^j$.*
2. *We have* $\max\{l_1, l_2\} = k$.
3. *For $l_1 \leq l_2$, we have* $\Delta^j = \begin{cases} \Delta_1^j \cup \Delta_2^j & \text{for } j = 1, \dots, l_1, \infty \\ \Delta_2^j & \text{for } j = l_1 + 1, \dots, k \end{cases}$.

Proof. **Ad 1.:** Because we can swap the indices 1, 2 in the syntax splitting, we can assume $i = 1$ without loss of generality. We will show that $\Delta_1^0 = \Delta^0 \cap \Delta_1$ for $\Delta_1 \neq \emptyset$. This implies $\Delta_1^j = \Delta^j \cap \Delta_1$ for

$j \in \{1, \ldots, l_1, \infty\}$ as the extended Z-partition can be constructed by recursively selecting the conditionals tolerated by all other conditionals in the belief base.

As Δ and therefore also Δ_2 is weakly consistent, every conditional $r \in \Delta_1$ is tolerated by all conditionals in Δ iff it is tolerated by all conditionals in Δ_1.

If $q \in \Delta_1^0$, then q is in Δ_1 and tolerated by every conditional in Δ_1. Hence, q is also in Δ and tolerated by every conditional in Δ (see above). Thus, $q \in \Delta^0 \cap \Delta_1$. If $p \in \Delta^0 \cap \Delta_1$, then p is in Δ_1 and it is tolerated by every conditional in Δ. Therefore, p is also tolerated by Δ_1. Thus, $p \in \Delta_1^0$. Together, we have $\Delta_1^0 = \Delta^0 \cap \Delta_1$.

Ad 2: As $\Delta_i \subseteq \Delta$ for $i = 1, 2$ we have $l_1, l_2 \leq k$. As Δ_k is not empty, it contains at least one conditional r. This r is either in Δ_1 or in Δ_2. Let $i \in \{1, 2\}$ be such that $r \in \Delta_i$. Then there is some m such that $r \in \Delta_i^m$. With (1.) we have $\Delta_i^m \subseteq \Delta^m$. As r can only be in one set of the extended Z-partition of Δ and $r \in \Delta^m$ and $r \in \Delta^k$ we have $m = k$. Therefore, the extended Z-partition of Δ_i has at least k elements, i.e., $l_i = k$.

Ad 3: First, consider the case that $j \leq l_1$ and therefore also $j \leq l_2$. As $\Delta_i^j \subseteq \Delta^j$ for $i = 1, 2$ we get $\Delta^j \supseteq \Delta_1^j \cup \Delta_2^j$. Every $r \in \Delta^j$ is either in Δ_1 or in Δ_2. W.l.o.g. assume $r \in \Delta_1$. Then there is some m such that $r \in \Delta_1^m$. With (1.) we have $\Delta_1^m \subseteq \Delta^m$. As r can only be in one set of the extended Z-partition of Δ we have $m = j$. Therefore, $\Delta^j \subseteq \Delta_1^j \cup \Delta_2^j$ and thus $\Delta^j = \Delta_1^j \cup \Delta_2^j$.

Now consider $l_1 < j \leq k$. From (1.) we get $\Delta^j \supseteq \Delta_2^j$. Analogous to the first case, we know that every conditional $r \in \Delta^j$ is either in Δ_1^j or Δ_2^j. Because $j > l_1$ there is no Δ_1^j in the extended Z-partition of Δ_1, and thus we have $r \in \Delta_2^j$. Therefore, $\Delta^j \subseteq \Delta_2^j$ and thus $\Delta^j = \Delta_2^j$.

For $j = \infty$ the same argumentation as for the case $j \leq l_1$ applies. □

For $\Delta = \Delta_1 \bigcup_{\Sigma_1, \Sigma_2} \Delta_2$, if we have $\omega <_\Delta^{\mathsf{w}+} \omega'$ then this relation can also be obtained using only Δ_1 or only Δ_2.

Lemma 5.24. *Let* $\Delta = \Delta_1 \bigcup_{\Sigma_1, \Sigma_2} \Delta_2$ *be a weakly consistent belief base and let* $\omega, \omega' \in \Omega_\Delta^{feas}$. *If* $\omega <_\Delta^{\mathsf{w}+} \omega'$, *then* $\omega <_{\Delta_1}^{\mathsf{w}+} \omega'$ *or* $\omega <_{\Delta_2}^{\mathsf{w}+} \omega'$.

Proof. Let $EP(\Delta) = (\Delta^0, \ldots, \Delta^k, \Delta^\infty)$ and let ξ, ξ^i be the functions mapping worlds to the set of falsified conditionals for Δ as in Definition 5.2. Let $\omega, \omega' \in \Omega$ be feasible worlds with $\omega <_\Delta^{\mathsf{w}+} \omega'$. By definition of $<^{\mathsf{w}+}_{\Delta}$ there is an $m \in \{0, \dots, k\}$ such that $\xi^i(\omega) = \xi^i(\omega')$ for every $i = m+1, \dots, k, \infty$ and $\xi^m(\omega) \subsetneqq \xi^m(\omega')$. Therefore, there is an $r \in \Delta$ such that $r \in \xi^m(\omega')$ and $r \notin \xi^m(\omega)$. The conditional r is either in Δ_1 or Δ_2. Assume that $r \in \Delta_x$ with x being either 1 or 2. Let $EP(\Delta_x) = (\Delta_x^0, \dots, \Delta_x^{k_x}, \Delta_x^\infty)$ be the extended Z-partition of Δ_x. Let ξ_x, ξ_x^i for $i = 0, \dots, k_x, \infty$ be the functions mapping worlds to the set of falsified conditionals for Δ_x. Because $\Delta_x^i \subseteq \Delta^i$ (see Lemma 5.23) and $\xi^i(\omega) = \xi^i(\omega')$ for every $i = m+1, \dots, k, \infty$ we have $\xi_x^i(\omega) = \xi_x^i(\omega')$ for every $i = m+1, \dots, l$. Furthermore, because $r \in \xi_x^m(\omega')$ and $r \notin \xi_x^m(\omega)$ we have $\xi_x^m(\omega) \subsetneqq \xi_x^m(\omega')$. Therefore, $\omega <^{\mathsf{w}+}_{\Delta_x} \omega'$.

Hence, we have $\omega <^{\mathsf{w}+}_{\Delta_1} \omega'$ or $\omega <^{\mathsf{w}+}_{\Delta_2} \omega'$. □

Note that both $\omega <^{\mathsf{w}+}_{\Delta_1} \omega'$ and $\omega <^{\mathsf{w}+}_{\Delta_2} \omega'$ might be true.

The next two Lemmas 5.25 and 5.26 consider situations where we can infer properties of $(\Omega^{feas}_{\Delta}, <^{\mathsf{w}+}_{\Delta})$ from $(\Omega^{feas}_{\Delta_1}, <^{\mathsf{w}+}_{\Delta_1})$ for a belief base $\Delta = \Delta_1 \bigcup_{\Sigma_1,\Sigma_2} \Delta_2$.

Lemma 5.25. *Let $\Delta = \Delta_1 \bigcup_{\Sigma_1,\Sigma_2} \Delta_2$ be a weakly consistent belief base, let $i, j \in \{1, 2\}, i \neq j$, and let $\omega \in \Omega^{feas}_{\Delta_i}$. If there is a world $\omega' \in \Omega^{feas}_{\Delta_j}$ such that $\omega_{|\Sigma_j} = \omega'_{|\Sigma_j}$, then $\omega \in \Omega^{feas}_{\Delta}$.*

Proof. Because $\omega \in \Omega^{feas}_{\Delta_i}$, we have that ω does not falsify a conditional from Δ_i^∞. Because $\omega' \in \Omega^{feas}_{\Delta_j}$, we have that ω' does not falsify a conditional from Δ_j^∞. Because $\omega_{|\Sigma_j} = \omega'_{|\Sigma_j}$ and $\Delta_j \in \mathcal{L}_{\Sigma_j}$, the worlds ω and ω' falsify the same conditionals in Δ_j. Hence, also ω does not falsify any conditional in Δ_j^∞. In combination, ω does not falsify any conditional in $\Delta^\infty = \Delta_i^\infty \cup \Delta_j^\infty$ (see Lemma 5.23). Therefore, $\omega \in \Omega^{feas}_{\Delta}$. □

Lemma 5.26. *Let $\Delta = \Delta_1 \bigcup_{\Sigma_1,\Sigma_2} \Delta_2$ be a weakly consistent belief base let $\omega, \omega' \in \Omega^{feas}_{\Delta}$, and let $i, j \in \{1, 2\}, i \neq j$. If $\omega <^{\mathsf{w}+}_{\Delta_i} \omega'$ and $\omega_{|\Sigma_j} = \omega'_{|\Sigma_j}$, then $\omega <^{\mathsf{w}+}_{\Delta} \omega'$.*

Proof. Because we can swap the indices 1, 2 in the syntax splitting, we can assume $i = 1$ and $j = 2$ without loss of generality.

Let ω, ω' be feasible worlds w.r.t. Δ such that $\omega <^{\mathsf{w}}_{\Delta_1} \omega'$ and $\omega_{|\Sigma_2} = \omega'_{|\Sigma_2}$. Let $EP(\Delta) = (\Delta^0, \dots, \Delta^k, \Delta^\infty)$ and let ξ, ξ^i be the functions mapping worlds to sets of falsified conditionals as in Definition 5.2. Let

$EP(\Delta_1) = (\Delta_1^0, \ldots, \Delta_1^{k_1}, \Delta_1^\infty)$ be the extended Z-partition of Δ_1 and let ξ_1, ξ_1^i for $i = 0, \ldots, k_1, \infty$ be the functions mapping worlds to the set of falsified conditionals for Δ_1. By the definition of $<_{\Delta_1}^{\mathsf{w}+}$ there is an $m \in \{0, \ldots, k_1\}$ such that $\xi_1^i(\omega) = \xi_1^i(\omega')$ for every $i = m+1, \ldots, k_1$ and $\xi_1^m(\omega) \subsetneqq \xi_1^m(\omega')$. With Lemma 5.23 we have $\xi_1^j(\omega^*) = \{r \in \Delta_1^j \mid \omega^* \text{ falsifies } r\} = \{r \in \Delta_1 \cap \Delta^j \mid \omega^* \text{ falsifies } r\} = \xi^j(\omega^*) \cap \Delta_1$ for every world ω^*, and $j = 0, \ldots, k_1, \infty$. This implies $\xi^i(\omega) \cap \Delta_1 = \xi_1^i(\omega) = \xi_1^i(\omega') = \xi^i(\omega') \cap \Delta_1$ for every $i = m+1, \ldots, k, \infty$ and $\xi^m(\omega) \cap \Delta_1 = \xi_1^m(\omega) \subsetneqq \xi_1^m(\omega) = \xi^m(\omega') \cap \Delta_1$.

Because $\omega_{|\Sigma_2} = \omega'_{|\Sigma_2}$, we have $\xi^i(\omega) \cap \Delta_2 = \xi^i(\omega') \cap \Delta_2$ for every $i = 0, \ldots, k, \infty$. Hence, we have $\xi^i(\omega) = \xi^i(\omega')$ for every $i = m+1, \ldots, k$ and $\xi^m(\omega) \subsetneqq \xi^m(\omega')$ and therefore $\omega <_\Delta^{\mathsf{w}+} \omega'$. □

The following Lemma 5.27 is a special case of Lemma 5.22 and describes that the variable assignment for variables that do not occur in the belief set has no influence on the position of a world in the resulting extended preferred structure on worlds.

Lemma 5.27. *Let $\Delta = \Delta_1 \bigcup_{\Sigma_1, \Sigma_2} \Delta_2$ be a weakly consistent belief base, $i \in \{1, 2\}$ and let $\omega^a, \omega^b, \omega' \in \Omega_\Sigma$ such that $\omega^a{}_{|\Sigma_i} = \omega^b{}_{|\Sigma_i}$. Then we have*

1. *$\omega^a \in \Omega_{\Delta_i}^{feas}$ iff $\omega^b \in \Omega_{\Delta_i}^{feas}$ and*
2. *if $\omega^a, \omega^b, \omega' \in \Omega^{feas}$ then $\omega^a <_{\Delta_i}^{\mathsf{w}+} \omega'$ iff $\omega^b <_{\Delta_i}^{\mathsf{w}+} \omega'$.*

Proof. This follows immediately from Lemma 5.22. □

Using these lemmas, we show that extended system W fulfils (Rel^{spo+}) and (Ind^{spo+}).

Proposition 5.28. *Extended system W fulfils (Rel^{spo+}).*

Proof. Let $\Delta = \Delta_1 \bigcup_{\Sigma_1, \Sigma_2} \Delta_2$ be a weakly consistent belief base with syntax splitting and $(\Omega_\Delta^{feas}, <_\Delta^{\mathsf{w}+})$ be the extended preferred structure on worlds induced by Δ. Let $EP(\Delta) = (\Delta^0, \ldots, \Delta^k, \Delta^\infty)$ be the extended Z-partition of Δ, and let $i, j \in \{1, 2\}, i \neq j$. Let $A, B, F \in \mathcal{L}_{\Sigma_i}$ be propositional formulas such that A, B are feasible for $(\Omega_\Delta^{feas}, <_\Delta^{\mathsf{w}+})$. We need to show that

$$Mod_\Sigma(F) \cap \Omega_\Delta^{feas} \neq \emptyset \quad \text{iff} \quad Mod_\Sigma(F) \cap \Omega_{\Delta_i}^{feas} \neq \emptyset \quad \text{and} \tag{5.3}$$

$$A <_\Delta^{\mathsf{w}+} B \quad \text{iff} \quad A <_{\Delta_i}^{\mathsf{w}+} B. \tag{5.4}$$

Because we can swap the indices 1, 2 in the syntax splitting, we can assume $i = 1$ and $j = 2$ without loss of generality.

Direction $\Rightarrow$ of (5.3): Assume that $Mod_\Sigma(F) \cap \Omega_\Delta^{feas} \neq \emptyset$. Then there is an $\omega \in Mod_\Sigma(F) \cap \Omega_\Delta^{feas}$; this ω does not falsify any conditional in Δ^∞. Especially ω does not falsify any conditionals in $\Delta_1^\infty \subseteq \Delta^\infty$ (see Lemma 5.23). Hence, $Mod_\Sigma(F) \cap \Omega_{\Delta_1}^{feas} \neq \emptyset$.

Direction $\Leftarrow$ of (5.3): Assume that $Mod_\Sigma(F) \cap \Omega_{\Delta_1}^{feas} \neq \emptyset$. Then there is at least one world $\omega \in Mod_\Sigma(F) \cap \Omega_{\Delta_1}^{feas}$. As Δ is weakly consistent, there is a world $\omega' \in \Omega_\Sigma$ that does not falsify any conditionals in Δ and thus does not satisfy any conditional in Δ_2^∞. Let $\omega^* := \omega_{|\Sigma_1}\omega'_{|\Sigma_2}$. As falsification of a conditional can only be influenced by the atoms occurring in a conditional and the valuations of the atoms from Σ_1 in ω^* coincide with their valuation in ω, the world ω^* does not falsify a conditional in Δ_1^∞. Analogously, ω^* does not falsify any conditional in Δ_2^∞, because ω' does not falsify a conditional in Δ_2^∞. In combination, ω^* does not falsify any conditional in $\Delta^\infty = \Delta_1^\infty \cup \Delta_2^\infty$ (see Lemma 5.23) and therefore $\omega^* \in \Omega_\Delta^{feas}$. Because ω^* coincides with ω on Σ_1, it is also a model of F. Hence, $Mod_\Sigma(F) \cap \Omega_\Delta^{feas} \neq \emptyset$.

Direction $\Rightarrow$ of (5.4): Assume that $A <_\Delta^{\mathsf{w}+} B$. We need to show that $A <_{\Delta_1}^{\mathsf{w}+} B$. Let ω' be any world in $Mod_\Sigma(B) \cap \Omega_\Delta^{feas}$. Now choose a feasible $\omega'_{min} \in \Omega_\Delta^{feas}$ such that

1. $\omega'_{min} \leq_\Delta^{\mathsf{w}+} \omega'$,
2. $\omega'_{|\Sigma_1} = \omega'_{min|\Sigma_1}$, and
3. there is no world $\omega'_{min2} \in \Omega_\Delta^{feas}$ with $\omega'_{min2} <_\Delta^{\mathsf{w}+} \omega'_{min}$ that fulfils (1.) and (2.).

Such an ω'_{min} exists because ω' fulfils properties (1.) and (2.), $<_\Delta^{\mathsf{w}+}$ is irreflexive and transitive, and there are only finitely many worlds in Ω_Δ^{feas}.

Because of (2.) and because $\omega' \models B$ we have that $\omega'_{min} \models B$. Because $A <_\Delta^{\mathsf{w}+} B$, there is a feasible world $\omega \in \Omega_\Delta^{feas}$ such that $\omega \models A$ and $\omega <_\Delta^{\mathsf{w}+} \omega'_{min}$. Because $\omega, \omega'_{min} \in \Omega_\Delta^{feas}$ it also holds that $\omega, \omega'_{min} \in \Omega_{\Delta_1}^{feas}$ and $\omega, \omega'_{min} \in \Omega_{\Delta_2}^{feas}$. Lemma 5.24 yields that $\omega <_{\Delta_1}^{\mathsf{w}+} \omega'_{min}$ or $\omega <_{\Delta_2}^{\mathsf{w}+} \omega'_{min}$.

The case $\omega <_{\Delta_2}^{\mathsf{w}+} \omega'_{min}$ is not possible: Assuming $\omega <_{\Delta_2}^{\mathsf{w}+} \omega'_{min}$, it follows that for $\omega'_{min2} := \omega'_{min|\Sigma_1}\omega_{|\Sigma_2}$ we have $\omega'_{min2} \in \Omega_{\Delta_2}^{feas}$ and $\omega'_{min2} <_{\Delta_2}^{\mathsf{w}} \omega'_{min}$ with Lemma 5.27. With Lemma 5.25 it follows that $\omega'_{min2} \in \Omega_\Delta^{feas}$ and with Lemma 5.26 it follows that $\omega'_{min2} <_\Delta^{\mathsf{w}+} \omega'_{min}$.

This contradicts (3.). Hence, $\omega <^{\mathsf{w}}_{\Delta_1} \omega'_{min}$. Because of (2.) and Lemma 5.27 it follows that $\omega <^{\mathsf{w}+}_{\Delta_1} \omega'$. As we can find an $\omega \in \Omega^{feas}_{\Delta_1}$ such that $\omega <^{\mathsf{w}+}_{\Delta_1} \omega'$ and $\omega \models A$ for every $\omega' \in \Omega^{feas}_{\Delta_1}$ with $\omega' \models B$ we have that $A <^{\mathsf{w}+}_{\Delta_1} B$.

Direction $\Leftarrow$ of (5.4): Assume that $A <^{\mathsf{w}+}_{\Delta_1} B$. We need to show that $A <^{\mathsf{w}+}_{\Delta} B$. Let ω' be any world in $Mod_\Sigma(B) \cap \Omega^{feas}_{\Delta}$. Then it also holds that $\omega' \in \Omega^{feas}_{\Delta_1}$. Because $A <^{\mathsf{w}+}_{\Delta_1} B$, there is a world $\omega^* \in \Omega^{feas}_{\Delta_1}$ such that $\omega^* \models A$ and $\omega^* <^{\mathsf{w}+}_{\Delta_1} \omega'$. Let $\omega := \omega^*{}_{|\Sigma_1}\omega'{}_{|\Sigma_2}$. Because $\omega^* \models A$ we have that $\omega \models A$. Furthermore, with Lemma 5.27 it follows that $\omega \in \Omega^{feas}_{\Delta_1}$ and $\omega <^{\mathsf{w}+}_{\Delta_1} \omega'$. Thus, $\omega \in \Omega^{feas}_{\Delta}$ with Lemma 5.25 and $\omega <^{\mathsf{w}+}_{\Delta} \omega'$ with Lemma 5.26. As we can construct $\omega \in \Omega^{feas}_{\Delta}$ such that $\omega <^{\mathsf{w}}_{\Delta} \omega'$ and $\omega \models A$ for every $\omega' \in \Omega^{feas}_{\Delta_1}$ with $\omega' \models B$ we have that $A <^{\mathsf{w}}_{\Delta} B$. □

Proposition 5.29. *Extended System W fulfils* (Ind^{spo+}).

Proof. Let $\Delta = \Delta_1 \bigcup_{\Sigma_1,\Sigma_2} \Delta_2$ be a weakly consistent belief base with syntax splitting and let $(\Omega^{feas}_{\Delta}, <^{\mathsf{w}+}_{\Delta})$ be the limited SPO on worlds induced with system W. Let $EP(\Delta) = (\Delta^0, \ldots, \Delta^k, \Delta^\infty)$ be the extended Z-partition of Δ, and let $i, j \in \{1, 2\}, i \neq j$. Let $A, B, F \in \mathcal{L}_{\Sigma_i}$ and $D \in \mathcal{L}_{\Sigma_2}$ be formulas such that A, B, D are feasible for $(\Omega^{feas}_{\Delta}, <^{\mathsf{w}+}_{\Delta})$. We need to show that

$$Mod_\Sigma(F) \cap \Omega^{feas}_{\Delta} \neq \emptyset \quad \text{iff} \quad Mod_\Sigma(FD) \cap \Omega^{feas}_{\Delta} \neq \emptyset \quad \text{and} \tag{5.5}$$

$$A <^{\mathsf{w}+}_{\Delta} B \quad \text{iff} \quad AD <^{\mathsf{w}+}_{\Delta} BD. \tag{5.6}$$

Because we can swap the indices 1, 2 in the syntax splitting, we can assume $i = 1$ and $j = 2$ without loss of generality.

Direction $\Rightarrow$ of (5.5): Assume that $Mod_\Sigma(F) \cap \Omega^{feas}_{\Delta} \neq \emptyset$, i.e., there is at least one world $\omega \in Mod_\Sigma(F) \cap \Omega^{feas}_{\Delta}$. As D is feasible w.r.t. $(\Omega^{feas}_{\Delta}, <^{\mathsf{w}+}_{\Delta})$, there is a feasible world $\omega' \in Mod_\Sigma(D)$; this ω' does not falsify any conditional in Δ^∞_2. Let $\omega^* := \omega_{|\Sigma_1}\omega'{}_{|\Sigma_2}$. As the falsification of a conditional can only be influenced by the atoms occurring in a conditional and the valuations of the atoms from Σ_1 in ω^* coincide with their valuation in ω, the world ω^* does not falsify a conditional in Δ_1. Analogously, ω^* does not falsify any conditional in Δ^∞_2, because ω' does not falsify a conditional in Δ^∞_2. In combination, ω^* does not falsify any conditional in $\Delta^\infty = \Delta^\infty_1 \cup \Delta^\infty_2$ (see Lemma 5.23) and is therefore feasible w.r.t. $(\Omega^{feas}_{\Delta}, <^{\mathsf{w}+}_{\Delta})$. As ω^* coincides with ω on Σ_1 it is a model of F and as ω^* coincides with ω' on Σ_2 it is a model of D. Hence, FD is feasible w.r.t. $(\Omega_\Delta^{feas}, <_\Delta^{\mathsf{w}+})$.

Direction $\Leftarrow$ of (5.5): Assume that $Mod_\Sigma(FD) \cap \Omega_\Delta^{feas} \neq \emptyset$. Then there is an $\omega \in \Omega_\Delta^{feas}$ such that $\omega \models FD$. This ω also models F; therefore $Mod_\Sigma(F) \cap \Omega_\Delta^{feas} \neq \emptyset$.

Direction $\Rightarrow$ of (5.6): Assume that $A <_\Delta^{\mathsf{w}+} B$. We need to show that $AD <_\Delta^{\mathsf{w}+} BD$. Let ω' be any world in $Mod_\Sigma(BD) \cap \Omega_\Delta^{feas}$. Now choose a feasible $\omega'_{min} \in \Omega_\Delta^{feas}$ such that

1. $\omega'_{min} \preceq_\Delta^{\mathsf{w}+} \omega'$,
2. $\omega'_{|\Sigma_1} = \omega'_{min|\Sigma_1}$, and
3. there is no $\omega'_{min2} \in \Omega_\Delta^{feas}$ with $\omega'_{min2} <_\Delta^{\mathsf{w}+} \omega'_{min}$ that fulfils (1.) and (2.).

Such an ω'_{min} exists because ω' fulfils properties (1.) and (2.), $<_\Delta^{\mathsf{w}+}$ is irreflexive and transitive, and there are only finitely many worlds in Ω_Δ^{feas}. Because of (2.) and because $\omega' \models BD$ we have that $\omega'_{min} \models B$. Because $A <_\Delta^{\mathsf{w}+} B$, there is a world $\omega^* \in \Omega_\Delta^{feas}$ such that $\omega^* \models A$ and $\omega^* <_\Delta^{\mathsf{w}+} \omega'_{min}$. Because $\omega^*, \omega'_{min} \in \Omega_\Delta^{feas}$ it also holds that $\omega^*, \omega'_{min} \in \Omega_{\Delta_1}^{feas}$ and $\omega^*, \omega'_{min} \in \Omega_{\Delta_2}^{feas}$. Lemma 5.24 yields that either $\omega^* <_{\Delta_1}^{\mathsf{w}} \omega'_{min}$ or $\omega^* <_{\Delta_2}^{\mathsf{w}} \omega'_{min}$.

The case $\omega^* <_{\Delta_2}^{\mathsf{w}+} \omega'_{min}$ is not possible: Assuming $\omega^* <_{\Delta_2}^{\mathsf{w}+} \omega'_{min}$, it follows that for $\omega'_{min2} := \omega'_{min|\Sigma_1}\omega^*_{|\Sigma_2}$ we have $\omega'_{min2} \in \Omega_{\Delta_2}^{feas}$ and $\omega'_{min2} <_{\Delta_2}^{\mathsf{w}+} \omega'_{min}$ with Lemma 5.27. With Lemma 5.25 it follows that $\omega'_{min2} \in \Omega_\Delta^{feas}$ and with Lemma 5.26 it follows that $\omega'_{min2} <_\Delta^{\mathsf{w}+} \omega'_{min}$. This contradicts (3.). Hence, $\omega^* <_{\Delta_1}^{\mathsf{w}+} \omega'_{min}$. Let $\omega := \omega^*_{|\Sigma_1}\omega'_{|\Sigma_2}$. Because $\omega^* \models A$ we have that $\omega \models A$. Because $\omega' \models D$ we have that $\omega \models D$. Because of (2.) and Lemma 5.27 it follows that $\omega \in \Omega_{\Delta_1}^{feas}$ and $\omega <_{\Delta_1}^{\mathsf{w}+} \omega'$. With Lemma 5.25 we have that $\omega \in \Omega_\Delta^{feas}$ and thus with Lemma 5.26 it follows that $\omega <_\Delta^{\mathsf{w}+} \omega'$. As we can construct an ω for every ω', we have that $AD <_\Delta^{\mathsf{w}+} BD$.

Direction $\Leftarrow$ of (5.6): Assume that $AD <_\Delta^{\mathsf{w}+} BD$. We need to show that $A <_\Delta^{\mathsf{w}+} B$. Let ω' be any world in $Mod_\Sigma(B) \cap \Omega_\Delta^{feas}$. Now choose $\omega'_{min} \in \Omega_\Delta^{feas}$ such that

1. $\omega'_{min} \models D$
2. $\omega'_{|\Sigma_1} = \omega'_{min|\Sigma_1}$, and
3. there is no world ω'_{min2} with $\omega'_{min2} < \omega'_{min}$ that fulfils (1.) and (2.).

Such an ω'_{min} exists because D is consistent, $<_\Delta^{\mathsf{w}+}$ is irreflexive and transitive, and there are only finitely many worlds in Ω^{feas}_{Δ}. Because of (2.) and because $\omega' \models B$ we have that $\omega'_{min} \models B$. Because of (1.) we have that $\omega'_{min} \models D$. Because $AD <^{w+}_{\Delta} BD$, there is a world $\omega^* \in \Omega^{feas}_{\Delta}$ such that $\omega^* \models AD$ and $\omega^* <^{w+}_{\Delta} \omega'_{min}$. Because $\omega^*, \omega'_{min} \in \Omega^{feas}_{\Delta}$ it also holds that $\omega^*, \omega'_{min} \in \Omega^{feas}_{\Delta_1}$ and $\omega^*, \omega'_{min} \in \Omega^{feas}_{\Delta_2}$. Lemma 5.24 yields that either $\omega^* <^{w+}_{\Delta_1} \omega'_{min}$ or $\omega^* <^{w+}_{\Delta_2} \omega'_{min}$.

The case $\omega^* <^{w+}_{\Delta_2} \omega'_{min}$ is not possible: Assuming $\omega^* <^{w+}_{\Delta_2} \omega'_{min}$, it follows that for $\omega'_{min2} := \omega'_{min|\Sigma_1}\omega^*_{|\Sigma_2}$ we have that ω'_{min2} is feasible and $\omega'_{min2} <^{w+}_{\Delta_2} \omega'_{min}$ with Lemma 5.27. With Lemma 5.25 it follows that $\omega'_{min2} \in \Omega^{feas}_{\Delta}$ and with Lemma 5.26 it follows that $\omega'_{min2} <^{w+}_{\Delta} \omega'_{min}$. This contradicts (3.). Hence, $\omega^* <^{w}_{\Delta_1} \omega'_{min}$. Let $\omega := \omega^*_{|\Sigma_1}\omega'_{|\Sigma_2}$. Because $\omega^* \models A$ we have that $\omega \models A$. Because of (2.) and Lemma 5.27 it follows that $\omega \in \Omega^{feas}_{\Delta_1}$ and $\omega <^{w+}_{\Delta_1} \omega'$. With Lemma 5.25 we have that $\omega \in \Omega^{feas}_{\Delta}$ and thus with Lemma 5.26 we have $\omega <^{w+}_{\Delta} \omega'$. As we can construct an ω for every ω' we have that $A <^{w+}_{\Delta} B$. □

Combining Propositions 5.28 and 5.29 yields that extended system W fulfils (SynSplit^{spo+}). Using Propositions 5.19 and 5.20 we get that extended system W satisfies (Rel$^+$), (Ind$^+$), and thus (SynSplit$^+$).

Proposition 5.30. *Extended system W satisfies (SynSplit$^+$).*

Thus, analogously to system W, also extended system W fully complies with syntax splittings.

5.6. Extended c-Inference

After we extended system W in the previous sections of this chapter, we now want to see how c-inference can be extended to handle belief bases that are not strongly consistent. While system W is defined using a (full) SPO on worlds, c-inference relies on c-representations which are ranking functions. Therefore, to define extended c-inference we first introduce extended c-representations, an adapted notion of c-representations in Subsection 5.6.1. Then, in Subsection 5.6.2 we define extended c-inference.

5.6.1. Introducing Extended c-Representations

Ranking functions as introduced in Subsection 2.1.2 can already model weakly consistent belief bases by assigning rank ∞ to worlds that are considered infeasible. But as observed in Section 3.8, a belief base that is not strongly consistent has no c-representation if we only use finite impacts as suggested in Definition 3.44. Hence, to work with belief bases that are only weakly consistent we need a more general definition of c-representations. To model a belief base that is not strongly consistent a generalized definition of c-representations must assign rank ∞ to some worlds. In [Ker01; Ker04] the concept of c-representations is introduced in a much more general way that is not limited to finite ranking functions (or ranking functions at all). Using this more general concept of c-representations we can define extended c-representations that are also constructed as a sum of impacts (as in (3.6)) but allow for infinite impacts.

Definition 5.31 (extended c-representation). *An* extended c-representation *of a belief base* $\Delta = \{(B_1|A_1), \ldots, (B_n|A_n)\}$ *over* Σ *is a ranking function* $\kappa_{\vec{\eta}}$ *constructed from impacts* $\vec{\eta} = (\eta_1, \ldots, \eta_n)$ *with* $\eta_i \in \mathbb{N}_0 \cup \{\infty\}$, $i \in \{1, \ldots, n\}$ *assigned to each conditional* $(B_i|A_i)$ *such that* $\kappa_{\vec{\eta}}$ *models* Δ *and is given by:*

$$\kappa_{\vec{\eta}}(\omega) = \sum_{\substack{1 \leq i \leq n \\ \omega \models A_i \overline{B}_i}} \eta_i. \tag{5.7}$$

We denote the set of all extended c-representations of Δ *by* $Mod^{ec}_{\Sigma}(\Delta)$.

By comparing definitions, we can see that every c-representation of a belief base Δ is also an extended c-representation of Δ.

Lemma 5.32. *Let* Δ *be a strongly consistent belief base. Every c-representation* $\kappa_{\vec{\eta}}$ *of* Δ *is an extended c-representation of* Δ.

We can show that every weakly consistent belief base Δ has a trivial extended c-representation that assigns rank ∞ to any world that violates a conditional Δ.

Proposition 5.33. *Let* Δ *be a weakly consistent belief base. Then* $\kappa_{\vec{\eta}}$ *with* $\vec{\eta} = (\infty, \ldots, \infty)$ *is an extended c-representation of* Δ.

Proof. Because Δ is weakly consistent, there is at least one world $\omega \in \Omega_{\Sigma}$ that does not falsify any of the conditionals (see Lemma 2.2). This implies $\kappa_{\vec{\eta}}(\omega) = 0$. Thus, $\kappa_{\vec{\eta}}$ is a ranking function.

For every conditional $(B_i|A_i) \in \Delta$ it holds that $\kappa_{\vec{\eta}}(A_i\overline{B_i}) = \infty$ because every model of $A_i\overline{B_i}$ falsifies $(B_i|A_i)$ with impact $\eta_i = \infty$. For $\kappa_{\vec{\eta}}(A_iB_i)$ we have either (1.) $\kappa_{\vec{\eta}}(A_iB_i) = 0$ or (2.) $\kappa_{\vec{\eta}}(A_iB_i) = \infty$. In case (1.) we have $\kappa_{\vec{\eta}}(A_iB_i) = 0 < \infty = \kappa_{\vec{\eta}}(A_i\overline{B_i})$. In case (2.) we have $\kappa_{\vec{\eta}}(A_i) = \infty$. In both cases $\kappa_{\vec{\eta}}$ models $(B_i|A_i)$. Thus, $\kappa_{\vec{\eta}} \models \Delta$. □

Proposition 5.33 also illustrates that worlds may have rank infinity in extended c-representations without the belief base requiring this. We can show that an extended c-representation of Δ needs to assign rank infinity only to those worlds that have rank infinity in the extended z-ranking function κ^{z+}_{Δ} of Δ. Proposition 5.34 states that $\kappa^{z+}_{\Delta}(\omega) = \infty$ implies $\kappa_{\vec{\eta}}(\omega) = \infty$, and Proposition 5.35 states that we can construct an extended c-representation such that for all ω with $\kappa^{z+}_{\Delta}(\omega) < \infty$ we have $\kappa_{\vec{\eta}}(\omega) < \infty$.

Proposition 5.34. *Let Δ be a weakly consistent belief base. For a world ω, if $\kappa^{z+}_{\Delta}(\omega) = \infty$ then for all extended c-representations $\kappa_{\vec{\eta}}$ of Δ we have that $\kappa_{\vec{\eta}}(\omega) = \infty$.*

Proof. Assume that $\kappa^{z+}_{\Delta}(\omega) = \infty$. Let $EP(\Delta) = (\Delta^0, \dots, \Delta^m, \Delta^\infty)$ be the extended Z-partition of Δ. By definition of κ^{z+}_{Δ} there exists a conditional $(B|A) \in \Delta^\infty$ such that ω is applicable for $(B|A)$. By Lemma 3.18 we have that there is a conditional $(B'|A') \in \Delta^\infty$ that is falsified by ω. Towards a contradiction assume that there is an extended c-representation $\kappa_{\vec{\eta}}$ of Δ with $\kappa_{\vec{\eta}}(\omega) < \infty$. This implies $\kappa_{\vec{\eta}}(A') < \infty$ since $\omega \models A'$. Because $\kappa_{\vec{\eta}}$ is a model of Δ and thus also of $(B'|A')$ there must be a world ω^1 that verifies $(B'|A')$ and satisfies $\kappa_{\vec{\eta}}(\omega^1) < \kappa_{\vec{\eta}}(\omega)$. Because $(B'|A') \in \Delta^\infty$, the conditional $(B'|A')$ is not tolerated by Δ^∞ and there must be another conditional $(B^1|A^1) \in \Delta^\infty$ that is falsified by ω^1, and analogously another world ω_2 that verifies $(B^1|A^1)$ and satisfies $\kappa_{\vec{\eta}}(\omega^2) < \kappa_{\vec{\eta}}(\omega^1)$. By repeating this argumentation we obtain an infinite chain of worlds $\omega_1, \omega_2, \dots$ such that $\kappa_{\vec{\eta}}(\omega_1) > \kappa_{\vec{\eta}}(\omega_2) > \dots$. But as there are only finitely many worlds (and also because there are only finitely many ranks below $\kappa_{\vec{\eta}}(\omega_1)$) such a chain cannot exist. This is a contradiction. □

Proposition 5.35. *Let Δ be a weakly consistent belief base. There exists an extended c-representation $\kappa_{\vec{\eta}}$ of Δ such that for all worlds ω we have that $\kappa^{z+}_{\Delta}(\omega) < \infty$ implies $\kappa_{\vec{\eta}}(\omega) < \infty$.*

Proof. Let $\Delta = \{(B_1|A_1), \dots, (B_n|A_n)\}$ be a weakly consistent belief base. Let $EP(\Delta) = (\Delta^0, \dots, \Delta^m, \Delta^\infty)$ be the extended Z-partition of Δ. Construct the impact vector $\vec{\eta}$ for Δ as follows. Let $\mu^0 := 1$ and $\mu^j := |\Delta^0 \cup \cdots \cup \Delta^{j-1}| \cdot \mu^{j-1} + 1$ for $j = 1, \ldots, m$. For $(B_i|A_i)$ with $(B_i|A_i) \in \Delta^j$ let $\eta_i := \mu^j$ for $j < \infty$ and $\eta_j := \infty$ for $j = \infty$. By construction, for worlds ω that do not falsify a conditional from $\Delta^j \cup \cdots \cup \Delta^m \cup \Delta^\infty$ we have $\kappa_{\vec{\eta}}(\omega) < \mu^j$.

$\kappa_{\vec{\eta}}$ is an extended c-representation of Δ: Let $(B_i|A_i)$ be any conditional in Δ. If $(B_i|A_i) \in \Delta^\infty$ then $\kappa_{\vec{\eta}}(A_i) = \infty$ and therefore $\kappa_{\vec{\eta}} \models (B_i|A_i)$. Otherwise, we have $(B_i|A_i) \in \Delta^j$ with $j < \infty$. Then for any world ω' falsifying $(B_i|A_i)$ we have $\kappa_{\vec{\eta}}(\omega) > \mu^j$; hence $\kappa_{\vec{\eta}}(A_i\overline{B_i}) \geq \mu_j$. Because $(B_i|A_i) \in \Delta^j$, there is a world ω' that verifies $(B_i|A_i)$ and does not falsify a conditional in $\Delta^j \cup \cdots \cup \Delta^m \cup \Delta^\infty$. Therefore, $\kappa_{\vec{\eta}}(A_iB_i) < \mu_j$. Thus, $\kappa_{\vec{\eta}}(A_iB_i) < \mu_j \leq \kappa_{\vec{\eta}}(A_i\overline{B_i})$ and $\kappa_{\vec{\eta}} \models (B_i|A_i)$.

Furthermore, it holds that $\kappa_{\vec{\eta}}(\omega) = \infty$ iff ω falsifies a conditional in Δ^∞. Therefore, $\kappa_{\vec{\eta}}(\omega) < \infty$ for all worlds ω with $\kappa^{z+}_\Delta(\omega) < \infty$. □

Using Proposition 5.34 we can see that for all worlds ω the extended c-representation constructed in the proof of Proposition 5.35 satisfies that $\kappa_{\vec{\eta}}(\omega) < \infty$ iff $\kappa^{z+}_\Delta(\omega) < \infty$. Using Lemma 3.17 we have $\kappa_{\vec{\eta}}(\omega) < \infty$ iff ω does not entail $\perp$ with p-entailment.

Lemma 5.36. *Let Δ be a weakly consistent belief base. There is an extended c-representation $\kappa_{\vec{\eta}}$ of Δ such that for all $\omega \in \Omega$ we have $\kappa_{\vec{\eta}}(\omega) < \infty$ iff $\omega \not\mid\!\sim^p_\Delta \perp$.*

Another consequence of Propositions 5.34 and 5.35 is the following.

Proposition 5.37. *Let Δ be a weakly consistent belief base with $EP(\Delta) = \{\Delta^0, \ldots, \Delta^m, \Delta^\infty\}$, and let $\omega \in \Omega$. We have that $\kappa(\omega) = \infty$ for all $\kappa \in Mod^{ec}_\Delta$ iff $\omega \models A$ for some $(B|A) \in \Delta^\infty$.*

Proof. **Direction ⇒:** Assume that $\kappa(\omega) = \infty$ for all $\kappa \in Mod^{ec}_\Delta$. With Proposition 5.35 this implies $\kappa^{z+}_\Delta(\omega) = \infty$. By Definition 3.16 this is the case if a conditional in Δ^∞ is applicable for ω.

Direction ⇐: Assume that $\omega \models A$ for some $(B|A) \in \Delta^\infty$. Then $\kappa^{z+}_\Delta(\omega) = \infty$ and with Proposition 5.34 we have $\kappa(\omega) = \infty$ for all $\kappa \in Mod^{ec}_\Delta$. □

In the next subsection we will use extended c-representations to define extended c-inference.

5.6.2. Introducing Extended c-Inference

c-Inference is the sceptical inference over all c-representations of a belief base. Therefore, we define extended c-inference as the sceptical inference over all extended c-representations of a belief base Δ.

Definition 5.38 (extended c-inference, $\mid\!\sim^{ec}_{\Delta}$)**.** *Let Δ be a belief base and let $A, B \in \mathcal{L}$. Then B is an* extended c-inference *from A in the context of Δ, denoted by $A \mid\!\sim^{ec}_{\Delta} B$, iff $A \mid\!\sim_{\kappa} B$ holds for all extended c-representations κ of Δ.*

First, we verify that extended c-inference is indeed an inductive inference operator that coincides with c-inference for strongly consistent belief bases.

Proposition 5.39. *Extended c-inference is an inductive inference operator.*

Proof. We need to show that extended c-inference satisfies both (DI) and (TV).

(DI): Every extended c-representation of Δ accepts the conditionals in Δ by definition. Therefore, $A \mid\!\sim^{ec}_{\Delta} B$ for every $(B|A) \in \Delta$.

(TV): For $\Delta = \emptyset$ the only extended c-representation is κ^0 with $\kappa^0(\omega) = 0$ for all $\omega \in \Omega_\Sigma$ because there are no conditionals that can be falsified by worlds. In this case κ accepts only conditionals $(B|A)$ with $A\overline{B} = \bot$, which are exactly the conditionals with $A \models B$. □

Proposition 5.40. *For strongly consistent belief bases, extended c-inference coincides with c-inference.*

Proof. Let $\Delta = \{(B_1|A_1), \dots, (B_n|A_n)\}$ be a strongly consistent belief base and $C, D \in \mathcal{L}$. We need to show that $C \mid\!\sim^{ec}_{\Delta} D$ iff $C \mid\!\sim^{c}_{\Delta} D$.

Direction $\Rightarrow$: Let $C \mid\!\sim^{ec}_{\Delta} D$, i.e., every extended c-representation of Δ induces $C \mid\!\sim D$. As every c-representation is an extended c-representation (Lemma 5.32), every c-representation induces $C \mid\!\sim D$. Thus, $C \mid\!\sim^{c}_{\Delta} D$.

Direction $\Leftarrow$: Let $C \mid\!\sim^{c}_{\Delta} D$, i.e., every c-representation of Δ induces $C \mid\!\sim D$. We need to show that any extended c-representation $\kappa_{\vec{\eta}}$ of Δ induces $C \mid\!\sim_{\kappa_{\vec{\eta}}} D$.

If $\vec{\eta}$ contains only finite values it is a c-representation and thus $C \mid\!\sim_{\kappa_{\vec{\eta}}} D$ by assumption. Assume that $\vec{\eta}$ contains infinite entries.

Let $EP(\Delta) = (\Delta^0, \ldots, \Delta^m, \Delta^\infty)$ be the extended Z-partition of Δ. Because Δ is strongly consistent, we have $\Delta^\infty = \emptyset$. Let $\mathit{fin}(\vec{\eta}) = \{\eta_i \mid i \in \{0, \ldots, n\}, \eta_i < \infty\}$ be the multi-set of finite values in impact vector $\vec{\eta}$. Now construct $\vec{\eta}^f$ from $\vec{\eta}$ as follows.

- For $(B_i|A_i)$ with $\eta_i < \infty$ let $\eta_i^f := \eta_i$.
- Let $f_0 := 1 + |\mathit{fin}(\vec{\eta})| \cdot \max(\mathit{fin}(\vec{\eta}))$.
  For $(B_i|A_i) \in \Delta^0$ with $\eta_i = \infty$ let $\eta_i^f := f_0$.
- For $j \in \{1, \ldots, m\}$ let

  $$f_j := f_{j-1} \cdot \left(\left|\{(B_i|A_i) \in \Delta^{j-1} \mid \eta_i = \infty\}\right| + 1\right).$$

  For $(B_i|A_i) \in \Delta^j$ with $\eta_i = \infty$ let $\eta_i^f := f_j$.

By construction the sum of the impacts in $\mathit{fin}(\vec{\eta})$ is less than f_0 and the sum of the impacts of the conditionals in $\Delta^0 \cup \cdots \cup \Delta^{j-1}$ is less than f_j for $j = 0, \ldots, m$.

Let $\kappa^f := \kappa_{\vec{\eta}^f}$. Now verify that:

1. κ^f is a c-representation of Δ. For this we need to check that κ^f models all conditionals in Δ.
2. $\mathrel{|\!\sim}_{\kappa^f} \subseteq \mathrel{|\!\sim}_{\kappa_{\vec{\eta}}}$, i.e., every inference in $\mathrel{|\!\sim}_{\kappa^f}$ is also an inference in $\mathrel{|\!\sim}_{\kappa_{\vec{\eta}}}$.

From (1.) it follows that κ^f induces $C \mathrel{|\!\sim}_{\kappa^f} D$, because $C \mathrel{|\!\sim}^c_\Delta D$. With (2.) it follows that $\kappa_{\vec{\eta}}$ induces $C \mathrel{|\!\sim}_{\kappa_{\vec{\eta}}} D$.

Ad (1): Let $(B_i|A_i) \in \Delta$. We distinguish three cases.

<u>Case 1:</u> $\kappa_{\vec{\eta}}(A_iB_i) < \kappa_{\vec{\eta}}(A_i\overline{B_i}) < \infty$

In this case $\kappa^f(A_iB_i) < \kappa^f(A_i\overline{B_i}) < f_0$ and therefore $\kappa^f \models (B_i|A_i)$.

<u>Case 2:</u> $\kappa_{\vec{\eta}}(A_iB_i) < \infty$ and $\kappa_{\vec{\eta}}(A_i\overline{B_i}) = \infty$

In this case $\kappa^f(A_iB_i) < f_0 < \kappa^f(A_i\overline{B_i})$ and therefore $\kappa^f \models (B_i|A_i)$.

<u>Case 3:</u> $\kappa_{\vec{\eta}}(A_iB_i) = \infty$ and $\kappa_{\vec{\eta}}(A_i\overline{B_i}) = \infty$

Assume that $(B_i|A_i)$ is in Δ^j. Then there is a world ω such that $\omega \models A_iB_i$ and ω falsifies no conditional in $\Delta^j \cup \cdots \cup \Delta^m$. Therefore, $\kappa^f(\omega) < f_j$ and thus $\kappa^f(A_iB_i) < f_j$. Any model of $A_i\overline{B_i}$ falsifies $(B_i|A_i)$, therefore $\kappa^f(A_i\overline{B_i}) > f_j$. Thus, we have $\kappa^f(A_iB_i) < f_j < \kappa^f(A_i\overline{B_i})$ and therefore $\kappa^f \models (B_i|A_i)$.

Ad (2.): Assume that $X \mathrel{|\!\sim}_{\kappa^f} Y$. There are two cases.

<u>Case 1:</u> $\kappa^f(X\overline{Y}) < f_0$

In this case $\kappa^f(XY) < \kappa^f(X\overline{Y}) < f_0$ and therefore $\kappa_{\vec{\eta}}(XY) < \kappa_{\vec{\eta}}(X\overline{Y}) < \infty$. Hence, $X \mathrel{|\!\sim}_{\kappa_{\vec{\eta}}} Y$.

Case 2: $\kappa^f(X\overline{Y}) \geq f_0$
In this case $\kappa_{\vec{\eta}}(X\overline{Y}) = \infty$ and therefore $X \mathrel{|\!\sim}_{\kappa_{\vec{\eta}}} Y$. □

Furthermore, extended c-inference is a preferential inductive inference operator, i.e., it satisfies the system P postulates.

Proposition 5.41. *Extended c-inference satisfies system P.*

Proof. Extended c-inference is the sceptical inference over the extended c-representations of a belief base. Using the fact that the inference relation induced by a single ranking function is preferential and that the intersection of preferential inference relations is preferential again, we can show that extended c-inference is preferential analogously to the proof of [Bei+21, Proposition 11]. □

Proposition 5.41 implies that extended c-inference captures p-entailment, i.e., if $A \mathrel{|\!\sim}^p_\Delta B$ then $A \mathrel{|\!\sim}^{ec}_\Delta B$. In addition to that, extended c-inference satisfies (Classic Preservation), i.e., it coincides with p-entailment on entailments of the form $A \mathrel{|\!\sim} \bot$.

Proposition 5.42. *Extended c-inference satisfies (Classic Preservation).*

Proof. We need to show that $A \mathrel{|\!\sim}^{ec}_\Delta \bot$ iff $A \mathrel{|\!\sim}^p_\Delta \bot$. Using Lemma 3.17 it is sufficient to show that $A \mathrel{|\!\sim}^{ec}_\Delta \bot$ iff $\kappa^{z+}_\Delta(A) = \infty$.

Direction $\Leftarrow$**:** Let $\kappa^{z+}_\Delta(A) = \infty$, i.e., for every model $\omega \in Mod_\Sigma(A)$ of A we have $\kappa^{z+}_\Delta(\omega) = \infty$. For every extended c-representation $\kappa_{\vec{\eta}}(A)$ of Δ, with Proposition 5.34 it follows that $\kappa_{\vec{\eta}}(\omega) = \infty$ for every $\omega \in Mod_\Sigma(A)$ and thus $\kappa_{\vec{\eta}}(A) = \infty$. Thus, $A \mathrel{|\!\sim}^{ec}_\Delta \bot$.

Direction $\Rightarrow$**:** Let $A \mathrel{|\!\sim}^{ec}_\Delta \bot$, i.e., there is no extended c-representation $\kappa_{\vec{\eta}}$ of Δ s.t. $\kappa_{\vec{\eta}}(A) < \infty$. By Proposition 5.35 we have $\kappa^{z+}_\Delta(A) = \infty$. □

Extended c-inference does not satisfy *Rational Monotony (RM)* as c-inference already violates (RM). Because c-inference and extended c-inference coincide for strongly consistent belief bases, every instance where c-inference violates (RM) is also an example of extended c-inference violating (RM).

5.7. Characterization of Extended c-Representations by Constraint Satisfaction Problems

The c-representations of a belief base can conveniently be characterized by the solutions of a constraint satisfaction problem (CSP). The following modelling of c-representations as solutions of a CSP was introduced by Beierle, Kern-Isberner, and Södler [BKS11] and is based on the constraints characterizing c-revisions by Kern-Isberner [Ker01; Ker04]. For $\Delta = \{(B_1|A_1), \dots, (B_n|A_n)\}$ over Σ the constraint satisfaction problem for c-representations of Δ, denoted by $CR_\Sigma(\Delta)$, on the constraint variables $\{\eta_1, \dots, \eta_n\}$ ranging over $\mathbb{N}_0$ is given by the constraints cr_i^Δ for all $i \in \{1, \dots, n\}$:

$$\eta_i > \min_{\substack{\omega \in \Omega_\Sigma \\ \omega \models A_i B_i}} \sum_{\substack{j \neq i \\ \omega \models A_j \overline{B_j}}} \eta_j - \min_{\substack{\omega \in \Omega_\Sigma \\ \omega \models A_i \overline{B_i}}} \sum_{\substack{j \neq i \\ \omega \models A_j \overline{B_j}}} \eta_j. \qquad (cr_i^\Delta)$$

For each $i \in \{1, \dots, n\}$ the constraint cr_i^Δ ensures that $\kappa_{\vec{\eta}}$ is a model of the conditional $(B_i|A_i)$. The sum terms are induced by the worlds verifying and falsifying $(B_i|A_i)$, respectively. A solution of $CR_\Sigma(\Delta)$ is an n-tuple $(\eta_1, \dots, \eta_n) \in \mathbb{N}_0^n$. For a constraint satisfaction problem CSP, the set of solutions is denoted by $Sol(CSP)$. Thus, with $Sol(CR_\Sigma(\Delta))$ we denote the set of all solutions of $CR_\Sigma(\Delta)$ and each solution of $Sol(CR_\Sigma(\Delta))$ corresponds to a c-representations of Δ.

Proposition 5.43 (soundness and completeness of $CR_\Sigma(\Delta)$ [Bei+18]). *Let $\Delta = \{(B_1|A_1), \dots, (B_n|A_n)\}$ be a belief base over Σ. Then we have:*

$$Mod_\Sigma^c(\Delta) = \{\kappa_{\vec{\eta}} \mid \vec{\eta} \in Sol(CR_\Sigma(\Delta))\} \qquad (5.8)$$

Now we construct a similar CSP for extended c-representations. The extended c-representations characterized by this CSP can assign rank ∞ to some formulas and worlds. Therefore, we need to take into account that an extended c-representation $\kappa_{\vec{\eta}}$ accepts a conditional $(B|A)$ not only if $\kappa_{\vec{\eta}}(AB) < \kappa_{\vec{\eta}}(A\overline{B})$ but also if $\kappa_{\vec{\eta}}(A) = \infty$. Encoding this acceptance condition into a constraint yields the following CSP.

Definition 5.44 ($CR_\Sigma^{ex}(\Delta)$). *Let $\Delta = \{(B_1|A_1), \dots, (B_n|A_n)\}$ be a belief base over Σ. The constraint satisfaction problem for extended c-representations of Δ, denoted by $CR_\Sigma^{ex}(\Delta)$, on the constraint variables*

$\{\eta_1, \ldots, \eta_n\}$ ranging over $\mathbb{N}_0 \cup \{\infty\}$ is given by the constraints $cr_i^{ex\,\Delta}$ for all $i \in \{1, \ldots, n\}$:

$$\begin{array}{l} \min\limits_{\substack{\omega\in\Omega_\Sigma\\ \omega\models A_i}} \sum\limits_{\substack{1\leq j\leq n\\ \omega\models A_j\overline{B_j}}} \eta_j = \infty \qquad or \\ \eta_i > \min\limits_{\substack{\omega\in\Omega_\Sigma\\ \omega\models A_iB_i}} \sum\limits_{\substack{j\neq i\\ \omega\models A_j\overline{B_j}}} \eta_j - \min\limits_{\substack{\omega\in\Omega_\Sigma\\ \omega\models A_i\overline{B_i}}} \sum\limits_{\substack{j\neq i\\ \omega\models A_j\overline{B_j}}} \eta_j \end{array} \qquad (cr_i^{ex\,\Delta})$$

Again, for each $i \in \{1, \ldots, n\}$ the constraint $cr_i^{ex\,\Delta}$ corresponds to the conditional $(B_i|A_i)$.

Proposition 5.45 (soundness and completeness of $CR_\Sigma^{ex}(\Delta)$)**.** *Let $\Delta = \{(B_1|A_1), \ldots, (B_n|A_n)\}$ be a weakly consistent belief base over Σ. Then we have:*

$$Mod_\Sigma^{ec}(\Delta) = \{\kappa_{\vec{\eta}} \mid \vec{\eta} \in Sol(CR_\Sigma^{ex}(\Delta))\} \tag{5.9}$$

Proof. **Soundness:** Let $\vec{\eta}$ be an impact vector in $Sol(CR_\Sigma^{ex}(\Delta))$. Because Δ is weakly consistent, there is a world ω that does not falsify any conditional in Δ (Lemma 2.2); therefore $\kappa_{\vec{\eta}}(\omega) = 0$ and $\kappa_{\vec{\eta}}$ is a ranking function. It is left to show that $\kappa_{\vec{\eta}}$ models the conditionals in Δ.

Let $(B_i|A_i) \in \Delta$. There are three cases.

Case 1: $\kappa_{\vec{\eta}}(A_i\overline{B_i}) = \infty$ and $\kappa_{\vec{\eta}}(A_iB_i) = \infty$
In this case $\kappa_{\vec{\eta}}(A_i) = \infty$ and therefore $\kappa_{\vec{\eta}} \models (B_i|A_i)$.

Case 2: $\kappa_{\vec{\eta}}(A_i\overline{B_i}) = \infty$ and $\kappa_{\vec{\eta}}(A_iB_i) < \infty$
In this case $\kappa_{\vec{\eta}}(A_i\overline{B_i}) > \kappa_{\vec{\eta}}(A_iB_i)$ and therefore $\kappa_{\vec{\eta}} \models (B_i|A_i)$.

Case 3: $\kappa_{\vec{\eta}}(A_i\overline{B_i}) < \infty$
In this case

$$\min_{\substack{\omega\in\Omega_\Sigma\\ \omega\models A_i}} \sum_{\substack{1\leq j\leq n\\ \omega\models A_j\overline{B_j}}} \eta_j = \kappa_{\vec{\eta}}(A_i) < \kappa_{\vec{\eta}}(A_i\overline{B_i}) < \infty,$$

hence the condition in $cr_i^{ex\,\Delta}$ to the left of the *or* is not satisfied. Because $\vec{\eta} \in Sol(CR_\Sigma^{ex}(\Delta))$, the impacts must satisfy all constraints in $CR_\Sigma^{ex}(\Delta)$ including $cr_i^{ex\,\Delta}$. As the condition to the left of the *or* is violated, the condition to the right of the *or* must hold, i.e.,

$$\begin{aligned}
& \eta_i > \min_{\substack{\omega \in \Omega_\Sigma \\ \omega \models A_i B_i}} \sum_{\substack{j \neq i \\ \omega \models A_j \overline{B_j}}} \eta_j - \min_{\substack{\omega \in \Omega_\Sigma \\ \omega \models A_i \overline{B_i}}} \sum_{\substack{j \neq i \\ \omega \models A_j \overline{B_j}}} \eta_j \\
\Leftrightarrow \quad & \eta_i + \min_{\substack{\omega \in \Omega_\Sigma \\ \omega \models A_i \overline{B_i}}} \sum_{\substack{j \neq i \\ \omega \models A_j \overline{B_j}}} \eta_j > \min_{\substack{\omega \in \Omega_\Sigma \\ \omega \models A_i B_i}} \sum_{\substack{j \neq i \\ \omega \models A_j \overline{B_j}}} \eta_j \\
\Leftrightarrow \quad & \min_{\substack{\omega \in \Omega_\Sigma \\ \omega \models A_i \overline{B_i}}} \sum_{\substack{1 \leq j \leq n \\ \omega \models A_j \overline{B_j}}} \eta_j > \min_{\substack{\omega \in \Omega_\Sigma \\ \omega \models A_i B_i}} \sum_{\substack{1 \leq j \leq n \\ \omega \models A_j \overline{B_j}}} \eta_j \\
\Leftrightarrow \quad & \kappa_{\vec{\eta}}(A_i \overline{B_i}) > \kappa_{\vec{\eta}}(A_i B_i)
\end{aligned}$$

and therefore $\kappa_{\vec{\eta}} \models (B_i | A_i)$.

Completeness: Let $\kappa_{\vec{\eta}}$ be an extended c-representation of Δ with impact vector $\vec{\eta}$. We need to show that $\vec{\eta} \in Sol(CR_\Sigma^{ex}(\Delta))$, i.e., that $\vec{\eta}$ satisfies every constraint cr_i^Δ in $Sol(CR_\Sigma^{ex}(\Delta))$. Because $\kappa_{\vec{\eta}}$ is an extended c-representation of Δ, we have $\kappa_{\vec{\eta}} \models (B_i|A_i)$. This requires either (1.) $\kappa_{\vec{\eta}}(A_i) = \infty$ or (2.) $\kappa_{\vec{\eta}}(A_i\overline{B_i}) > \kappa_{\vec{\eta}}(A_i B_i)$. In case (1.) we have

$$\min_{\substack{\omega \in \Omega_\Sigma \\ \omega \models A_i}} \sum_{\substack{1 \leq j \leq n \\ \omega \models A_j \overline{B_j}}} \eta_j = \kappa_{\vec{\eta}}(A_i \overline{B_i}) = \infty$$

and the condition before the *or* in $cr_i^{ex\,\Delta}$ is satisfied.

In case (2.) we can see with the equivalence transformations in the *Soundness* part of this proof that the condition to the right of the *or* is satisfied. In both cases, $\vec{\eta}$ satisfies $cr_i^{ex\,\Delta}$. □

The requirement for weak consistency in Proposition 5.45 is necessary: a belief base Δ that is not weakly consistent has no extended c-representations, i.e., $Mod_\Sigma^{ec}(\Delta) = \emptyset$, but the set of solutions for $CR_\Sigma^{ex}(\Delta)$ is not empty as $Sol(CR_\Sigma^{ex}(\Delta)) = \{(\infty, \dots, \infty)\}$.

The CSP $CR_\Sigma^{ex}(\Delta)$ representing extended c-representations is more complex than the CSP $CR_\Sigma(\Delta)$ characterizing c-representations. However, for the computation of extended c-inference we can construct a simplified CSP $CRS_\Sigma^{ex}(\Delta)$ that still yields all extended c-representations necessary for extended c-inference. This simplification of the CSPs uses the extended Z-partition $EP(\Delta)$ and Propositions 5.34 and 5.35 to determine which impacts need to be infinite and which impacts can be restricted to finite values. The simplified CSP

$CRS^{ex}_{\Sigma}(\Delta)$ uses both fewer constraint variables and fewer constraints than $CR^{ex}_{\Sigma}(\Delta)$ for belief bases that are weakly consistent but not strongly consistent.

Before stating $CRS^{ex}_{\Sigma}(\Delta)$, we show two propositions that we will later use for proving the soundness and completeness of $CRS^{ex}_{\Sigma}(\Delta)$. One important observation is that we can assume the impacts of conditionals in Δ^{∞} to be infinity without changing the induced c-representation. Note that this does not imply that $\eta_i = \infty$ for every $(B_i|A_i) \in \Delta^{\infty}$. For example, if Δ^{∞} contains two conditionals $(B_i|A_i), (B_j|A_j)$ that falsify the same conditionals, then one of η_i, η_j could be finite.

Proposition 5.46. *Let Δ be a weakly consistent belief base with extended Z-partition $EP(\Delta) = (\Delta^0, \ldots, \Delta^m, \Delta^{\infty})$. Let $\vec{\eta}$ be impacts such that $\kappa_{\vec{\eta}}$ is an extended c-representation of Δ and let $\vec{\eta}'$ be the impact vector defined by, for $i = 1, \ldots, m$,*

$$\eta_i' := \begin{cases} \infty & \text{if } (B_i|A_i) \in \Delta^{\infty} \\ \eta_i & \text{otherwise.} \end{cases}$$

Then $\kappa_{\vec{\eta}} = \kappa_{\vec{\eta}'}$.

Proof. Let ω be a world. There are two cases.

Case 1: There is a conditional $(B_i|A_i) \in \Delta^{\infty}$ that is falsified by ω. Then $\kappa^{z+}_{\Delta}(\omega) = \infty$ and therefore $\kappa_{\vec{\eta}}(\omega) = \infty$ by Proposition 5.34. Because $\eta_i' = \infty$ we have

$$\kappa_{\vec{\eta}'}(\omega) = \sum_{\substack{1 \leq j \leq n \\ \omega \models A_j \overline{B}_j}} \eta_j' = \infty = \kappa_{\vec{\eta}}(\omega).$$

Case 2: There is no conditional in Δ^{∞} that is falsified by ω. Because $\eta_i = \eta_i'$ for all i with $\omega \models A_j \overline{B}_j$ we have

$$\kappa_{\vec{\eta}'}(\omega) = \sum_{\substack{1 \leq j \leq n \\ \omega \models A_j \overline{B}_j}} \eta_j' = \sum_{\substack{1 \leq j \leq n \\ \omega \models A_j \overline{B}_j}} \eta_j = \kappa_{\vec{\eta}}(\omega).$$

□

A further observation is that for extended c-inference it is sufficient to take only a subset of all extended c-representations of a belief base into account. The set $CMod^{ec}_{\Sigma}(\Delta)$ defined below contains all c-representations from $Mod^{ec}_{\Sigma}(\Delta)$ that only assign rank ∞ to a world if this is required by Proposition 5.34. We can show that sceptical inference over $CMod^{ec}_{\Sigma}(\Delta)$ yields that same inference relation as sceptical inference over $Mod^{ec}_{\Sigma}(\Delta)$.

Definition 5.47 ($CMod^{ec}_{\Sigma}(\Delta)$)**.** *For a belief base Δ, $CMod^{ec}_{\Sigma}(\Delta)$ is the set of extended c-representations $\kappa_{\vec{\eta}}$ of Δ with $\kappa_{\vec{\eta}}(\omega) < \infty$ for all worlds ω with $\kappa^{z+}_{\Delta}(\omega) < \infty$.*

Proposition 5.48. *Let Δ be a belief base. Then $A \mathrel{|\!\sim}_{\kappa_{\vec{\eta}}} B$ holds for all extended c-representations $\kappa_{\vec{\eta}}$ in $CMod^{ec}_{\Sigma}(\Delta)$ iff $A \mathrel{|\!\sim}_{\kappa_{\vec{\eta}}} B$ holds for all extended c-representations $\kappa_{\vec{\eta}}$ in Mod^{ec}_{Δ}.*

Proof. **Direction $\Leftarrow$:** Observe that $CMod^{ec}_{\Sigma}(\Delta) \subseteq Mod^{ec}_{\Sigma}(\Delta)$. Therefore, if $A \mathrel{|\!\sim}_{\kappa} B$ holds for all extended c-representations in $Mod^{ec}_{\Sigma}(\Delta)$, then $A \mathrel{|\!\sim}_{\kappa} B$ holds for all extended c-representations in $CMod^{ec}_{\Sigma}(\Delta)$.

Direction $\Rightarrow$: Show this direction by contraposition. Assume that there is a $\kappa \in Mod^{ec}_{\Sigma}(\Delta)$ with $A \mathrel{|\!\not\sim}_{\kappa} B$. We will construct an extended c-representation $\kappa' \in CMod^{ec}_{\Sigma}(\Delta)$ such that $A \mathrel{|\!\not\sim}_{\kappa'} B$.

Let $\vec{\eta}$ be an impact vector inducing κ. Let $EP(\Delta) = (\Delta^0, \dots, \Delta^m, \Delta^\infty)$ be the extended Z-partition of Δ. Let $fin(\vec{\eta}) := \{\eta_i \mid i \in \{0, \dots, n\}, \eta_i < \infty\}$ be the set of finite values in impact vector $\vec{\eta}$. Now construct $\vec{\eta}'$ from $\vec{\eta}$ as follows.

- For $(B_i|A_i)$ with $\eta_i < \infty$ let $\eta'_i := \eta_i$.
- Let $f_0 := 1 + |fin(\vec{\eta})| \cdot \max(fin(\vec{\eta}))$.
  For $(B_i|A_i) \in \Delta^0$ with $\eta_i = \infty$ let $\eta'_i := f_0$.
- For $j \in \{1, \dots, m\}$ let

$$f_j := f_{j-1} \cdot \left(\left|\{(B_i|A_i) \in \Delta^{j-1} \mid \eta_i = \infty\}\right| + 1\right).$$

  For $(B_i|A_i) \in \Delta^j$ with $\eta_i = \infty$ let $\eta'_i := f_j$.
- For every $(B_i|A_i) \in \Delta^\infty$ with $\eta_i = \infty$ let $\eta'_i := \infty$.

By construction the sum of the impacts in $fin(\vec{\eta})$ is less than f_0 and the sum of the impacts of the conditionals in $\Delta^0 \cup \dots \cup \Delta^j$ is less than f_j for $j = 0, \dots, m$.

Let $\kappa' := \kappa_{\vec{\eta}'}$. Now we verify that:

1. κ' is an extended c-representation of Δ.
2. For $\omega \in \Omega_\Sigma$, we have that $\kappa^{z+}_{\Delta}(\omega) < \infty$ implies $\kappa_{\vec{\eta}'}(\omega) < \infty$.

3. $A \not\mid\!\sim_{\kappa'} B$

From (1.) and (2.) it then follows that $\kappa' \in CMod^{ec}_{\Sigma}(\Delta)$.

Ad (1): Let $(B_i|A_i) \in \Delta$. We distinguish three cases.

Case 1: $\kappa_{\vec{\eta}}(A_iB_i) < \kappa_{\vec{\eta}}(A_i\overline{B_i}) < \infty$

In this case $\kappa'(A_iB_i) < \kappa'(A_i\overline{B_i}) < f_0$ and therefore $\kappa' \models (B_i|A_i)$.

Case 2: $\kappa_{\vec{\eta}}(A_iB_i) < \infty$ and $\kappa_{\vec{\eta}}(A_i\overline{B_i}) = \infty$

In this case $\kappa'(A_iB_i) < f_0 < \kappa'(A_i\overline{B_i})$ and therefore $\kappa' \models (B_i|A_i)$.

Case 3: $\kappa_{\vec{\eta}}(A_iB_i) = \infty$ and $\kappa_{\vec{\eta}}(A_i\overline{B_i}) = \infty$

Assume that $(B_i|A_i)$ is in Δ^j.

Case 3(a): $j < \infty$ Then there is a world ω s.t. $\omega \models A_iB_i$ and ω does not falsify any conditional in $\Delta^0 \cup \cdots \cup \Delta^j$. Therefore, $\kappa'(\omega) < f_j$ and thus $\kappa'(A_iB_i) < f_j$. Any model of $A_i\overline{B_i}$ falsifies $(B_i|A_i)$, therefore $\kappa'(A_i\overline{B_i}) > f_j$. Thus, we have $\kappa'(A_iB_i) < f_j < \kappa'(A_i\overline{B_i})$ and therefore $\kappa' \models (B_i|A_i)$.

Case 3(b): $j = \infty$ For every world ω s.t. $\omega \models A_i\overline{B_i}$ we have $\kappa'(\omega) = \infty$ and thus $\kappa(A\overline{B}) = \infty$. If $\kappa(AB) < \infty$ then $(B_i|A_i)$ holds. Otherwise, if $\kappa(AB) < \infty$ then $\kappa'(A) = \infty$ and $(B_i|A_i)$ also holds.

Ad (2.): If $\kappa^{z+}_{\Delta}(\omega) < \infty$ then ω does not falsify a conditional in Δ^∞. Then $\kappa_{\vec{\eta}'}(\omega)$ is the sum of only finite impacts and therefore $\kappa_{\vec{\eta}'}(\omega) < \infty$.

Ad (3.): Towards a contradiction, assume that $A \mid\!\sim_{\kappa'} B$. There are two cases.

Case 1: $\kappa'(A\overline{B}) < f_0$

In this case $\kappa'(AB) < \kappa'(A\overline{B}) < f_0$ and therefore $\kappa_{\vec{\eta}}(AB) < \kappa_{\vec{\eta}}(A\overline{B}) < \infty$. Hence, $A \mid\!\sim_{\kappa_{\vec{\eta}}} B$, a contradiction to $A \not\mid\!\sim_{\kappa} B$.

Case 2: $\kappa^f(A\overline{B}) \geq f_0$

In this case $\kappa_{\vec{\eta}}(A\overline{B}) = \infty$ and therefore $A \not\mid\!\sim_{\kappa_{\vec{\eta}}} B$, a contradiction to $A \mid\!\sim_{\kappa} B$.

As both cases lead to contradictions, we get $A \not\mid\!\sim_{\kappa'} B$. □

The extended c-representations in $CMod^{ec}_{\Sigma}(\Delta)$ that were just shown to be sufficient to describe extended c-inference from Δ, can be characterized by the following CSP $CRS^{ex}_{\Sigma}(\Delta)$.

Definition 5.49 ($CRS^{ex}_{\Sigma}(\Delta)$, J_Δ). *Let $\Delta = \{(B_1|A_1), \ldots, (B_n|A_n)\}$ be a belief base over Σ with the extended tolerance partition $EP(\Delta) = (\Delta^0, \ldots, \Delta^m, \Delta^\infty)$. Let*

$$J_\Delta := \Big\{ i \;\Big|\; (B_i|A_i) \in \Delta \setminus \Delta^\infty \text{ s.t. } A_i\overline{B_i} \wedge \Big(\bigwedge_{(D|C) \in \Delta^\infty} (\overline{C} \vee D) \Big) \not\equiv \bot \Big\}.$$

For $J_\Delta = \{i_1, \dots, i_l\}$, *the* simplified constraint satisfaction problem $CRS^{ex}_\Sigma(\Delta)$ *for extended c-inference of* Δ *on the constraint variables* $\{\eta_{i_1}, \dots, \eta_{i_l}\}$ *ranging over* $\mathbb{N}_0$ *is given by the constraints* $crs^{ex\,\Delta}_i$ *for all* $i \in J_\Delta$*:*

$$\eta_i > \min_{\substack{\omega\in\Omega_\Sigma \\ \omega\models A_iB_i}} \sum_{\substack{j\in J_\Delta \\ j\neq i \\ \omega\models A_j\overline{B_j}}} \eta_j - \min_{\substack{\omega\in\Omega_\Sigma \\ \omega\models A_i\overline{B}_i}} \sum_{\substack{j\in J_\Delta \\ j\neq i \\ \omega\models A_j\overline{B_j}}} \eta_j. \qquad (crs^{ex\,\Delta}_j)$$

The condition $A_j\overline{B_j} \wedge \left(\bigwedge_{(D|C)\in\Delta^\infty}(\overline{C} \vee D)\right) \not\equiv \bot$ in the definition of J_Δ is equivalent to the existence of a world $\omega \in \Omega_{A_j\overline{B_j}}$ that does not falsify a conditional in Δ^∞. This way J_Δ contains all $i \in \{1, \dots, n\}$ for which selecting $(\eta_j = \infty$ for all $j \in \{1, \dots, n\}$ with $(A_j|B_j) \in \Delta^\infty)$ does not imply $\kappa_{\vec{\eta}} \models (B_i|A_i)$.

As only conditionals $(B_i|A_i) \in \Delta$ with $i \in J_\Delta$ have a constraint variable η_i in $CRS^{ex}_\Sigma(\Delta)$, we need to add impacts for the conditionals $(B_j|A_j) \in \Delta$ with $j \notin J_\Delta$ to obtain a full impact vector for Δ. For those conditionals we choose $\eta_j = \infty$ as every world falsifying $(B_j|A_j)$ also falsifies a conditional in Δ^∞ and thus has rank ∞ in any extended c-representation of Δ.

Definition 5.50 ($\vec{\eta}^{J+\infty}, Sol^{J+\infty}_\Delta$)**.** *Let* Δ *be a belief base,* $n := |\Delta|$*, and let* J_Δ *be defined as in Definition 5.49. For every* $\vec{\eta}^J \in Sol(CRS^{ex}_\Sigma(\Delta))$ *let* $\vec{\eta}^{J+\infty} \in (\mathbb{N}_0 \cup \{\infty\})^n$ *be the impact vector defined by*

$$\eta^{J+\infty}_i := \begin{cases} \eta_i & \text{for } i \in J_\Delta \\ \infty & \text{otherwise.} \end{cases}$$

Then $Sol^{J+\infty}_\Delta := \{\vec{\eta}^{J+\infty} \mid \vec{\eta}^J \in Sol(CRS^{ex}_\Sigma(\Delta))\}$*.*

Now we can show that the solutions in $Sol^{J+\infty}_\Delta$ correspond to the extended c-representations in $CMod^{ec}_\Sigma(\Delta)$.

Proposition 5.51 (soundness and completeness of $CRS^{ex}_\Sigma(\Delta)$)**.** *Let* Δ *be a weakly consistent belief base over* Σ*. Then*

$$CMod^{ec}_\Sigma(\Delta) = \{\kappa_{\vec{\eta}} \mid \vec{\eta} \in Sol^{J+\infty}_\Delta\}. \qquad (5.10)$$

Proof. Let $EP(\Delta) = (\Delta^0, \dots, \Delta^k, \Delta^\infty)$, and let J_Δ be defined as in Definition 5.49.

Soundness: Let $\vec{\eta}$ be an impact vector in $Sol_{\Delta}^{J+\infty}$. By definition, there is a vector $\vec{\eta}^J \in Sol(CRS_{\Sigma}^{ex}(\Delta))$ such that $\vec{\eta} = \vec{\eta}^{J+\infty}$.

Because $\eta_i = \infty$ for every $(B_i|A_i) \in \Delta^\infty$ and due to Lemma 3.18, all worlds ω for which one of the conditionals in Δ^∞ is applicable have rank $\kappa_{\vec{\eta}}(\omega) = \infty$. Therefore, $\kappa_{\vec{\eta}}$ is a model of all conditionals in Δ^∞.

For any conditional $(B_i|A_i) \in \Delta \setminus \Delta^\infty$ there is at least one world ω that verifies $(B_i|A_i)$ without falsifying a conditional in Δ^∞ (otherwise $(B_i|A_i)$ would not be tolerated by Δ^∞). Because every world that falsifies a conditional $(B_j|A_j)$ with $j \notin J_\Delta$ also falsifies a conditional in Δ^∞, the world ω does not falsify any such conditional $(B_j|A_j)$ with impact ∞. Therefore, $\kappa_{\vec{\eta}}(A_iB_i) < \infty$. If $\kappa_{\vec{\eta}}(A_i\overline{B_i}) = \infty$ then $\kappa_{\vec{\eta}} \models (B_i|A_i)$. Otherwise, for $\kappa_{\vec{\eta}}(A_i\overline{B_i}) < \infty$, there is a world that falsifies $(B_i|A_i)$ without falsifying a conditional in Δ^∞. In this case we have $i \in J_\Delta$ and the CSP $CRS_{\Sigma}^{ex}(\Delta)$ contains the constraint $crs_i^{ex\,\Delta}$ which must hold for $\vec{\eta}^J$:

$$\begin{aligned}
& \eta_i > \min_{\substack{\omega\in\Omega_\Sigma\\ \omega\models A_iB_i}} \sum_{\substack{j\in J_\Delta\\ j\neq i\\ \omega\models A_j\overline{B_j}}} \eta_j - \min_{\substack{\omega\in\Omega_\Sigma\\ \omega\models A_i\overline{B_i}}} \sum_{\substack{j\in J_\Delta\\ j\neq i\\ \omega\models A_j\overline{B_j}}} \eta_j \\
\Leftrightarrow\quad & \eta_i + \min_{\substack{\omega\in\Omega_\Sigma\\ \omega\models A_i\overline{B_i}}} \sum_{\substack{j\in J_\Delta\\ j\neq i\\ \omega\models A_j\overline{B_j}}} \eta_j > \min_{\substack{\omega\in\Omega_\Sigma\\ \omega\models A_iB_i}} \sum_{\substack{j\in J_\Delta\\ j\neq i\\ \omega\models A_j\overline{B_j}}} \eta_j \\
\Leftrightarrow\quad & \min_{\substack{\omega\in\Omega_\Sigma\\ \omega\models A_i\overline{B_i}}} \sum_{\substack{j\in J_\Delta\\ \omega\models A_j\overline{B_j}}} \eta_j > \min_{\substack{\omega\in\Omega_\Sigma\\ \omega\models A_iB_i}} \sum_{\substack{j\in J_\Delta\\ \omega\models A_j\overline{B_j}}} \eta_j \\
\overset{(*)}{\Leftrightarrow}\quad & \min_{\substack{\omega\in\Omega_\Sigma\\ \omega\models A_i\overline{B_i}}} \sum_{\substack{1\leq j\leq n\\ \omega\models A_j\overline{B_j}}} \eta_j > \min_{\substack{\omega\in\Omega_\Sigma\\ \omega\models A_iB_i}} \sum_{\substack{1\leq j\leq n\\ \omega\models A_j\overline{B_j}}} \eta_j \\
\Leftrightarrow\quad & \kappa_{\vec{\eta}}(A_i\overline{B_i}) > \kappa_{\vec{\eta}}(A_iB_i).
\end{aligned}$$

Therefore, $\kappa_{\vec{\eta}} \models (B_i|A_i)$. The equivalence $(*)$ holds, because there is a model for each A_iB_i and $A_i\overline{B_i}$ that does not falsify a conditional in Δ^∞, we have $\eta_j = \infty$ for all $(B_j|A_j)$ with $j \notin J_\Delta$, and therefore

$$\min_{\substack{\omega\in\Omega_\Sigma\\ \omega\models A_iB_i}} \sum_{\substack{j\in J_\Delta\\ \omega\models A_j\overline{B_j}}} \eta_j = \min_{\substack{\omega\in\Omega_\Sigma\\ \omega\models A_iB_i}} \sum_{\substack{1\leq j\leq n\\ \omega\models A_j\overline{B_j}}} \eta_j$$

$$\text{and} \quad \min_{\substack{\omega\in\Omega_\Sigma\\ \omega\models A_i\overline{B_i}}} \sum_{\substack{j\in J_\Delta\\ \omega\models A_j\overline{B_j}}} \eta_j = \min_{\substack{\omega\in\Omega_\Sigma\\ \omega\models A_i\overline{B_i}}} \sum_{\substack{1\leq j\leq n\\ \omega\models A_j\overline{B_j}}} \eta_j.$$

For any world ω with $\kappa^{z+}_{\Delta}(\omega) < \infty$ it holds that all conditionals in Δ^{∞} are not applicable in ω. Therefore, $\kappa_{\vec{\eta}}(\omega)$ is the sum of some of the impacts in $\vec{\eta}^J$; and because $\vec{\eta}^J \in \mathbb{N}_0^l$ we have $\kappa_{\vec{\eta}}(\omega) < \infty$.

In summary, $\kappa_{\vec{\eta}} \in CMod^{ec}_{\Delta}$.

Completeness: Let $\kappa \in CMod^{ec}_{\Sigma}(\Delta)$ be an extended c-representation. Let $\vec{\eta} \in (\mathbb{N}_0 \cup \infty)^n$ be an impact vector such that $\kappa = \kappa_{\vec{\eta}}$. Because of Proposition 5.46, w.l.o.g. we can assume $\eta_i = \infty$ for all $(B_i|A_i) \in \Delta^{\infty}$. Furthermore, w.l.o.g., we can assume $\eta_i = \infty$ for all conditionals $(B_i|A_i) \in \Delta \setminus \Delta^{\infty}$ which are falsified only by worlds ω that also falsify a conditional in Δ^{∞} – all worlds for which these impacts apply already have rank ∞ because of the impacts for the conditionals in Δ^{∞}.

The vector $\vec{\eta}$ is a combination of a vector $\vec{\eta}^J$ of impacts η_j for conditionals $(B_j|A_j)$ with $j \in J_{\Delta}$, and a vector $(\infty, \ldots, \infty)$ of size $n - |J_{\Delta}|$ of impacts for conditionals $(B_j|A_j)$ with $j \notin J_{\Delta}$.

For every conditional $(B_i|A_i)$ with $i \in J_{\Delta}$, by construction of J_{Δ} there is at least one world ω falsifying $(B_i|A_i)$ without falsifying a conditional in Δ^{∞}. Therefore, $\kappa^{z+}_{\Delta}(\omega) < \infty$ because ω falsifies no conditionals in Δ^{∞} and due to Lemma 3.18. This implies $\eta_i < \kappa_{\vec{\eta}}(\omega) < \infty$ because $\kappa_{\vec{\eta}} \in CMod^{ec}_{\Sigma}(\Delta)$. Hence, $\vec{\eta}^J \in \mathbb{N}_0^{|J_{\Delta}|}$.

It is left to show that $\vec{\eta}^J$ is a solution of $CRS^{ex}_{\Sigma}(\Delta)$, i.e., that for every $i \in J_{\Delta}$ it satisfies the constraint $crs_i^{ex\,\Delta}$. As $\kappa_{\vec{\eta}}$ is a model of Δ, it models the conditional $(B_i|A_i) \in \Delta$. By construction of J_{Δ}, there is at least one world ω falsifying $(B_i|A_i)$ without falsifying a conditional in Δ^{∞}. As established above, the rank of such a world in $\kappa_{\vec{\eta}}$ is finite, and thus $\kappa_{\vec{\eta}}(A)$ is finite. To satisfy $(B_i|A_i)$ it is necessary that $\kappa_{\vec{\eta}}(A_i\overline{B_i}) > \kappa_{\vec{\eta}}(A_iB_i)$. Using the equivalence transformation in the *Soundness* part of this proof, we obtain that $crs_i^{ex\,\Delta}$ holds for $\vec{\eta}^J$. □

In combination, Propositions 5.48 and 5.51 imply the following result.

Proposition 5.52. *Let Δ be a weakly consistent belief base. Then $A \mathrel{|\!\sim}^{ec}_{\Delta} B$ iff $A \mathrel{|\!\sim}_{\kappa_{\vec{\eta}}} B$ for every $\vec{\eta} \in Sol^{J+\infty}_{\Delta}$.*

The following example illustrates how $CRS^{ex}_{\Sigma}(\Delta)$ is constructed from a belief base Δ, and that it is simpler than $CR^{ex}_{\Sigma}(\Delta)$.

Example 5.53. *Let $\Sigma := \{a, b, c\}$ and $\Delta := \{(\bot|a), (\overline{a}|b), (b|c)\}$. The*

CSP $CR^{ex}_{\Sigma}(\Delta)$ *over* $\eta_1, \eta_2, \eta_3 \in \mathbb{N}_0 \cup \{\infty\}$ *contains the constraints*

$$\min_{\substack{\omega\in\Omega_\Sigma \\ \omega\models a}} \sum_{\substack{1\leq j\leq n \\ \omega\models A_j\overline{B_j}}} \eta_j = \infty \qquad or$$

$$\eta_1 > \min_{\substack{\omega\in\Omega_\Sigma \\ \omega\models a\wedge\bot}} \sum_{\substack{j\neq 1 \\ \omega\models A_j\overline{B_j}}} \eta_j - \min_{\substack{\omega\in\Omega_\Sigma \\ \omega\models a\wedge\top}} \sum_{\substack{j\neq 1 \\ \omega\models A_j\overline{B_j}}} \eta_j, \tag{$cr^{ex}_1\Delta$}$$

$$\min_{\substack{\omega\in\Omega_\Sigma \\ \omega\models b}} \sum_{\substack{1\leq j\leq n \\ \omega\models A_j\overline{B_j}}} \eta_j = \infty \qquad or$$

$$\eta_i > \min_{\substack{\omega\in\Omega_\Sigma \\ \omega\models b\overline{a}}} \sum_{\substack{j\neq 2 \\ \omega\models A_j\overline{B_j}}} \eta_j - \min_{\substack{\omega\in\Omega_\Sigma \\ \omega\models ba}} \sum_{\substack{j\neq 2 \\ \omega\models A_j\overline{B_j}}} \eta_j, \tag{$cr^{ex}_2\Delta$}$$

$$\min_{\substack{\omega\in\Omega_\Sigma \\ \omega\models c}} \sum_{\substack{1\leq j\leq n \\ \omega\models A_j\overline{B_j}}} \eta_j = \infty \qquad or$$

$$\eta_i > \min_{\substack{\omega\in\Omega_\Sigma \\ \omega\models cb}} \sum_{\substack{j\neq 3 \\ \omega\models A_j\overline{B_j}}} \eta_j - \min_{\substack{\omega\in\Omega_\Sigma \\ \omega\models c\overline{b}}} \sum_{\substack{j\neq 3 \\ \omega\models A_j\overline{B_j}}} \eta_j. \tag{$cr^{ex}_3\Delta$}$$

The extended Z-partition of Δ *is* $EP(\Delta) = (\Delta^0, \Delta^\infty)$ *with* $\Delta^0 = \{(\overline{a}|b), (b|c)\}$ *and* $\Delta^\infty = \{(\bot|a)\}$. *The conditional* $(\overline{a}|b)$ *cannot be falsified without also falsifying* $(\bot|a) \in \Delta^\infty$. *Therefore,* $J_\Delta = \{3\}$ *and the CSP* $CRS^{ex}_{\Sigma}(\Delta)$ *over* $\eta_3 \in \mathbb{N}_0$ *contains only the constraint*

$$\eta_3 > \min_{\substack{\omega\in\Omega_\Sigma \\ \omega\models bc}} \sum_{\substack{j\in J_\Delta \\ j\neq 3 \\ \omega\models A_j\overline{B_j}}} \eta_j - \min_{\substack{\omega\in\Omega_\Sigma \\ \omega\models b\overline{c}}} \sum_{\substack{j\in J_\Delta \\ j\neq 3 \\ \omega\models A_j\overline{B_j}}} \eta_j \tag{$crs^{ex}_3\Delta$}$$

which simplifies to $\eta_3 > 0$. *For* $\vec{\eta} \in Sol^{J+\infty}_{\Delta}$ *it holds that* $\eta_1 = \eta_2 = \infty$ *and* $\eta_3 \in Sol(CRS^{ex}_{\Sigma}(\Delta))$.

In the next section we use the CSP $CRS^{ex}_{\Sigma}(\Delta)$ to characterize extended c-inference.

5.8. Characterizing Extended c-Inference with CSPs

The CSP $CR_{\Sigma}(\Delta)$ can be used to compute c-inference by checking a CSP for unsolvability [Bei+18]. The idea of this approach is that in order to check whether $A \mid\!\sim^{c}_{\Delta} B$ holds, a constraint encoding that $A \mid\!\sim_{\kappa_{\vec{\eta}}} B$ does not hold is added to $CR_{\Sigma}(\Delta)$. If the resulting CSP is unsolvable, $A \mid\!\sim_{\kappa_{\vec{\eta}}} B$ holds for all solutions $\vec{\eta}$ of $CR_{\Sigma}(\Delta)$. Based on this idea, we develop a method that tests for extended c-inference by checking a CSP for unsolvability. For this, we first define a constraint expressing that a conditional $(B|A)$ does not hold in an extended c-representation.

Definition 5.54 ($\neg CRS^{ex}_{\Delta}(B|A)$). *Let $\Delta = \{(B_1|A_1), \ldots, (B_n|A_n)\}$ be a belief base and let J_Δ be defined as in Definition 5.49. The constraint $\neg CRS^{ex}_{\Delta}(B|A)$ is given by*

$$\min_{\omega \models AB} \sum_{\substack{i \in J_\Delta \\ \omega \models A_i \overline{B_i}}} \eta_i \geq \min_{\omega \models A\overline{B}} \sum_{\substack{i \in J_\Delta \\ \omega \models A_i \overline{B_i}}} \eta_i. \tag{5.11}$$

Now we can show how $A \mid\!\sim^{ec}_{\Delta} B$ corresponds to the unsolvability of $CRS^{ex}_{\Sigma}(\Delta) \cup \{\neg CRS^{ex}_{\Delta}(B|A)\}$. Contrary to the approach for c-inference, we have to take into account that also for formulas A, B with $A, A\overline{B}$ consistent an inference $A \mid\!\sim^{ec}_{\Delta} B$ might hold only because for every extended c-representation $\kappa_{\vec{\eta}}$ of Δ we have either $\kappa_{\vec{\eta}}(A) = \infty$ or $\kappa_{\vec{\eta}}(A\overline{B}) = \infty$ and $\kappa_{\vec{\eta}}(AB) < \infty$.

Proposition 5.55. *Let Δ be a weakly consistent belief base. Then $A \mid\!\sim^{ec}_{\Delta} B$ iff either*

- $\kappa^{z+}_{\Delta}(A\overline{B}) = \infty$ *or*
- $\kappa^{z+}_{\Delta}(AB) < \infty$ *and* $CRS^{ex}_{\Sigma}(\Delta) \cup \{\neg CRS^{ex}_{\Delta}(B|A)\}$ *is unsolvable.*

Proof. **Direction $\Rightarrow$:** Assume that $A \mid\!\sim^{ec}_{\Delta} B$ and that $\kappa^{z+}_{\Delta}(A\overline{B}) < \infty$. Then, for all $\kappa \in CMod^{ec}_{\Sigma}(\Delta)$, we have $\kappa(A\overline{B}) < \infty$ by the definition of $CMod^{ec}_{\Sigma}(\Delta)$. Therefore, $\kappa(A) < \infty$ for all $\kappa \in CMod^{ec}_{\Sigma}(\Delta)$. Furthermore, $A \mid\!\sim^{ec}_{\Delta} B$ implies that for every $\kappa \in CMod^{ec}_{\Sigma}(\Delta)$, we have $A \mid\!\sim_{\kappa} B$. Therefore, $\kappa(AB) < \kappa(A\overline{B})$ for every $\kappa \in CMod^{ec}_{\Sigma}(\Delta)$, and because of Proposition 5.51 we have $\kappa_{\vec{\eta}}(AB) < \kappa_{\vec{\eta}}(A\overline{B})$ for every $\vec{\eta} \in Sol^{J+\infty}_{\Delta}$. Hence, we have

$$\begin{aligned}
& \kappa_{\vec{\eta}}(AB) < \kappa_{\vec{\eta}}(A\overline{B}) \\
\Leftrightarrow \quad & \min_{\omega \models AB} \sum_{\substack{1 \leq i \leq n \\ \omega \models A_i \overline{B_i}}} \eta_i < \min_{\omega \models A\overline{B}} \sum_{\substack{1 \leq i \leq n \\ \omega \models A_i \overline{B_i}}} \eta_i \\
\overset{(*)}{\Leftrightarrow} \quad & \min_{\omega \models AB} \sum_{\substack{i \in J_\Delta \\ \omega \models A_i \overline{B_i}}} \eta_i < \min_{\omega \models A\overline{B}} \sum_{\substack{i \in J_\Delta \\ \omega \models A_i \overline{B_i}}} \eta_i.
\end{aligned}$$

Equivalence $(*)$ holds because the ranks of the minimal models of AB and $A\overline{B}$ are finite and therefore do not violate a conditional $(B_i|A_i)$ with $i \notin J_\Delta$.

Therefore, $\neg CRS_\Delta^{ex}(B|A)$ does not hold for any solution of $CRS_\Sigma^{ex}(\Delta)$, implying that $CRS_\Sigma^{ex}(\Delta) \cup \{\neg CRS_\Delta^{ex}(B|A)\}$ is unsolvable.

Direction $\Leftarrow$: Assume that we have either $\kappa_\Delta^{z+}(A\overline{B}) = \infty$ or $\left(\ \kappa_\Delta^{z+}(AB) < \infty \text{ and } CRS_\Sigma^{ex}(\Delta) \cup \{\neg CRS_\Delta^{ex}(B|A)\} \text{ is unsolvable }\right)$. There are three cases.

<u>Case 1:</u> $\kappa_\Delta^{z+}(AB) = \infty$ and $\kappa_\Delta^{z+}(A\overline{B}) = \infty$
Then $\kappa_\Delta^z(A) = \infty$ and, by Proposition 5.34, $\kappa(A) = \infty$ for every $\kappa \in Mod_\Sigma^{ec}(\Delta)$. Therefore, $A \mid\!\sim_\Delta^{ec} B$.

<u>Case 2:</u> $\kappa_\Delta^{z+}(AB) < \infty$ and $\kappa_\Delta^{z+}(A\overline{B}) = \infty$
Then, by the definition of $CMod_\Sigma^{ec}(\Delta)$, we have $\kappa(AB) < \infty$ and, by Proposition 5.34, $\kappa(A\overline{B}) = \infty$ for every $\kappa \in CMod_\Sigma^{ec}(\Delta)$. Therefore, $\kappa(AB) < \kappa(A\overline{B})$ for every $\kappa \in CMod_\Sigma^{ec}(\Delta)$ and hence $A \mid\!\sim_\Delta^{ec} B$ by Proposition 5.48.

<u>Case 3:</u> $\kappa_\Delta^{z+}(A\overline{B}) < \infty$
Then, by assumption, $\kappa_\Delta^{z+}(AB) < \infty$ and $CRS_\Sigma^{ex}(\Delta) \cup \{\neg CRS_\Delta^{ex}(B|A)\}$ is unsolvable. This implies that $\neg CRS_\Delta^{ex}(B|A)$ is violated for every $\vec{\eta}^J \in Sol(CRS_\Sigma^{ex}(\Delta))$. In this case, using the equivalence transformations in the part of the proof for *Direction* $\Rightarrow$, we have $\kappa_{\vec{\eta}}(AB) < \kappa_{\vec{\eta}}(A\overline{B})$ for every $\vec{\eta} \in Sol_\Delta^{J+\infty}$. With Proposition 5.52 it follows that $A \mid\!\sim_\Delta^{ec} B$. □

This realization of extended c-inference by a CSP gives us a starting point for an implementation of extended c-inference using a CSP solver [BEK17; KB21a], or as a SAT or SMT problem [BBS22; BSB23].

5.9. Extended c-Inference Satisfies Syntax Splitting

Besides system W, c-inference is one of the other few inductive inference operators that satisfy (SynSplit). In this section we will consider syntax splitting postulates for extended c-inference and prove that extended c-inference satisfies (SynSplit$^+$). To show that extended c-inference complies with syntax splitting, we will first show some lemmas on the behaviour of extended c-representations in the context of a syntax splitting $\Delta = \Delta_1 \bigcup_{\Sigma_1,\Sigma_2} \Delta_2$. Later we will use these lemmas in the proofs for (Rel$^+$) and (Ind$^+$).

Differing from the proof that c-inference satisfies (SynSplit) in [KBB20], in the following proofs we argue about the sets of extended c-inferences $Mod^{ec}_{\Sigma}(\Delta)$ directly instead of the sets of solutions of the corresponding CSPs. This is mainly because the CSPs characterizing all extended c-representations are somewhat more involved than the CSPs for c-representations.

Lemma 5.56 states that the combination of any extended c-inference of Δ_1 with an extended c-inference of Δ_2 is an extended c-inference of Δ.

Lemma 5.56. *Let $\Delta = \Delta_1 \bigcup_{\Sigma_1,\Sigma_2} \Delta_2$ be a weakly consistent belief base with syntax splitting. Let $\kappa_1 \in Mod^{ec}_{\Sigma_1}(\Delta_1)$ and $\kappa_2 \in Mod^{ec}_{\Sigma_2}(\Delta_2)$. Then $\kappa_\oplus := \kappa_1 \oplus \kappa_2$ is an extended c-representation of Δ, i.e., $\kappa_\oplus \in Mod^{ec}_{\Sigma}(\Delta)$.*

Proof. Let $(B_1|A_1), \ldots, (B_k|A_k)$ be the conditionals in Δ_1 and let $(B_{k+1}|A_{k+1}), \ldots, (B_n|A_n)$ be the conditionals in Δ_2. Let $\vec{\eta}^1$ be an impact vector inducing κ_1 and let $\vec{\eta}^2$ be an impact vector inducing κ_2. Let ω be any world in Ω_Σ. Because of the syntax splitting, $\omega_{|\Sigma_1}$ falsifies the same worlds in Δ_1 as ω and $\omega_{|\Sigma_2}$ falsifies the same worlds in Δ_2 as ω. Let $\vec{\eta}$ be the impact vector for Δ that combines the impacts from $\vec{\eta}^1$ and $\vec{\eta}^2$. We have that

$$\begin{aligned}
\kappa_\oplus &= \kappa_1(\omega_{|\Sigma_1}) + \kappa_2(\omega_{|\Sigma_2}) \\
&= \sum_{\substack{1 \leq i \leq k \\ \omega_{|\Sigma_1} \models A_i \overline{B_i}}} \eta_i + \sum_{\substack{k+1 \leq i \leq n \\ \omega_{|\Sigma_2} \models A_i \overline{B_i}}} \eta_i \\
&= \sum_{\substack{1 \leq i \leq n \\ \omega \models A_i \overline{B_i}}} \eta_i = \kappa_{\vec{\eta}}.
\end{aligned} \tag{5.12}$$

Additionally, because $\kappa_1 = \kappa_{\oplus|\Sigma_1}$ and $\kappa_2 = \kappa_{\oplus|\Sigma_2}$ (see Lemma 2.10), Lemma 2.6 yields that $\kappa_\oplus$ models the conditionals in Δ_1 and in Δ_2. Therefore, $\kappa_\oplus$ is an extended c-representation of Δ. □

In the other direction, Lemma 5.57 shows how an extended c-representation of Δ splits for certain formulas. Using $X \equiv X \wedge \top$, Lemma 5.57 can be seen as a more general version of [KBB20, Proposition 10].

Lemma 5.57. *Let* $\Delta = \Delta_1 \bigcup_{\Sigma_1,\Sigma_2} \Delta_2$ *be a weakly consistent belief base with syntax splitting. Let* $\kappa_{\vec{\eta}} \in Mod_\Sigma^{ec}(\Delta)$ *be an extended c-representation induced by impact vector* $\vec{\eta}$. *Let* $\vec{\eta}^1$ *be the impact vector containing the impacts from* $\vec{\eta}$ *for* Δ_1 *and let* $\vec{\eta}^2$ *be the impact vector containing the impacts from* $\vec{\eta}$ *for* Δ_2. *Then, for* $X \in \mathcal{L}_{\Sigma_1}, Y \in \mathcal{L}_{\Sigma_2}$ *we have* $\kappa_{\vec{\eta}}(XY) = \kappa_{\vec{\eta}^1}(X) + \kappa_{\vec{\eta}^2}(Y)$.

Proof. Let $(B_1|A_1), \ldots, (B_k|A_k)$ be the conditionals in Δ_1 and let $(B_{k+1}|A_{k+1}), \ldots, (B_n|A_n)$ be the conditionals in Δ_2. For any $\omega \in \Omega_\Sigma$ we have that

$$\kappa(\omega) = \sum_{\substack{1\leq i\leq n \\ \omega\models A_i\overline{B_i}}} \eta_i = \sum_{\substack{1\leq i\leq k \\ \omega\models A_i\overline{B_i}}} \eta_i + \sum_{\substack{k+1\leq i\leq n \\ \omega\models A_i\overline{B_i}}} \eta_i = \kappa_{\vec{\eta}^1}(\omega) + \kappa_{\vec{\eta}^2}(\omega).$$

Because $X \in \mathcal{L}_{\Sigma_1}$ and $Y \in \mathcal{L}_{\Sigma_2}$ we have that $Mod_\Sigma(XY) = \{\omega^x\omega^y \mid \omega^x \in Mod_{\Sigma_1}(X), \omega^y \in Mod_{\Sigma_2}(Y)\}$. In summary, we have that

$$\begin{aligned}
&\kappa(XY)\\
&= \min\{\kappa(\omega) \mid \omega \in Mod_\Sigma(XY)\}\\
&= \min\{\kappa(\omega^x\omega^y) \mid \omega^x \in Mod_{\Sigma_1}(X), \omega^y \in Mod_{\Sigma_1}(Y)\}\\
&= \min\{\kappa_{\vec{\eta}^1}(\omega^x) + \kappa_{\vec{\eta}^2}(\omega^y) \mid \omega^x \in Mod_{\Sigma_1}(X), \omega^y \in Mod_{\Sigma_2}(Y)\}\\
&= \min\{\kappa_{\vec{\eta}^1}(\omega^x) \mid \omega^x \in Mod_{\Sigma_2}(X)\} + \min\{\kappa_{\vec{\eta}^2}(\omega^y) \mid \omega^y \in Mod_{\Sigma_2}(Y)\}\\
&= \kappa_{\vec{\eta}^1}(X) + \kappa_{\vec{\eta}^2}(Y).
\end{aligned} \tag{5.13}$$

□

Lemma 5.58 states that marginalizing an extended c-representation of Δ to the subsignature Σ_i, $i \in \{1, 2\}$, leads to an extended c-representation of Δ_i.

Lemma 5.58. *Let* $\Delta = \Delta_1 \bigcup_{\Sigma_1,\Sigma_2} \Delta_2$ *be a weakly consistent belief base with syntax splitting and let* $i \in \{1, 2\}$. *If* $\kappa \in Mod_\Sigma^{ec}(\Delta)$ *then* $\kappa_{|\Sigma_i} \in Mod_{\Sigma_i}^{ec}(\Delta_i)$.

Proof. Because we can swap the indices 1, 2 in the syntax splitting, we can assume $i = 1$ without loss of generality.

Let $\kappa \in Mod_\Sigma^{ec}(\Delta)$. By Lemma 2.6, $\kappa_{|\Sigma_1}$ models the same conditionals in $(\mathcal{L}|\mathcal{L})_{\Sigma_1}$ as κ. Especially, $\kappa_{|\Sigma_1}$ models all conditionals in

Δ_1. It remains to be shown that $\kappa_{|\Sigma_1}$ can be constructed from integer impacts.

For this let $(B_1|A_1), \dots, (B_k|A_k)$ be the conditionals in Δ_1 and let $(B_{k+1}|A_{k+1}), \dots, (B_n|A_n)$ be the conditionals in Δ_2. Let $\vec{\eta}$ be an impact vector inducing κ, and let $\vec{\eta}^1$ be the impact vector containing the impacts from $\vec{\eta}$ for Δ_1. Let $\omega^0 \in \Omega_\Sigma$ be a world that does not falsify any conditional in Δ (see Lemma 2.2). Let ω' be any world in Ω_{Σ_1}. All worlds ω with $\omega_{|\Sigma_1} = \omega'$ falsify the same worlds in Δ_1. The world $\omega^* := \omega' {\omega^0}_{|\Sigma_2}$ falsifies no conditional in Δ_2 and is thus one of the worlds with the lowest rank in κ that coincides with ω' on Σ_1. We have that

$$\begin{aligned}
\kappa_{|\Sigma_1}(\omega') &= \min\{\kappa(\omega) \mid \omega_{|\Sigma_1} = \omega'\} \\
&= \min\{ \sum_{\substack{1 \leq i \leq n \\ \omega \models A_i \overline{B_i}}} \eta_i \mid \omega_{|\Sigma_1} = \omega'\} \\
&= \sum_{\substack{1 \leq i \leq n \\ \omega^* \models A_i \overline{B_i}}} = \sum_{\substack{1 \leq i \leq k \\ \omega' \models A_i \overline{B_i}}} \eta_i = \kappa_{\vec{\eta}^1}(\omega').
\end{aligned}$$

Therefore, $\kappa_{|\Sigma_1}$ is an extended c-representation of Δ_1. □

One of the key observations for proving that c-inference satisfies (SynSplit) in [KBB20] is [KBB20, Proposition 8]. Given a belief base with syntax splitting $\Delta = \Delta_1 \bigcup\limits_{\Sigma_1, \Sigma_2} \Delta_2$, this proposition states that the c-representations of Δ are exactly the combinations of the c-representations of Δ_1 with the c-representations of Δ_2. In combination, the Lemmas 5.56, 5.57, and 5.58 yield a corresponding observation for extended c-representations as expressed in the following lemma.

Proposition 5.59. *Let $\Delta = \Delta_1 \bigcup\limits_{\Sigma_1, \Sigma_2} \Delta_2$ be a weakly consistent belief base with syntax splitting. Then $\kappa \in Mod^{ec}_\Sigma(\Delta)$ iff there are $\kappa_1 \in Mod^{ec}_{\Sigma_1}(\Delta_1)$ and $\kappa_2 \in Mod^{ec}_{\Sigma_2}(\Delta_2)$ such that $\kappa = \kappa_1 \oplus \kappa_2$.*

Proof. Direction $\Leftarrow$ follows from Lemma 5.57. In the other direction $\Rightarrow$, with Lemma 5.57 we can see that there are $\kappa_1 : \Omega_{\Sigma_1} \to \mathbb{N} \cup \{\infty\}$ and $\kappa_1 : \Omega_{\Sigma_1} \to \mathbb{N} \cup \{\infty\}$ such that $\kappa = \kappa_1 \oplus \kappa_2$. By Lemma 2.10 we have that $\kappa_i = (\kappa_1 \oplus \kappa_2)_{|\Sigma_i} = \kappa_{|\Sigma_i}$ for $i \in \{1, 2\}$ and therefore, with Lemma 5.58, that $\kappa_1 \in Mod^{ec}_{\Sigma_1}(\Delta_1)$ and $\kappa_2 \in Mod^{ec}_{\Sigma_1}(\Delta_1)$. □

Similarly to extended system W (see Lemma 5.21), also extended c-inference does not change if unused atoms are added to or removed from the signature. This is captured by the following Lemma 5.60.

Lemma 5.60. *Let Σ be a signature, $\Sigma' \subseteq \Sigma$, and Δ be a belief base over Σ'. For $A, B \in \mathcal{L}_{\Sigma'}$ we have $A \mathrel{|\!\sim}^{ec}_{\Delta} B$ with respect to Σ iff $A \mathrel{|\!\sim}^{ec}_{\Delta} B$ with respect to Σ'.*

Proof. Show both directions of the *iff*.

Direction $\Rightarrow$: Let $A \mathrel{|\!\sim}^{ec}_{\Delta} B$ with respect to Σ. Let $\kappa' \in Mod^{ec}_{\Sigma'}(\Delta)$. We can see Δ as a belief base with syntax splitting $\Delta = \Delta \bigcup_{\Sigma', \Sigma \setminus \Sigma'} \emptyset$. The only extended c-representation in $Mod^{ec}_{\Sigma \setminus \Sigma'}(\emptyset)$ is κ^0 with $\kappa^0(\omega) = 0$ for all $\omega \in \Omega_{\Sigma \setminus \Sigma'}$. By Lemma 5.56, $\kappa_{\oplus} = \kappa' \oplus \kappa^0$ is in $Mod^{ec}_{\Sigma}(\Delta)$, and therefore $A \mathrel{|\!\sim}_{\kappa_{\oplus}} B$. By Lemma 3.4 this implies that $A \mathrel{|\!\sim}_{\kappa'} B$ because $\kappa' = \kappa_{\oplus | \Sigma'}$ (see Lemma 2.10). Hence, in summary we have that $A \mathrel{|\!\sim}^{ec}_{\Delta} B$ with respect to Σ'.

Direction $\Leftarrow$: Let $A \mathrel{|\!\sim}^{ec}_{\Delta} B$ with respect to Σ'. Let $\kappa \in Mod^{ec}_{\Sigma}(\Delta)$ be an extended c-representation. Again, we can see Δ as a belief base with syntax splitting $\Delta = \Delta \bigcup_{\Sigma', \Sigma \setminus \Sigma'} \emptyset$. By Lemma 5.58, $\kappa' := \kappa_{|\Sigma'}$ is an extended c-representation in $Mod^{ec}_{\Sigma'}(\Delta)$, and therefore $A \mathrel{|\!\sim}_{\kappa'} B$. Then Lemma 3.4 implies that $A \mathrel{|\!\sim}_{\kappa} B$. Hence, in summary we have that $A \mathrel{|\!\sim}^{ec}_{\Delta} B$ with respect to Σ. □

Using the lemmas above, we can now show that extended c-inference satisfies (Rel$^+$). Observe that the proofs for these lemmas and also the proof for the next Proposition 5.61 do not need to deal explicitly with the case that a formula/world is infeasible (i.e., has rank ∞). In these proofs, all situations where a world or formula has rank ∞ are already covered by the underlying definitions and results. E.g., in (5.12) the world ω can have rank ∞ in $\kappa_{\oplus}$, and in (5.13) the formulas X, Y can have rank ∞ in κ.

Proposition 5.61. *Extended c-inference satisfies (Rel$^+$).*

Proof. Let $\Delta = \Delta_1 \bigcup_{\Sigma_1, \Sigma_2} \Delta_2$ be a weakly consistent belief base with syntax splitting. Let $i \in \{1, 2\}$ and $A, B \in \mathcal{L}_{\Sigma_i}$. We need to show that $A \mathrel{|\!\sim}^{ec}_{\Delta} B$ iff $A \mathrel{|\!\sim}^{ec}_{\Delta_i} B$. Because we can swap the indices 1, 2 in the syntax splitting, we can assume $i = 1$ without loss of generality.

Direction $\Rightarrow$: Assume that $A \mathrel{|\!\!\sim}^{ec}_{\Delta} B$. Because of Lemma 5.60 it suffices to show that $A \mathrel{|\!\!\sim}^{ec}_{\Delta_1} B$ w.r.t. Σ_1. Let $\kappa_1 \in Mod^{ec}_{\Sigma_1}(\Delta_1)$ be any extended c-representation of Δ_1. We need to show that $A \mathrel{|\!\!\sim}_{\kappa_1} B$.

Let $\kappa_2 \in Mod^{ec}_{\Sigma_2}(\Delta_2)$ and $\kappa_\oplus := \kappa_1 \oplus \kappa_2$. By Lemma 5.56 we have $\kappa_\oplus \in Mod^{ec}_{\Sigma}(\Delta)$. Therefore, by assumption we have $A \mathrel{|\!\!\sim}_{\kappa_\oplus} B$. Because $\kappa_1 = \kappa_{\oplus|\Sigma_1}$ (see Lemma 2.10), with Lemma 3.4 we have that $A \mathrel{|\!\!\sim}_{\kappa_1} B$.

Direction $\Leftarrow$: Assume that $A \mathrel{|\!\!\sim}^{ec}_{\Delta_1} B$ (w.r.t. Σ). Let $\kappa \in Mod^{ec}_{\Sigma}(\Delta)$ be any extended c-representation of Δ. We need to show that $A \mathrel{|\!\!\sim}_{\kappa} B$.

With Lemma 5.58 we have that $\kappa_1 := \kappa_{|\Sigma_1}$ is an extended c-representation of Δ_1. With Lemma 5.60 we have that $A \mathrel{|\!\!\sim}^{ec}_{\Delta_1} B$ w.r.t. Σ_1, and therefore $A \mathrel{|\!\!\sim}_{\kappa_1} B$. Using Lemma 3.4 we have that $A \mathrel{|\!\!\sim}_{\kappa} B$. □

Next we show that extended c-inference also satisfies (Ind$^+$). Here, in contrast to proving (Rel$^+$) in Proposition 5.61, we have to distinguish explicitly between the case that an entailment $A \mathrel{|\!\!\sim}_{\kappa} B$ holds because its antecedent is infeasible ($\kappa(A) = \infty$) and the case that an entailment holds because its verification has a lower rank than its falsification ($\kappa(AB) < \kappa(A\overline{B})$).

Proposition 5.62. *Extended c-inference satisfies (Ind$^+$).*

Proof. Let $\Delta = \Delta_1 \bigcup_{\Sigma_1,\Sigma_2} \Delta_2$ be a weakly consistent belief base with syntax splitting. Let $i, j \in \{1,2\}, i \neq j$ and let $A, B \in \mathcal{L}_{\Sigma_i}, D \in \mathcal{L}_{\Sigma_j}$ such that $D \not\mathrel{|\!\!\sim}^{ec}_{\Delta} \bot$. We need to show that $A \mathrel{|\!\!\sim}^{ec}_{\Delta} B$ iff $AD \mathrel{|\!\!\sim}^{ec}_{\Delta} B$. Because we can swap the indices 1, 2 in the syntax splitting, we can assume $i = 1$ and $j = 2$ without loss of generality.

Direction $\Rightarrow$: Assume that $A \mathrel{|\!\!\sim}^{ec}_{\Delta} B$. We show that $AD \mathrel{|\!\!\sim}_{\kappa} B$ for every $\kappa \in Mod^{ec}_{\Sigma}(\Delta)$.

Let $\kappa \in Mod^{ec}_{\Sigma}(\Delta)$ be any extended c-representation of Δ. Because $A \mathrel{|\!\!\sim}^{ec}_{\Delta} B$ we have that $A \mathrel{|\!\!\sim}_{\kappa} B$. Let $\vec{\eta}$ be the impact vector inducing κ, i.e., $\kappa = \kappa_{\vec{\eta}}$. Because $\Delta = \Delta_1 \cup \Delta_2$, we can sort the impacts in $\vec{\eta}$ into an impact vector $\vec{\eta}^1$ for Δ_1 and an impact vector $\vec{\eta}^2$ for Δ_2.

We can distinguish three cases.

<u>Case 1:</u> $\kappa_{\vec{\eta}}(A) = \infty$

Applying Lemma 5.57, we have that $\kappa_{\vec{\eta}}(A) = \kappa_{\vec{\eta}}(A \wedge \top) = \kappa_{\vec{\eta}^1}(A) + \kappa_{\vec{\eta}^2}(\top)$. Because Δ is weakly consistent, with Lemma 2.2 there is at least one world ω that does not falsify a conditional in Δ. Therefore, we have that $\kappa_{\vec{\eta}^2}(\top) = 0$. Hence, $\kappa_{\vec{\eta}^1}(A) = \infty$. This implies that $\kappa_{\vec{\eta}} = \kappa_{\vec{\eta}^1}(A) + \kappa_{\vec{\eta}^2}(D) = \infty + \kappa_{\vec{\eta}^2}(D) = \infty$. Thus, $AD \mid\!\sim_{\kappa} B$.

Case 2: $\kappa_{\vec{\eta}}(A) < \infty$ and $\kappa_{\vec{\eta}}(D) = \infty$
With a similar argumentation as in *Case 1*, we have that $\kappa_{\vec{\eta}^2}(D) = \infty$. This implies that $\kappa_{\vec{\eta}}(AD) = \kappa_{\vec{\eta}^1}(A) + \kappa_{\vec{\eta}^2}(D) = \kappa_{\vec{\eta}^1}(A) + \infty = \infty$. Thus, $AD \mid\!\sim_{\kappa_{\vec{\eta}}} B$.

Case 3: $\kappa_{\vec{\eta}}(A) < \infty$ and $\kappa_{\vec{\eta}}(D) < \infty$
Because $A \mid\!\sim_{\kappa_{\vec{\eta}}} B$ in this case it is necessary that $\kappa_{\vec{\eta}}(AB) < \kappa_{\vec{\eta}}(A\overline{B})$.

Applying Lemma 5.57, we have that $\kappa_{\vec{\eta}}(AB) = \kappa_{\vec{\eta}}(AB \wedge \top) = \kappa_{\vec{\eta}^1}(AB) + \kappa_{\vec{\eta}^2}(\top)$. Because Δ is weakly consistent, with Lemma 2.2 there is at least one world ω that does not falsify a conditional in Δ. Therefore, we have that $\kappa_{\vec{\eta}^2}(\top) = 0$. Hence, $\kappa_{\vec{\eta}^1}(AB) = \kappa_{\vec{\eta}}(AB)$. Analogously, $\kappa_{\vec{\eta}^1}(A\overline{B}) = \kappa_{\vec{\eta}}(A\overline{B})$ and $\kappa_{\vec{\eta}^2}(D) = \kappa_{\vec{\eta}}(D) < \infty$. Therefore, $\kappa_{\vec{\eta}^1}(AB) < \kappa_{\vec{\eta}^1}(A\overline{B})$.

Lemma 5.57 also yields that $\kappa_{\vec{\eta}}(ABD) = \kappa_{\vec{\eta}^1}(AB) + \kappa_{\vec{\eta}^2}(D)$ and $\kappa_{\vec{\eta}}(A\overline{B}D) = \kappa_{\vec{\eta}^1}(A\overline{B}) + \kappa_{\vec{\eta}^2}(D)$.

Together, we have that $\kappa_{\vec{\eta}}(ABD) = \kappa_{\vec{\eta}^1}(AB) + \kappa_{\vec{\eta}^2}(D) < \kappa_{\vec{\eta}^1}(A\overline{B}) + \kappa_{\vec{\eta}^2}(D) = \kappa_{\vec{\eta}}(A\overline{B}D)$ and thus $AD \mid\!\sim_{\kappa_{\vec{\eta}}} B$.

Direction $\Leftarrow$: Assume that $AD \mid\!\sim^{ec}_{\Delta} B$. We show that $A \mid\!\sim_{\kappa} B$ for every $\kappa \in Mod^{ec}_{\Sigma}(\Delta)$.

Let $\kappa \in Mod^{ec}_{\Sigma}(\Delta)$ be any extended c-representation of Δ. Because $AD \mid\!\sim^{ec}_{\Delta} B$ we have that $AD \mid\!\sim_{\kappa} B$.

Because $D \not\mid\!\sim^{ec}_{\Delta} \bot$, there is a $\kappa' \in Mod^{ec}_{\Sigma}(\Delta)$ such that $D \not\mid\!\sim_{\kappa'} \bot$ which implies $\kappa'(D) < \infty$. Using Lemma 5.58 we have that $\kappa'_{|\Sigma_2} \in Mod^{ec}_{\Sigma_2}(\Delta_2)$. With Lemma 2.5 we have that $\kappa'_{|\Sigma_2}(D) = \kappa'(D)$. Analogously, we have that $\kappa_{|\Sigma_1} \in Mod^{ec}_{\Sigma_1}(\Delta_1)$ and $\kappa_{|\Sigma_1}(A) = \kappa(A)$ and $\kappa_{|\Sigma_1}(AB) = \kappa(AB)$ and $\kappa_{|\Sigma_1}(A\overline{B}) = \kappa(A\overline{B})$. Let $\kappa_{\oplus} := \kappa_{|\Sigma_1} \oplus \kappa'_{|\Sigma_2}$. With Lemma 5.56 we have that $\kappa_{\oplus} \in Mod^{ec}_{\Sigma}(\Delta)$. Because $AD \mid\!\sim^{ec}_{\Delta} B$ this entails that $AD \mid\!\sim_{\kappa_{\oplus}} B$. We can distinguish two cases.

Case 1: $\kappa_{\oplus}(AD) = \infty$
Because of Lemma 2.9 we have that $\kappa_{\oplus}(AD) = \kappa_{|\Sigma_1}(A) + \kappa'_{|\Sigma_2}(D)$, and with $\kappa'_{|\Sigma_2}(D) = \kappa'(D) < \infty$ we have that $\kappa_{|\Sigma_1}(A) = \infty$. Therefore, $\kappa(A) = \kappa_{|\Sigma_1}(A) = \infty$ and thus $A \mid\!\sim_{\kappa} B$.

Case 2: $\kappa_{\oplus}(AD) < \infty$
Because $AD \mid\!\sim_{\kappa_{\oplus}} B$ we have that $\kappa_{\oplus}(ABD) < \kappa_{\oplus}(A\overline{B}D)$. With Lemma 2.9 we have that $\kappa_{\oplus}(ABD) = \kappa_{|\Sigma_1}(AB) + \kappa'_{|\Sigma_2}(D)$ and $\kappa_{\oplus}(A\overline{B}D) = \kappa_{|\Sigma_1}(A\overline{B}) + \kappa'_{|\Sigma_2}(D)$. This implies that $\kappa_{|\Sigma_1}(AB) + \kappa'_{|\Sigma_2}(D) < \kappa_{|\Sigma_1}(A\overline{B}) + \kappa'_{|\Sigma_2}(D)$ and therefore that $\kappa(AB) < \kappa(A\overline{B})$. Thus, $A \mid\!\sim_{\kappa} B$. □

Note that for *Direction* $\Leftarrow$ of the proof of Proposition 5.62, for showing $A \mathrel{|\!\!\sim}_{\kappa} B$ we had to pay special attention to the case where $\kappa(D) = \infty$ even though $D \mathrel{|\!\!\not\sim}^{ec}_{\Delta} \bot$. Therefore, in the proof we employ the extended c-representation $\kappa_{\oplus}$ derived from κ that satisfies $\kappa_{\oplus}(D) < \infty$ and is used to show that $A \mathrel{|\!\!\sim}_{\kappa} B$.

Combining Proposition 5.61 and Proposition 5.62 yields that extended c-inference satisfies (SynSplit$^+$).

Proposition 5.63. *Extended c-inference satisfies (SynSplit$^+$).*

Thus, extended c-inference fully complies with syntax splittings.

In summary, in this chapter we explored inference from weakly consistent belief bases that employs the idea of infeasible worlds. First we observed that a preferential inference operator must map only weakly consistent belief bases to inference relations that consider some worlds to be completely infeasible. Then we extended the definition of system W, which is initially defined as a SCA-inductive inference operator, to the universal inductive inference operator *extended* system W which is also defined for only weakly consistent belief bases. We showed that extended system W satisfies similar properties as system W; especially extended system W complies with syntax splitting.

We also extended the definition of c-inference to cover inference from all weakly consistent belief bases. This first required us to define a more general version of c-representations, which are then used to define extended c-inference. We investigated the properties of extended c-inference and showed that extended c-inference, similar to c-inference, complies with syntax splitting.

Chapter 6

Relations among Inductive Inference Operators

In this section we want to investigate relations among different inductive inference operators with a special focus on the inference operators around (extended) system W. To do this we connect the inference operators mentioned in this thesis with the "captures" and "strictly extends" relationships. In Section 6.1 we recall previous results on the relationships among p-entailment, c-inference, system Z, and system W from the literature. Then we establish the relation between extended system W and extended system Z in Section 6.2 and the relation between extended system W and extended c-inference in Section 6.3. We also show that extended system W is captured by adapted lexicographic inference in Section 6.4. In Section 6.5 we show that MP-closure coincides with extended system W. Then we proceed to introduce approximations of extended system W in Section 6.6. Section 6.7 summarizes the results of this section and gives an overview over the resulting landscape of inductive inference operators.

It was already shown in [KB22] that system W captures c-inference and system Z. In [Hal+23a] it was first shown that also extended system W captures extended system Z. The proof that extended system W captures extended c-inference is new in this thesis. The connection between system W and lexicographic inference was initially established in [HB22c], and in [Hal+23a] it was shown that extended system W is captured by adapted lexicographic inference. The result that MP-closure coincides with system W on strongly consistent belief bases was first given in [HB22a], and the more general result that MP-closure coincides with extended system W presented here

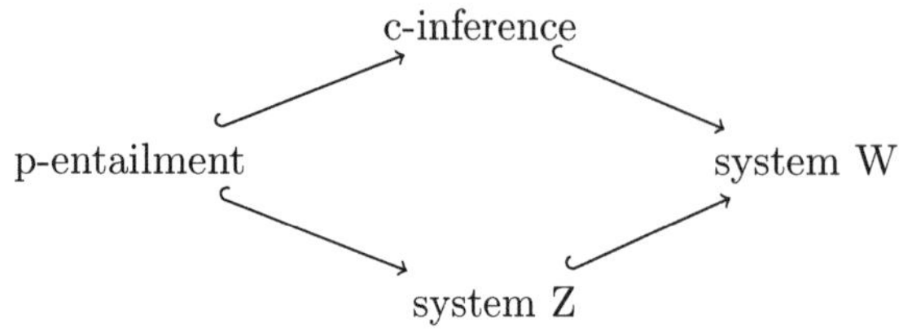

Figure 6.1. Overview of relationships among inference operators shown in [KB22] or known before that. An arrow $I_1 \hookrightarrow I_2$ indicates that inductive inference operator I_1 is captured and strictly extended by I_2.

originates from [Hal+23a]. The approximations of extended system W in Section 6.6 are generalizations of the approximations of system W in [HB23a].

6.1. Previous Results: System W Captures System Z and c-Inference

Previous works already established some relationships among inductive inference operators. For example, c-inference and system Z both satisfy system P [Pea90; BEK16] and therefore capture p-entailment. In [KB22] it was shown that system W captures c-inference as well as system Z.

Proposition 6.1 ([KB22]). *System W captures system Z, i.e., for a strongly consistent belief base Δ and $A, B \in \mathcal{L}_\Sigma$ it holds that $A \mathrel{|\!\!\sim}^{z}_{\Delta} B$ implies $A \mathrel{|\!\!\sim}^{\mathsf{w}}_{\Delta} B$.*

System W captures c-inference, i.e., for a strongly consistent belief base Δ and $A, B \in \mathcal{L}_\Sigma$ it holds that $A \mathrel{|\!\!\sim}^{c}_{\Delta} B$ implies $A \mathrel{|\!\!\sim}^{\mathsf{w}}_{\Delta} B$.

As p-entailment does not coincide with either system Z or c-inference, the latter two strictly extend p-entailment. Furthermore, system W strictly extends both c-inference and system Z [KB22]. An overview over these relationships is given in Figure 6.1.

In the next sections we will extend these results to the extended versions of c-inference, system Z, and system W. Additionally, we will add the relations between system W and (adapted) lexicographic closure as well as MP-closure.

6.2. Extended System W Captures Extended System Z

While the investigation of relations among inductive inference operators in this chapter has weakly consistent belief bases in mind, the results on relations among universal inductive inference operator in this chapter technically cover all belief bases, even those that are not even weakly consistent. This is actually a trivial observation: Because all inductive inference operators considered here are preferential, they map belief bases which are not weakly consistent to the inference relation $\mathcal{L}_\Sigma \times \mathcal{L}_\Sigma$ which contains every pair of formulas (cf. Proposition 3.10).

In this section we show that extended system W captures extended system Z and thus rational closure. Unlike the proof that system W captures system Z in [KB22] we need to consider the case that an inference $A \mathrel{|\!\sim}^{z+}_\Delta B$ only holds because $\kappa^{z+}_\Delta(A) = \infty$.

Proposition 6.2. *Extended system W captures extended system Z, i.e., for a belief base* Δ *and* $A, B \in \mathcal{L}_\Sigma$ *it holds that* $A \mathrel{|\!\sim}^{z+}_\Delta B$ *implies* $A \mathrel{|\!\sim}^{\mathsf{w}+}_\Delta B$.

Proof. Observing Definition 3.16 of the extended Z-ranking function κ^{z+}_Δ and Definition 5.2 of the extended preferred structure on worlds $(\Omega^{feas}_\Delta, <^{\mathsf{w}+}_\Delta)$ we see that

1. for any $\omega \in \Omega_\Sigma$ we have that $\kappa^{z+}_\Delta(\omega) = \infty$ iff $\omega \notin \Omega^{feas}_\Delta$ and
2. for $\omega, \omega' \in \Omega^{feas}_\Delta$ we have $\kappa^{z+}_\Delta(\omega) < \kappa^{z+}_\Delta(\omega')$ implies $\omega <^{\mathsf{w}+}_\Delta \omega'$.

If $A \mathrel{|\!\sim}^{z+}_\Delta B$ then either $\kappa^{z+}_\Delta(A) = \infty$ or $\kappa^{z+}_\Delta(AB) < \kappa^{z+}_\Delta(A\overline{B})$. In the first case, (1.) implies that A has no model in Ω^{feas}_Δ, and therefore $A\overline{B}$ has no model in Ω^{feas}_Δ. Trivially, $A \mathrel{|\!\sim}^{\mathsf{w}+}_\Delta B$.

In the second case, there is an $\omega \in Mod_\Sigma(AB)$ with a smaller z-rank than any $\omega' \in Mod_\Sigma(A\overline{B})$. Especially, $\kappa^{z+}_\Delta(\omega) < \infty$ and with (1.) we have that $\omega \in \Omega^{feas}_\Delta$. Then (2.) implies that for any $\omega' \in Mod_\Sigma(AB) \cap \Omega^{feas}_\Delta$ we have $\omega <^{\mathsf{w}+}_\Delta \omega'$. Therefore, $A \mathrel{|\!\sim}^{\mathsf{w}+}_\Delta B$. □

We already know that system W strictly extends system Z, i.e., there is a (strongly consistent) belief base Δ such that $\mathrel{|\!\sim}^{z}_\Delta \subsetneq \mathrel{|\!\sim}^{\mathsf{w}}_\Delta$. Because extended system Z and system Z, as well as extended system W and system W coincide for strongly consistent belief bases, we have that $\mathrel{|\!\sim}^{z+}_\Delta \subsetneq \mathrel{|\!\sim}^{\mathsf{w}+}_\Delta$ for Δ; and thus extended system W strictly extends extended system Z.

6.3. Extended System W Captures Extended c-Inference

Generalizing the result in Section 6.1, in this section we show that extended system W captures extended c-inference. To do this, we take a similar course as the corresponding proof that system W captures c-inference in [KB22]. Before we can show this main result in Proposition 6.6, we show some lemmas used in its proof.

The following Lemma 6.3 and its proof loosely correspond to [KB22, Proposition 5], but they are stated without the CSPs used in [KB22]. The lemma states that ranking functions induced by impacts satisfying inequation (6.1) are extended c-representations. Note that (6.1) does not coincide with the inequations characterizing (extended) c-representations (see Section 5.7). Instead (6.1) is a stronger requirement on the impacts that takes the tolerance partition of the belief base Δ into account, and is only satisfied by a subset of all c-representations.

Lemma 6.3. *Let $\Delta = \{(B_1|A_1), \dots, (B_n|A_n)\}$ be a weakly consistent belief base with extended Z-partition $EP(\Delta) = (\Delta^0, \dots, \Delta^k, \Delta^\infty)$. Let $\vec{\eta} = (\eta_1, \dots, \eta_n)$ be an impact vector for Δ such that for every $m \in \{0, \dots, k\}$ and for every $(B_i|A_i) \in \Delta^m$ it holds that*

$$\eta_i > \sum_{\substack{q \in \{1,\dots,n\}, \\ (B_q|A_q) \in \bigcup_{p=0}^{m-1} \Delta^p}} \eta_q \tag{6.1}$$

and for every $(B_i|A_i) \in \Delta^\infty$ it holds that $\eta_i = \infty$. Then $\kappa_{\vec{\eta}}$ is an extended c-representation for Δ.

Proof. We need to show that for every $(B_i|A_i) \in \Delta$ it holds that $\kappa_{\vec{\eta}} \models (B_i|A_i)$. For $(B_i|A_i) \in \Delta^\infty$ we have that $\eta_i = \infty$ and therefore, with Lemma 3.18, $\kappa_{\vec{\eta}}(A_i) = \infty$; implying that $\kappa_{\vec{\eta}} \models (B_i|A_i)$.

Now consider any $i \in \{1, \dots, n\}$ with $\kappa_{\vec{\eta}}(A_i) < \infty$. There is some $m \in \{0, \dots, k\}$ with $(B_i|A_i) \in \Delta^m$. By the definition of the extended Z-partition, there is some ω such that $\omega \models A_i B_i$ and ω does not falsify any conditional in $\bigcup_{l=m}^{k} \Delta^l$. We have that

$$\begin{aligned}
\kappa_{\vec{\eta}}(\omega) = \sum_{\substack{q \in \{1,\dots,n\},\\ \omega \models A_q\overline{B_q}}} \eta_q &\overset{(*)}{=} \sum_{\substack{q \in \{1,\dots,n\},\\ (B_q|A_q) \in \bigcup_{r=0}^{m-1} \Delta^r,\\ \omega \models A_q\overline{B_q}}} \eta_q \\
&\leq \sum_{\substack{q \in \{1,\dots,n\},\\ (B_q|A_q) \in \bigcup_{r=0}^{m-1} \Delta^r}} \eta_q \overset{(6.1)}{<} \eta_i.
\end{aligned}$$

Equation $(*)$ holds because ω does not falsify any conditional in Δ^l for $l = m, \dots, k$. In summary, $\kappa_{\vec{\eta}}(A_i B_i) < \eta_i$. Additionally, $\kappa_{\vec{\eta}}(\omega') = \sum_{\substack{q \in \{1,\dots,n\},\\ \omega' \models A_q\overline{B_q}}} \eta_q \geq \eta_i$ for every $\omega' \models A_i\overline{B_i}$. Therefore, $\kappa_{\vec{\eta}}(A_i\overline{B_i}) \geq \eta_i$. Hence, $\kappa_{\vec{\eta}}(A_i B_i) < \eta_i \leq \kappa_{\vec{\eta}}(A_i\overline{B_i})$ which implies that $\kappa_{\vec{\eta}} \models (B_i|A_i)$. □

The next Lemma 6.4 and its proof are adaptions of [KB22, Lemma 4]. The lemma states that for c-representations $\kappa_{\vec{\eta}}$ satisfying a certain condition the order on worlds induced by the ranks of $\kappa_{\vec{\eta}}$ refine the extended preferred structure on worlds. The lemma thus connects the extended preferred structure on worlds with c-inference.

Lemma 6.4. *Let $\Delta = \{(B_1|A_1), \dots, (B_n|A_n)\}$ be a weakly consistent belief base with extended Z-partition $EP(\Delta) = (\Delta^0, \dots, \Delta^k, \Delta^\infty)$. Let $\vec{\eta} = (\eta_1, \dots, \eta_n)$ be an impact vector for Δ such that for every $m \in \{0, \dots, k\}$ and for every $(B_i|A_i) \in \Delta^m$ it holds that $\eta_i \in \mathbb{N}_0$ and*

$$\eta_i > \sum_{\substack{q \in \{1,\dots,n\},\\ (B_q|A_q) \in \bigcup_{p=0}^{m-1} \Delta^p}} \eta_q. \tag{6.2}$$

Then, for $\omega, \omega' \in \Omega_\Delta^{feas}$ it holds that $\omega <_\Delta^{w+} \omega'$ implies $\kappa_{\vec{\eta}}(\omega) < \kappa_{\vec{\eta}}(\omega')$.

Proof. Let $\omega, \omega' \in \Omega_\Delta^{feas}$ such that $\omega <_\Delta^{w+} \omega'$. By definition, there is an $m \in \{0, \dots, k\}$ such that $\xi^i(\omega) = \xi^i(\omega')$ for $i = m+1, \dots, k$ and $\xi^m(\omega) \subsetneq \xi^m(\omega')$. Hence, there is a $(B_p|A_p) \in \xi^m(\omega') \setminus \xi^m(\omega)$. Because $\omega, \omega' \in \Omega_\Delta^{feas}$ and $\eta_i \in \mathbb{N}_0$ for $(B_i|A_i) \notin \Delta^\infty$ all conditionals falsified by ω or ω' have finite impact. Therefore, $\kappa(\omega), \kappa(\omega')$ are finite. We have that

$$
\begin{aligned}
&\kappa_{\vec{\eta}}(\omega') - \kappa_{\vec{\eta}}(\omega) \\
&= \sum_{\substack{q\in\{1,\dots,n\},\\ \omega'\models A_q\overline{B_q}}} \eta_q - \sum_{\substack{q\in\{1,\dots,n\},\\ \omega\models A_q\overline{B_q}}} \eta_q \\
&\overset{(*a)}{=} \sum_{\substack{q\in\{1,\dots,n\},\\ (B_q|A_q)\in\bigcup_{r=0}^{m}\Delta^r,\\ \omega'\models A_q\overline{B_q}}} \eta_q - \sum_{\substack{q\in\{1,\dots,n\},\\ (B_q|A_q)\in\bigcup_{r=0}^{m}\Delta^r,\\ \omega\models A_q\overline{B_q}}} \eta_q \\
&= \sum_{\substack{q\in\{1,\dots,n\},\\ (B_q|A_q)\in\Delta^m,\\ \omega'\models A_q\overline{B_q}}} \eta_q + \sum_{\substack{q\in\{1,\dots,n\},\\ (B_q|A_q)\in\bigcup_{r=0}^{m-1}\Delta^r,\\ \omega'\models A_q\overline{B_q}}} \eta_q - \sum_{\substack{q\in\{1,\dots,n\},\\ (B_q|A_q)\in\Delta^m,\\ \omega\models A_q\overline{B_q}}} \eta_q - \sum_{\substack{q\in\{1,\dots,n\},\\ (B_q|A_q)\in\bigcup_{r=0}^{m-1}\Delta^r,\\ \omega\models A_q\overline{B_q}}} \eta_q \\
&\overset{(*b)}{\geq} \eta_p + \sum_{\substack{q\in\{1,\dots,n\},\\ (B_q|A_q)\in\bigcup_{r=0}^{m-1}\Delta^r,\\ \omega'\models A_q\overline{B_q}}} \eta_q - \sum_{\substack{q\in\{1,\dots,n\},\\ (B_q|A_q)\in\bigcup_{r=0}^{m-1}\Delta^r,\\ \omega\models A_q\overline{B_q}}} \eta_q \\
&\geq \eta_p - \sum_{\substack{q\in\{1,\dots,n\},\\ (B_q|A_q)\in\bigcup_{r=0}^{m-1}\Delta^r,\\ \omega\models A_q\overline{B_q}}} \eta_q \\
&\overset{(6.2)}{>} 0.
\end{aligned}
$$

The equation $(*a)$ holds because $\xi^i(\omega) = \xi^i(\omega')$ for $i > m$. The inequation $(*b)$ holds because $\xi^m(\omega) \subseteq \xi^m(\omega^j)$ and $(B_p|A_p) \in \xi^m(\omega') \setminus \xi^m(\omega)$. In summary, we have $\kappa_{\vec{\eta}}(\omega) < \kappa_{\vec{\eta}}(\omega')$. □

Using Lemmas 6.3 and 6.4 we show now Lemma 6.5 which is central for proving that extended system W captures extended c-inference. It states that for worlds with $\omega \not<^{\mathsf{w}}_{\Delta} \omega'$ we can find an extended c-representation $\kappa_{\vec{\eta}}$ with $\kappa_{\vec{\eta}}(\omega') \leq \kappa_{\vec{\eta}}(\omega)$. Lemma 6.5 and its proof are adaptions of [KB22, Lemma 5].

Lemma 6.5. *Let Δ be a weakly consistent belief base, let $\omega' \in \Omega^{feas}_{\Delta}$, and let $\Omega^X \subseteq \Omega^{feas}_{\Delta}$ be a set of feasible worlds. If for all $\omega \in \Omega^X$ it holds that $\omega \not<^{\mathsf{w}+}_{\Delta} \omega'$, then there is an extended c-representation $\kappa_{\vec{\eta}}$ of Δ such that for all $\omega \in \Omega^X$ it holds that $\kappa_{\vec{\eta}}(\omega') \leq \kappa_{\vec{\eta}}(\omega)$.*

Proof. Let $(B_1|A_1), \dots, (B_n|A_n)$ be the conditionals in Δ and let

$EP(\Delta) = (\Delta^0, \ldots, \Delta^k, \Delta^\infty)$ be the extended Z-partition of Δ. Furthermore, let

$$\Omega^Y := \{\omega \in \Omega^X \mid \omega' \not<^{\mathsf{w+}}_\Delta \omega \text{ and } \xi(\omega) \neq \xi(\omega')\}.$$

Let $\omega^1, \ldots, \omega^l$ be the worlds in Ω^Y. Because, for every $j \in \{1, \ldots, l\}$, it holds that $\xi(\omega^j) \neq \xi(\omega')$, there is an $m_j \in \{0, \ldots, k\}$ such that $\xi^{m_j}(\omega) \neq \xi^{m_j}(\omega')$ and $\xi^i(\omega) = \xi^i(\omega)$ for $i \in \{m_j + 1, \ldots, k\}$. Because $\omega^j \not<^{\mathsf{w+}}_\Delta \omega'$ by assumption and $\omega' \not<^{\mathsf{w+}}_\Delta \omega^j$ by definition of Ω^Y, we have that $\xi^{m_j}(\omega^j) \not\subseteq \xi^{m_j}(\omega')$ and $\xi^{m_j}(\omega') \not\subseteq \xi^{m_j}(\omega^j)$. Define the set

$$I := \bigcup_{j=1}^{l} (\xi^{m_j}(\omega_j) \setminus \xi^{m_j}(\omega')).$$

Because $\xi^{m_j}(\omega^j) \not\subseteq \xi^{m_j}(\omega')$ the set I is not empty.

Now we define an extended c-representation of Δ that we will then show to satisfy $\kappa_{\vec{\eta}}(\omega') \leq \kappa_{\vec{\eta}}(\omega)$. We do this by iteratively defining the impacts for the conditionals in Δ^m, for $m = 0, \ldots, k, \infty$. For $m \in \{1, \ldots, k\}$, for any $(B_i|A_i) \in \Delta^m$, we have either $(B_i|A_i) \in I$ or $(B_i|A_i) \notin I$. If $(B_i|A_i) \notin I$, define

$$\eta_i := 1 + \sum_{\substack{q \in \{1,\ldots,n\}, \\ (B_q|A_q) \in \bigcup_{r=0}^{m-1} \Delta^r}} \eta_q. \tag{6.3}$$

If $(B_i|A_i) \in I$, then define

$$\eta_i := |\Delta^m| \cdot (1 + \sum_{\substack{q \in \{1,\ldots,n\}, \\ (B_q|A_q) \in \bigcup_{r=0}^{m-1} \Delta^r}} \eta_q). \tag{6.4}$$

For $m = \infty$, for any $(B_i|A_i) \in \Delta^m$ define $\eta_i = \infty$.

By construction for all $m = 0, \ldots, k, \infty$ and $(B_i|A_i) \in \Delta^m$ it holds that

$$\eta_i > \sum_{\substack{q \in \{1,\ldots,n\}, \\ (B_q|A_q) \in \bigcup_{p=0}^{m-1} \Delta^p}} \eta_q.$$

With Lemma 6.3 we see that $\kappa_{\vec{\eta}}$ is an extended c-representation of Δ.

Now we have to show that $\kappa_{\vec{\eta}}(\omega') \leq \kappa_{\vec{\eta}}(\omega)$ for all $\omega \in \Omega^X$. For all $\omega \in \Omega^X$ we have $\omega \not<^{\mathsf{w+}}_\Delta \omega'$ and one of the following three cases holds:

1. $\omega' <^{\mathsf{w+}}_\Delta \omega$

2. $\xi(\omega) = \xi(\omega')$
3. $\omega' \not<^{\mathsf{w}+}_{\Delta} \omega$ and $\xi(\omega) \neq \xi(\omega')$.

In case (1.), by Lemma 6.4 we have $\kappa_{\vec{\eta}}(\omega') < \kappa_{\vec{\eta}}(\omega)$ because $\kappa_{\vec{\eta}}$ is an extended c-representation of Δ. In case (2.), we trivially have $\kappa_{\vec{\eta}}(\omega') = \kappa_{\vec{\eta}}(\omega)$ for any extended c-representation $\kappa_{\vec{\eta}}$. In case (3.), we have to show that $\kappa_{\vec{\eta}}(\omega') \leq \kappa_{\vec{\eta}}(\omega)$ for all $\omega \in \Omega^Y$.

This means we need to show that $\kappa_{\vec{\eta}}(\omega') \leq \kappa_{\vec{\eta}}(\omega^j)$ for each $j = 1, \ldots, n$. First note, that because $\omega' \in \Omega_{\Delta}^{feas}$ and $\Omega^Y \subseteq \Omega^X \subseteq \Omega_{\Delta}^{feas}$ no world $\omega^j \in \Omega^Y$ nor ω' falsifies any conditional in Δ^∞. The world ω' falsifies at most $|\Delta^{m_j}| - 1$ conditionals in Δ^{m_j}, because otherwise we could not have $\xi^{m_j}(\omega^j) \not\subseteq \xi^{m_j}(\omega')$. For every $(B_i|A_i) \in \Delta^{m_j}$ with $\omega' \models A_i\overline{B_i}$ we have $(B_i|A_i) \in \xi^{m_j}(\omega')$ and therefore $(B_i|A_i) \notin I$; hence, η_i is defined as in (6.3). We have

$$\sum_{\substack{q\in\{1,\ldots,n\},\\ (B_q|A_q)\in\Delta^{m_j},\\ \omega'\models A_q\overline{B_q}}} \eta_q \quad \leq \quad (|\Delta^{m_j}| - 1)(1 + \sum_{\substack{q\in\{1,\ldots,n\},\\ (B_q|A_q)\in\bigcup_{r=0}^{m-1}\Delta^r}} \eta_q). \tag{6.5}$$

Now choose $(B_p|A_p) \in \xi^{m_j}(\omega^j) \setminus \xi^{m_j}(\omega')$. We have $(B|A) \in I$ and therefore the impact η_p is defined as in (6.4). Because $\omega^j, \omega' \in \Omega_{\Delta}^{feas}$ we have $\xi^\infty(\omega') = \xi^\infty(\omega^j) = \emptyset$ and both $\kappa_{\vec{\eta}}(\omega_j)$ and $\kappa_{\vec{\eta}}(\omega')$ are finite. Therefore, we have

$$\begin{aligned}
&\kappa_{\vec{\eta}}(\omega_j) - \kappa_{\vec{\eta}}(\omega') \\
&= \sum_{\substack{q\in\{1,\ldots,n\},\\ \omega_j\models A_q\overline{B_q}}} \eta_q - \sum_{\substack{q\in\{1,\ldots,n\},\\ \omega'\models A_q\overline{B_q}}} \eta_q \\
&\overset{(*a)}{=} \sum_{\substack{q\in\{1,\ldots,n\},\\ (B_q|A_q)\in\bigcup_{r=0}^{m_j}\Delta^r,\\ \omega_j\models A_q\overline{B_q}}} \eta_q - \sum_{\substack{q\in\{1,\ldots,n\},\\ (B_q|A_q)\in\bigcup_{r=0}^{m_j}\Delta^r,\\ \omega'\models A_q\overline{B_q}}} \eta_q \\
&\overset{(*b)}{\geq} \eta_p - \sum_{\substack{q\in\{1,\ldots,n\},\\ (B_q|A_q)\in\bigcup_{r=0}^{m_j}\Delta^r,\\ \omega'\models A_q\overline{B_q}}} \eta_q
\end{aligned}$$

$$
\begin{aligned}
&= \eta_p - \sum_{\substack{q \in \{1,\dots,n\},\\ (B_q|A_q) \in \Delta^{m_j},\\ \omega' \models A_q\overline{B_q}}} \eta_q - \sum_{\substack{q \in \{1,\dots,n\},\\ (B_q|A_q) \in \bigcup_{r=0}^{m_j-1} \Delta^r,\\ \omega' \models A_q\overline{B_q}}} \eta_q \\
&\overset{(6.4)}{=} |\Delta^{m_j}| \cdot (1 + \sum_{\substack{q \in \{1,\dots,n\},\\ (B_q|A_q) \in \bigcup_{r=0}^{m_j-1} \Delta^r}} \eta_q) - \sum_{\substack{q \in \{1,\dots,n\},\\ (B_q|A_q) \in \Delta^{m_j},\\ \omega' \models A_q\overline{B_q}}} \eta_q - \sum_{\substack{q \in \{1,\dots,n\},\\ (B_q|A_q) \in \bigcup_{r=0}^{m_j-1} \Delta^r,\\ \omega' \models A_q\overline{B_q}}} \eta_q \\
&\overset{(6.5)}{\geq} |\Delta^{m_j}| \cdot (1 + \sum_{\substack{q \in \{1,\dots,n\},\\ (B_q|A_q) \in \bigcup_{r=0}^{m_j-1} \Delta^r}} \eta_q) - (|\Delta^{m_j}| - 1)(1 + \sum_{\substack{q \in \{1,\dots,n\},\\ (B_q|A_q) \in \bigcup_{r=0}^{m-1} \Delta^r}} \eta_q) \\
&\qquad - \sum_{\substack{q \in \{1,\dots,n\},\\ (B_q|A_q) \in \bigcup_{r=0}^{m_j-1} \Delta^r,\\ \omega' \models A_q\overline{B_q}}} \eta_q \\
&= 1 + \sum_{\substack{q \in \{1,\dots,n\},\\ (B_q|A_q) \in \bigcup_{r=0}^{m_j-1} \Delta^r}} \eta_q - \sum_{\substack{q \in \{1,\dots,n\},\\ (B_q|A_q) \in \bigcup_{r=0}^{m_j-1} \Delta^r,\\ \omega' \models A_q\overline{B_q}}} \eta_q \\
&\geq 1.
\end{aligned}
$$

The equation $(*a)$ holds because $\xi^i(\omega) = \xi^i(\omega^j)$ for $i > m_j$. The inequation $(*b)$ holds because $(B_p|A_p) \in \Delta^{m_j}$ and ω_j falsifies $(B_p|A_p)$. In summary, we have $\kappa_{\vec{\eta}}(\omega_j) - \kappa_{\vec{\eta}}(\omega') \geq 1$ and therefore $\kappa_{\vec{\eta}}(\omega) \leq \kappa_{\vec{\eta}}(\omega_j)$. □

Now we can finally prove that extended system W captures extended c-inference. This proposition corresponds to [KB22, Proposition 11].

Proposition 6.6. *Extended system W captures extended c-inference, i.e., for a belief base Δ and $A, B \in \mathcal{L}_\Sigma$ it holds that $A \mathrel{|\!\!\sim}^{ec}_{\Delta} B$ implies $A \mathrel{|\!\!\sim}^{\mathsf{w}+}_{\Delta} B$.*

Proof. Let Δ be any belief base and let $A, B \in \mathcal{L}_\Sigma$. We show that $A \mathrel{|\!\!\sim}^{ec}_{\Delta} B$ implies $A \mathrel{|\!\!\sim}^{\mathsf{w}+}_{\Delta} B$ by contraposition, which means we have to show that $A \not\mathrel{|\!\!\sim}^{\mathsf{w}+}_{\Delta} B$ implies $A \not\mathrel{|\!\!\sim}^{ec}_{\Delta} B$.

Assume that $A \not\mathrel{|\!\!\sim}^{\mathsf{w}+}_{\Delta} B$. In this case Δ must be weakly consistent, because otherwise $A \mathrel{|\!\!\sim}^{\mathsf{w}+}_{\Delta} B$ would hold for any A, B. Because we have $A \not\mathrel{|\!\!\sim}^{\mathsf{w}+}_{\Delta} B$, there is an $\omega' \in \Omega^{feas}_{\Delta} \cap Mod_\Sigma(A\overline{B})$ such that for every

$\omega \in \Omega_\Delta^{feas} \cap Mod_\Sigma(AB)$ we have $\omega \not<_\Delta^{\mathsf{w}+} \omega'$. Let $\Omega^X := Mod_\Sigma(AB) \cap \Omega_\Delta^{feas}$. By Lemma 6.5 there is an extended c-representation $\kappa_{\vec{\eta}}$ of Δ such that, for every $\omega \in \Omega^X$ we have $\kappa_{\vec{\eta}}(\omega') \leq \kappa_{\vec{\eta}}(\omega)$. Therefore, $\kappa_{\vec{\eta}}(A\overline{B}) \leq \kappa_{\vec{\eta}}(AB)$ and thus $A \not\mid\!\sim_\Delta^{ec} B$. □

Analogously to system W and system Z we can see that extended system W strictly also extends extended c-inference because system W strictly extends c-inference.

6.4. Extended System W is Captured by Lexicographic Inference

We will now investigate and establish the relationship between extended system W and the (adapted) lexicographic inference as presented in Section 3.6. The connection between system W and lexicographic inference was first established in [HB22c]. There it was shown that system W is captured by lexicographic inference. Here we prove the more general result that extended system W is captured by adapted lexicographic inference.

The next Lemma 6.7 connects the order $<_\Delta^{\mathsf{w}+}$ used in the definition of system W with the order $<_\Delta^{lex}$ that is used to define lexicographic inference.

Lemma 6.7. *Let Δ be a belief base and ω, ω' be worlds. Then*

1. *$\omega \in \Omega_\Delta^{feas}$ iff $\xi^\infty(\omega) \neq \emptyset$, and*
2. *for $\omega, \omega' \in \Omega_\Delta^{feas}$ we have that $\omega <_\Delta^{\mathsf{w}+} \omega'$ implies $\omega <_\Delta^{lex} \omega'$.*

Proof. (1.) follows directly from the definition of $(\Omega_\Delta^{feas}, <_\Delta^{\mathsf{w}+})$.

For (2.), let $\omega, \omega' \in \Omega^{feas}$ be with $\omega <_\Delta^{\mathsf{w}} \omega'$. Then there is a k such that $\xi^k(\omega) \subsetneqq \xi^k(\omega')$ and $\xi^i(\omega) = \xi^i(\omega')$ for $i > k$. This implies that $|\xi^k(\omega)| < |\xi^k(\omega')|$ and $|\xi^i(\omega)| = |\xi^i(\omega')|$ for $i > k$. Hence, $\omega <_\Delta^{lex} \omega'$. □

Using Lemma 6.7, we can show that adapted lexicographic inference captures extended system W. To take into account that an inference $A \mid\!\sim_\Delta^{\mathsf{w}+} B$ might only hold because A or $A\overline{B}$ are infeasible we distinguish different cases in the proof.

Proposition 6.8. *Adapted lexicographic inference captures extended system W, i.e., for a belief base Δ and formulas $A, B \in \mathcal{L}_\Sigma$ it holds that if $A \mid\!\sim_\Delta^{\mathsf{w}+} B$ then $A \mid\!\sim_\Delta^{alex} B$.*

Proof. Let $A \mathrel{|\!\sim}^{\mathsf{w+}}_{\Delta} B$. We can distinguish three cases.

Case 1: $Mod_{\Sigma}(A) \cap \Omega^{feas}_{\Delta} = \emptyset$ Then $\xi^{\infty}(\omega) \neq \emptyset$ for all $\omega \in Mod_{\Sigma}(A)$ and therefore $A \mathrel{|\!\sim}^{alex}_{\Delta} B$ by the definition of $\mathrel{|\!\sim}^{alex}_{\Delta}$.

Case 2: $Mod_{\Sigma}(A) \cap \Omega^{feas}_{\Delta} \neq \emptyset$ and $Mod_{\Sigma}(A\overline{B}) \cap \Omega^{feas}_{\Delta} = \emptyset$ Then AB must have a model $\omega \in \Omega^{feas}_{\Delta}$. It holds that $|\xi^{\infty}(\omega)| = 0$ and $|\xi^{\infty}(\omega)| > 0$ for every $\omega' \in Mod_{\Sigma}(A\overline{B})$. Therefore, $AB <^{lex}_{\Delta} A\overline{B}$ and hence $A \mathrel{|\!\sim}^{alex}_{\Delta} B$.

Case 3: $Mod_{\Sigma}(A) \cap \Omega^{feas}_{\Delta} \neq \emptyset$ and $Mod_{\Sigma}(A\overline{B}) \cap \Omega^{feas}_{\Delta} \neq \emptyset$ Because $Mod_{\Sigma}(A\overline{B}) \cap \Omega^{feas}_{\Delta} \neq \emptyset$ and because $|\xi^{\infty}(\omega')| = 0$ for every $\omega' \in \Omega^{feas}_{\Delta}$ and $|\xi^{\infty}(\omega')| > 0$ for every $\omega' \in \Omega^{feas}_{\Delta}$ we have that $\min(Mod_{\Sigma}(A\overline{B}), <^{lex}_{\Delta}) \subseteq \Omega^{feas}_{\Delta}$. Because $A \mathrel{|\!\sim}^{\mathsf{w+}}_{\Delta} B$, for every $\omega' \in Mod_{\Sigma}(A\overline{B}) \cap \Omega^{feas}_{\Delta}$ there is another world $\omega \in Mod_{\Sigma}(AB) \cap \Omega^{feas}_{\Delta}$ such that $\omega <^{\mathsf{w+}}_{\Delta} \omega'$, and therefore $\omega <^{lex}_{\Delta} \omega'$ with Lemma 6.7. This implies that $\min(Mod_{\Sigma}(AB), <^{lex}_{\Delta}) <^{lex}_{\Delta} \min(Mod_{\Sigma}(A\overline{B}), <^{lex}_{\Delta})$. Hence, $AB <^{lex}_{\Delta} A\overline{B}$ and therefore $A \mathrel{|\!\sim}^{alex}_{\Delta} B$. □

Moreover, adapted lexicographic inference strictly extends extended system W, i.e., some adapted lexicographic inferences are not licensed by extended system W.

Proposition 6.9. *There are belief bases Δ such that $\mathrel{|\!\sim}^{\mathsf{w+}}_{\Delta} \subsetneq \mathrel{|\!\sim}^{alex}_{\Delta}$.*

Proof. Proposition 6.8 establishes that $\mathrel{|\!\sim}^{\mathsf{w+}}_{\Delta} \subseteq \mathrel{|\!\sim}^{alex}_{\Delta}$ for all Δ. We show that there are belief bases where $\mathrel{|\!\sim}^{\mathsf{w+}}_{\Delta} \neq \mathrel{|\!\sim}^{alex}_{\Delta}$.

Consider the belief base Δ_{ve} from Example 3.48 with $OP(\Delta_{ve}) = (\Delta^0, \Delta^1)$ where $\Delta^0 = \{(g|m), (t|b)\}$ and $\Delta^1 = \{(m|e), (\overline{g}|me)\}$ (cf. Example 4.24). Furthermore, consider the worlds $\omega := mbetg$ and $\omega' := \overline{m}be\overline{t}g$. We have that $(|\xi^0_{\Delta_{ve}}(\omega)|, |\xi^1_{\Delta_{ve}}(\omega)|) = (0, 1)$ and we have $(|\xi^0_{\Delta_{ve}}(\omega')|, |\xi^1_{\Delta_{ve}}(\omega')|) = (1, 1)$ Hence, $\omega <^{lex}_{\Delta_{ve}} \omega'$ and therefore $\omega \vee \omega' \mathrel{|\!\sim}^{alex}_{\Delta_{ve}} \omega$. But $\omega \not<^{\mathsf{w+}}_{\Delta_{ve}} \omega'$, and therefore $\omega \vee \omega' \mathrel{|\!\sim}^{\mathsf{w+}}_{\Delta_{ve}} \omega$. □

These propositions allow us to establish further relationships among inductive inference operators.

Proposition 6.10. *Adapted lexicographic inference captures and strictly extends extended c-inference, i.e., every extended c-inference is also an adapted lexicographic inference but there are adapted lexicographic inferences that are not extended c-inferences.*

Proof. Because extended system W captures extended c-inference (Proposition 6.6), this follows from Propositions 6.8 and 6.9. □

Similarly, because extended system W captures extended system Z, Propositions 6.2, 6.8, and 6.9 imply that adapted lexicographic inference captures and strictly extends extended system Z.

6.5. Multipreference-Closure Coincides with System W

Multipreference closure (MP-closure) [GG21] for conditional inference was introduced in the context of description logics with typicality independently of system W [KB20] with quite a different definition. In [HB22a] it was shown that MP-closure coincides with system W for strongly consistent belief bases. Now we extend this result and show that MP-closure coincides with extended system W for all belief bases.

By Propositions 5.15 and 5.18 we already know that for every Δ, the inference relation $\mid\!\sim^{\mathsf{w}+}_{\Delta}$ yielded by extended system W is also induced by the preferential model $\mathcal{M}^{\mathsf{w}}(\Delta) := \langle \Omega^{feas}_{\Delta}, \mathrm{id}, <^{\mathsf{w}+}_{\Delta} \rangle$ where $(\Omega^{feas}_{\Delta}, <^{\mathsf{w}}_{\Delta})$ is the preferred structure on worlds induced by Δ.

Lemma 6.11. *For every belief base Δ, the extended system W inference relation $\mid\!\sim^{\mathsf{w}+}_{\Delta}$ is induced by the preferential model $\mathcal{M}^{\mathsf{w}}(\Delta) := \langle \Omega^{feas}_{\Delta}, \mathrm{id}, <^{\mathsf{w}+}_{\Delta} \rangle$.*

To use the characterization theorem in Proposition 3.42 by [GG21], that connects MP-closure with MP-models, we now show that $\mathcal{M}^{\mathsf{w}}(\Delta)$ is an MP-model of Δ. As a first step for this, we observe that $\mathcal{M}^{\mathsf{w}}(\Delta)$ is a canonical model (see Definition 3.38) of Δ.

Proposition 6.12. *The preferential model $\mathcal{M}^{\mathsf{w}}(\Delta)$ is a canonical model of Δ.*

Proof. Because system W satisfies direct inference, Lemma 6.11 implies that $\mathcal{M}^{\mathsf{w}}(\Delta)$ is a model of Δ.

A world $\omega \in \Omega_\Sigma$ is compatible with Δ iff $\omega \not\mid\!\sim^{z+}_{\Delta} \bot$ which is equivalent to $\kappa^{z+}_{\Delta}(\omega) < \infty$. In Section 5.2 we saw that Ω^{feas}_{Δ} contains the worlds $\omega \in \Omega_\Sigma$ with $\kappa^{z+}_{\Delta}(\omega) = \infty$. Therefore, Ω^{feas}_{Δ} is the set of worlds that are compatible with Δ.

By construction, $\mathcal{M}^{\mathsf{w}}(\Delta)$ has the state $s = \omega$ with $l(s) \models \omega$ for every world $\omega \in \Omega^{feas}_{\Delta}$. Therefore, $\mathcal{M}^{\mathsf{w}}(\Delta)$ is a canonical model. □

While extended system W utilizes the extended Z-partition of a belief base that is based on the notion of tolerance, the MP-seriousness ordering (Definition 3.32) is defined based on the notion of exceptional conditionals (Definition 3.30). The next step to connect extended system W and MP-closure is showing that a belief base Δ tolerating a conditional $(B|A)$ is the opposite of $(B|A)$ being exceptional for Δ. A similar observation has been made but stated less explicitely in [GP90].

Proposition 6.13. *Let Δ be a belief base and $(B|A)$ be a conditional in Δ. Δ tolerates $(B|A)$ iff $(B|A)$ is not exceptional for Δ.*

Proof. We will prove both directions of the "iff".

Direction $\Rightarrow$: Assume $(B|A)$ is tolerated by Δ. By definition there is a world $\omega \in \Omega_\Sigma$ such that $\omega \models AB$ and ω does not falsify any conditional in Δ. Now take a preferential model $\mathcal{M}$ of Δ and obtain a new model $\mathcal{M}'$ by adding a minimal state s associated with ω. Because ω does not falsify any conditional in Δ the new model $\mathcal{M}'$ also models Δ. Because for the minimal state s the world $l(s) = \omega$ does not model $\neg A$ we have that $\top \not\mid\!\sim^p_\Delta \neg A$. Hence $(B|A)$ is not exceptional for Δ.

Direction $\Leftarrow$: Assume $(B|A)$ is not exceptional for Δ. Then $\top \not\mid\!\sim^p_\Delta \neg A$, i.e., there is a preferential model $\mathcal{M} = \langle S, l, \prec \rangle$ of Δ and a state $s \in S$ such that s is minimal and $l(s) \models A$. Because $\mathcal{M}$ models all conditionals in Δ including $(B|A)$, state s is minimal, and $l(s) \models A$, we have $l(s) \models AB$. As s is minimal, it cannot falsify any of the conditionals in Δ. In summary, the world $l(s)$ verifies $(B|A)$ and falsifies none of the other conditionals in Δ, yielding that $(B|A)$ is tolerated by Δ. □

Using Proposition 6.13 we can show that the extended Z-partition of a belief base groups conditionals according to their rank as defined in Definition 3.31.

Lemma 6.14. *Let Δ be a consistent belief base of order l and $EP(\Delta) = (\Delta^0, \dots, \Delta^k, \Delta^\infty)$ be the extended Z-partition of Δ. Then for $i = 0, \dots, k, \infty$ the conditionals $(B|A) \in \Delta^i$ have rank i, and furthermore $k = l - 1$.*

Proof. For $i = 0, \dots, k$ the conditionals in Δ^i are those that are tolerated by $\bigcup_{j \geq i} \Delta^j$ but not tolerated by $\bigcup_{j \geq i-1} \Delta^j$. Let the sets $C_0, C_1, \dots$ be constructed from Δ as in Definition 3.31. The conditionals in Δ with rank i are those that are not exceptional for C_i but exceptional for C_{i-1}; these are the conditionals in $C_i \setminus C_{i+1}$. We prove that $\Delta^i = C_i \setminus C_{i+1}$ by induction on i.

Base case: We have $C_0 = \Delta$ and $C_1 = E(\Delta)$. $C_0 \setminus C_1 = \Delta \setminus E(\Delta)$ is the set of conditionals in Δ that is not exceptional for Δ. By Proposition 6.13 this is the maximal set of conditionals that are tolerated by Δ. Therefore, $\Delta^0 = C_0 \setminus C_1$.

Induction step: Let $i > 0$. With $C_j \supseteq C_{j+1}$ for $j = 0, \dots, l$ and the induction hypothesis we have $C_i = \Delta \setminus \bigcup_{j<i} \Delta^j = \bigcup_{j \geq i} \Delta^j$. Analogously to the base case we show that $C_i \setminus C_{i+1}$ is the set of conditionals from C_i that are tolerated by C_i. By construction of $EP(\Delta)$ this is Δ^i.

By construction of $EP(\Delta)$, in $C_{k+1} = \Delta \setminus \bigcup_{j=0,\dots,k} \Delta^j = \Delta^\infty$ there are no conditionals that are tolerated by C_{k+1}. Therefore, $C_{k+2} = E(C_{k+1}) = C_{k+1}$. Hence, the order of Δ is $l = k+1$. Furthermore, the conditionals in Δ^∞ are exceptional for all C_j (with $j \in \mathbb{N}_0$) and therefore have rank ∞. □

Based on Lemma 6.14, the next lemma states that the MP-seriousness ordering of the sets of conditionals falsified by each world corresponds to the extended preferred structure on worlds.

Lemma 6.15. *Let Δ be a belief base. For all $\omega, \omega' \in \Omega_\Delta^{feas}$ it holds that*

$$\xi(\omega) \prec_\Delta^{MP} \xi(\omega') \quad \textit{iff} \quad \omega <_\Delta^{w+} \omega'.$$

Proof. Let l be the order of Δ, let $D := \xi(\omega)$, and let $D' := \xi(\omega')$. Let $(D_\infty, D_l, \dots, D_0)_D$ be the tuple of sets such that D_i is the set of conditionals in D with rank i; and let $(D'_\infty, D'_l, \dots, D'_0)_{D'}$ be the corresponding tuple of subsets of D'. Because $\omega, \omega' \in \Omega_\Delta^{feas}$ we have $D_\infty = D'_\infty = \emptyset$. Because a belief base with order l does not contain conditionals with rank l we have $D_l = D'_l = \emptyset$. Using Lemma 6.14, for $i = 0, \dots, k$ the set D_i of conditionals that are falsified by ω and have rank i equals the set $\xi^i(\omega)$ of conditionals that are falsified by ω and are in Δ^i. Analogously, $D'_i = \xi^i(\omega')$ for $i = 0, \dots, k$. We have that

$$
\begin{aligned}
& D \prec_\Delta^{MP} D' \\
\text{iff} \quad & (D_\infty, D_l, D_k, \dots, D_0)_D \ll (D'_\infty, D'_l, D'_k, \dots, D'_0)_{D'} \\
\text{iff} \quad & (\emptyset, \emptyset, \xi^k(\omega), \dots, \xi^0(\omega)) \ll (\emptyset, \emptyset, \xi^k(\omega'), \dots, \xi^0(\omega')) \\
\text{iff} \quad & \text{there is an } m \in \{0, \dots, k\} \text{ such that} \\
& \qquad \xi^i(\omega) = \xi^i(\omega') \quad \forall i \in \{m+1, \dots, k\} \text{ and}
\end{aligned}
$$

$$\xi^m(\omega) \subsetneq \xi^m(\omega')$$
$$\text{iff} \quad \omega <^{\mathsf{w}+}_{\Delta} \omega'.$$

□

The proof that MP-closure coincides with extended system W uses the characterization of MP-closure with MP-models. It relies on the observation that the system W preferential model $\mathcal{M}^{\mathsf{w}}(\Delta)$ of a belief base Δ is also an MP-model of Δ.

Proposition 6.16. *For a belief base Δ the preferential model $\mathcal{M}^{\mathsf{w}}(\Delta) = \langle \Omega^{feas}_{\Delta}, \mathrm{id}, <^{\mathsf{w}+}_{\Delta} \rangle$ is an MP-model of Δ.*

Proof. Let $<^{z}$ be the ordering on Ω^{feas}_{Δ} that is induced by the Z-ranking function κ^{z+}_{Δ} of Δ given by $\omega <^{z} \omega'$ iff $\kappa^{z+}_{\Delta}(\omega) < \kappa^{z+}_{\Delta}(\omega')$ for $\omega, \omega' \in \Omega^{feas}_{\Delta}$. Consider the preferential model $\mathcal{U} := \langle \Omega^{feas}_{\Delta}, \mathrm{id}, <^{z} \rangle$. The preferential model $\mathcal{U}$ is a canonical ranked model of Δ as the ordering $<^{z}$ is compatible with Δ and Ω^{feas}_{Δ} and id are the same as in $\mathcal{M}^{\mathsf{w}}(\Delta)$, which is canonical. As $<_{FIMS}$ (Definition 3.37) only relates models with the same set of states and the same valuation function and because there are only finitely many ranked models with a given set of states and valuation function, there is a model $\mathcal{V} = \langle \Omega^{feas}_{\Delta}, \mathrm{id}, \prec_{V} \rangle$ that is a minimal canonical ranked model of Δ.

Now let $\mathcal{W} = \langle S_W, l_W, \prec_W \rangle := \mathcal{F}_{\Delta}(\mathcal{V})$ (Definition 3.40) By definition, $\mathcal{W}$ is an MP-model of Δ. As $\mathcal{F}_{\Delta}$ leaves the set of states and the valuation function unchanged, we have $S_W = \Omega^{feas}_{\Delta}$ and $l_W = \mathrm{id}$. By the definition of $\mathcal{F}_{\Delta}$ it holds that $\omega \prec_W \omega'$ iff $\xi(\omega) \prec^{MP}_{\Delta} \xi(\omega')$. Using Lemma 6.15 yields that $\omega \prec_W \omega'$ iff $\omega <^{\mathsf{w}}_{\Delta} \omega'$. Hence $\mathcal{W} = \mathcal{M}^{\mathsf{w}}(\Delta)$.

Because $\mathcal{W}$ is an MP-model of Δ and $\mathcal{W} = \mathcal{M}^{\mathsf{w}}(\Delta)$ we have that $\mathcal{M}^{\mathsf{w}}(\Delta)$ is an MP-model of Δ. □

Using Proposition 6.16, we can show that the MP-closure of Δ coincides with the inference relation induced by $\mathcal{M}^{\mathsf{w}}(\Delta)$. This entails that MP-closure coincides with extended system W.

Proposition 6.17. *For every consistent belief base Δ and formulas $A, B \in \mathcal{L}_{\Sigma}$ it holds that:*

- $A \mathrel{|\!\sim}^{MP}_{\Delta} B$ *iff* $A \mathrel{|\!\sim}_{\mathcal{M}^{\mathsf{w}}(\Delta)} B$.
- $A \mathrel{|\!\sim}^{MP}_{\Delta} B$ *iff* $A \mathrel{|\!\sim}^{\mathsf{w}+}_{\Delta} B$.

Proof. The characterization result in Proposition 3.42 by [GG21] states that $A \mid\!\sim^{MP}_{\Delta} B$ iff $A \mid\!\sim_{\mathcal{M}^{MP}} B$ for every MP-model $\mathcal{M}^{MP}$ of Δ. For any MP-model $\mathcal{M}^{MP*}$ of Δ, because all MP-models of Δ induce the same inference relation [GG21], $A \mid\!\sim_{\mathcal{M}^{MP}} B$ holds for every MP-model $\mathcal{M}^{MP}$ iff $A \mid\!\sim_{\mathcal{M}^{MP*}} B$.

With this and because $\mathcal{M}^{\mathsf{w}}(\Delta)$ is an MP-model of Δ (see Proposition 6.16), we have that $\mid\!\sim_{\mathcal{M}^{\mathsf{w}}(\Delta)}$ is the MP-closure of Δ.

As $\mid\!\sim_{\mathcal{M}^{\mathsf{w}}(\Delta)}$ coincides with the extended system W inference $\mid\!\sim^{\mathsf{w}+}_{\Delta}$ (see Lemma 6.11), MP-closure coincides with extended system W. □

Thus, extended system W provides a semantic definition of MP-closure that is less complex than MP-closure's definition in [GG21]. The coincidence of extended system W and MP-closure allows transferring properties proven for system W (e.g., the syntax splitting postulates, see Section 5.5) to MP-closure and vice versa. Whenever we consider extended system W or MP-closure we can now use the more suitable of the two rather different definitions.

6.6. Approximations of System W

In the previous sections 6.2 and 6.3 we saw that extended system W captures both extended system Z and c-inference. Inspired by this, we address the question of whether there are other inductive inference operators that approximate extended system W and extend both extended system Z and extended c-inference.

Towards this goal, we introduce the combination of two inference operators by their union. Additionally, we introduce the closure of an inductive inference operator under a set of properties. An example of the latter is the minimal closure under system P.

We construct the least inference relation that satisfies system P and captures both extended c-inference and extended system Z; and we show that system W captures and strictly extends this approximation, which negates the previously open question whether system W can be characterized by the union (with closure under p-entailment) of system Z and c-inference.

In the other direction, we saw that system W is captured and strictly extended by adapted lexicographic inference. But lexicographic inference is not the least extension of extended system W. We present another inductive inference operator C^{wl} and show that it extends system W while also being extended by lexicographic inference.

6.6.1. Combining and Extending Inductive Inference Operators

A straightforward way of combining inductive inference operators is to consider the union of the inference relations induced by them.

Definition 6.18 (union of inference operators). *Let* $C^1 : \Delta \mapsto |\!\!\sim^1_\Delta$ *and* $C^2 : \Delta \mapsto |\!\!\sim^2_\Delta$ *be inductive inference operators. The* union *of* C^1 *and* C^2*, denoted by* $C = C^1 \uplus C^2$*, is the mapping* $C : \Delta \mapsto |\!\!\sim_\Delta$ *with* $|\!\!\sim_\Delta := |\!\!\sim^1_\Delta \cup |\!\!\sim^2_\Delta$.

This means that for any $A, B \in \mathcal{L}_\Sigma$ we have $A \,|\!\!\sim_\Delta\, B$ iff $A \,|\!\!\sim^1_\Delta\, B$ or $A \,|\!\!\sim^2_\Delta\, B$ (with C^1, C^2, C as in Definition 6.18). Uniting two inductive inference operators yields again an inductive inference operator.

Proposition 6.19. *The union* $C_1 \uplus C_2$ *of two inductive inference operators* C_1, C_2 *is an inductive inference operator.*

Proof. Let $C^1 : \Delta \mapsto |\!\!\sim^1_\Delta$ and $C^2 : \Delta \mapsto |\!\!\sim^2_\Delta$ be inductive inference operators, and let $C : \Delta \mapsto |\!\!\sim_\Delta$ be the union of them. To show that C is an inductive inference operator, we need to show that it satisfies (DI) and (TV).

Let $(B|A) \in \Delta$. Then we have $A \,|\!\!\sim^1_\Delta\, B$ because C^1 satisfies (DI). This entails $A \,|\!\!\sim_\Delta\, B$. Hence C satisfies (DI).

Let $\Delta := \emptyset$ and $A, B \in \mathcal{L}_\Sigma$ such that $A \,|\!\!\sim_\Delta\, B$. Then $A \,|\!\!\sim^1_\Delta\, B$ or $A \,|\!\!\sim^2_\Delta\, B$. As C^1 and C^2 satisfy (TV), we have that $A \models B$ in both cases. Therefore, C satisfies (TV). □

Usually certain properties are desired for inductive inference operators. The desired properties can be stated in the form of postulates and vary depending on the context or application of the inductive inference operator. In this thesis we already saw examples for such postulates, examples are system P (see Section 3.1), (RM), (Classic Preservation), the postulates in Figure 4.1, and more complex postulates like (Ind), (Rel), or (SynSplit) in Section 3.9.

While the postulates of system P consider an inference relation on its own, more complex postulates like (Ind) can relate the inference relations induced by different belief bases.

If an inductive inference operator C fails to satisfy a (set of) postulate(s), compliance with these postulates can sometimes be achieved by adding additional pairs to the inference relations induced by C.

Definition 6.20 (Closure under a set of postulates). *Let $C : \Delta \mapsto \mathrel{|\!\sim}_\Delta$ be an inductive inference operator. Let X be a set of postulates for inductive inference operators. An inductive inference operator $C^X : \Delta \mapsto \mathrel{|\!\sim}^X_\Delta$ is a* closure *of C under X if $\mathrel{|\!\sim}_\Delta \subseteq \mathrel{|\!\sim}^X_\Delta$ and $\mathrel{|\!\sim}^X_\Delta$ satisfies X.*

$C^X : \Delta \mapsto \mathrel{|\!\sim}^X_\Delta$ is a minimal closure *of C under X if it is a closure of C under X, and if there is no other closure C' of C under X such that $C'(\Delta) \subsetneq C^X(\Delta)$ for every Δ.*

Thus, the minimal closures are inclusion minimal with respect to the induced inference relations. To simplify notation, for a single property P we say that C^P is a closure of C under P if it is the closure of C under $\{P\}$. Depending on X, a closure of C under X might not always exist.

Example 6.21. *Consider the postulate (Classic Preservation). For an inductive inference operator $C : \Delta \mapsto \mathrel{|\!\sim}_\Delta$, a belief base Δ, and $A \in \mathcal{L}_\Sigma$ with $A \mathrel{|\!\sim}_\Delta \bot$ and $A \not\mathrel{|\!\sim}^p_\Delta \bot$, this violation of (Classic Preservation) cannot be fixed by adding inferences to $\mathrel{|\!\sim}_\Delta$.*

Even if a closure exists, the minimal closure might not be unique.

Proposition 6.22. *The minimal closure of an inductive inference operator under a set of postulates is not necessarily unique.*

Proof. Consider the postulate (RM). Now we want to find a minimal closure of p-entailment under system P and (RM). The combination of system P and (RM) characterizes exactly the inference relations that are induced by ranking functions [LM92]. For the belief base $\Delta := \{(b|p), (f|b), (\overline{f}|p)\}$ the ranking functions κ_1, κ_2 defined as

	bpf	$bp\overline{f}$	$b\overline{p}f$	$b\overline{p}\overline{f}$	$\overline{b}pf$	$\overline{b}p\overline{f}$	$\overline{b}\overline{p}f$	$\overline{b}\overline{p}\overline{f}$
κ_1 :	2	1	0	**1**	2	2	0	0
κ_2 :	2	1	0	**2**	2	2	0	0

each induce an inference relation extending $\mathrel{|\!\sim}^p_\Delta$ and comply with system P and (RM). The induced inference relations are not equal and neither of them captures the other one, because $b\overline{p}\overline{f} \vee \overline{b}pf \mid\!\sim_{\kappa_1} \overline{b}pf$ and $\overline{b}f \not\mid\!\sim_{\kappa_1} \overline{p}$ for κ_1, but $b\overline{p}\overline{f} \vee \overline{b}pf \not\mid\!\sim_{\kappa_2} \overline{b}pf$ and $\overline{b}f \mid\!\sim_{\kappa_2} \overline{p}$ for κ_2. Furthermore, $\mid\!\sim_{\kappa_1}$ and $\mid\!\sim_{\kappa_2}$ are both inclusion minimal among the inference relations that extend $\mid\!\sim^{p}_{\Delta}$ and comply with system P and (RM), i.e., a minimal closure of C^p under system P and (RM) could map Δ to $\mid\!\sim_{\kappa_1}$ or to $\mid\!\sim_{\kappa_2}$. □

Note that the intersection of all minimal closures is not necessarily a minimal closure itself because in some cases it violates the property we closed under. For example, taking up the example in the proof of Proposition 6.22, the intersection of all minimal closures of C^p under system P and (RM) would yield p-entailment again which violates (RM). But in some cases the closure of inductive inference operators behaves quite well. Any inductive inference operator has a unique minimal closure under system P.

Proposition 6.23 (Closure under system P). *For any inductive inference operator C there is a unique minimal closure of C under system P.*

Proof. The unique minimal closure $C' : \Delta \mapsto \mid\!\sim'_{\Delta}$ of $C : \Delta \mapsto \mid\!\sim_{\Delta}$ under system P can be obtained by

$$C' : \Delta \mapsto \{A \mid\!\sim'_{\Delta} B \mid A \mid\!\sim B \text{ is derivable from } \mid\!\sim_{\Delta} \text{ by iteratively applying system P axioms}\}.$$

Every inference in $C'(\Delta)$ needs to be in any closure of C under system P, as C' only adds inferences that are required to be included by the system P axioms. Furthermore, $C'(\Delta)$ satisfies system P: Whenever the antecedent of one of the system P axioms is satisfied, the inference required by the conclusion is included by definition. Hence, C' is the unique minimal completion of C under system P. □

More generally, the argumentation in the proof of Proposition 6.23 can be applied to every set of axioms of the form

$$A_1 \mid\!\sim B_1 \text{ and } \dots \text{ and } A_n \mid\!\sim B_n \quad \text{implies} \quad A_{n+1} \mid\!\sim B_{n+1}. \tag{6.6}$$

These axioms have the shape of Horn clauses, and corresponding to the existence of minimal models for sets of Horn clauses, we observe that every inductive inference operator has a unique closure under a set of such axioms.

Proposition 6.24. *Let X be a set of postulates of the form* (6.6)*. For any inductive inference operator C there is a unique minimal closure of C under X.*

Note that the closure of an inductive inference operator under any set of postulates of any form is again an inductive inference operator as long as it does not violate (TV), i.e., as long as the empty belief base induces only trivial inferences.

Proposition 6.25. *Let X be a set of postulates. If the closure C' of an inductive inference operator C under X exists and does not violate (TV), then C' is an inductive inference operator.*

Proof. We only need to show that the closure C' of an inference operator C satisfies (DI). This holds trivially, as C satisfies (DI) and $C(\Delta) \subseteq C'(\Delta)$ for any Δ. □

In the following we will consider the union of extended system Z and extended c-inference as well as this union's closure under system P as approximations for system W.

6.6.2. Inductive Inference Operators around System W

To better understand the relationship between extended system W on the one side and extended system Z and extended c-inference on the other side we introduce two approximations C^{cZ} and $C^{P(cZ)}$ for extended system W based on extended system Z and extended c-inference. Here we consider the extended versions of these inference operators. Limiting the work in this section to strongly consistent belief bases would yield corresponding results for system Z, c-inference, and system W.

The inference operators C^{cZ} and $C^{P(cZ)}$ lie "between" extended c-inference and extended system Z on the one side and system W on the other side. In the other direction, we will introduce the inductive inference operator C^{wl} between extended system W and (adapted) lexicographic inference.

For this section, the inductive inference operator extended system Z will be denoted by C^Z and extended c-inference will be denoted by C^c. To approximate system W with system Z and c-inference, we first consider the union of both inference operators:

$$C^{cZ} : \Delta \mapsto {\mid\!\sim}^{cZ}_{\Delta}, \qquad C^{cZ} := C^c \uplus C^Z.$$

By definition, C^{cZ} is the smallest inductive inference operator to capture extended system Z and extended c-inference.

Proposition 6.26. *Every inductive inference operator C' capturing extended system Z and extended c-inference also captures C^{cZ}.*

C^{cZ} is illustrated by the following Example 6.27. Additionally, this example shows that C^{cZ} does not satisfy system P, despite extended system Z and extended c-inference satisfying system P.

Example 6.27. *Let $\Sigma := \{a, b, c, d, e, f\}$ and*

$$\Delta := \{(ab|a \vee b), (\overline{a}b|\overline{a}b \vee a\overline{b}), (ab|ab \vee \overline{a}\overline{b}), (c|d), (e|c), (\overline{e}|d), (f|c)\}.$$

We have $\overline{b}d \mathrel{|\!\sim}^{z}_{\Delta} \overline{a}$ and $\overline{b}d \mathrel{|\!\sim}^{c}_{\Delta} f$ and therefore $\overline{b}d \mathrel{|\!\sim}^{cZ}_{\Delta} \overline{a}$ and $\overline{b}d \mathrel{|\!\sim}^{cZ}_{\Delta} f$. Furthermore, $\overline{b}d \mathrel{|\!\not\sim}^{z}_{\Delta} \overline{a}f$ and $\overline{b}d \mathrel{|\!\not\sim}^{c}_{\Delta} \overline{a}f$ and therefore $\overline{b}d \mathrel{|\!\not\sim}^{cZ}_{\Delta} \overline{a}f$. Note that this violates (AND)*; therefore C^{cZ} does not satisfy system P.*

Because the result of naively combining extended system Z and extended c-inference does not satisfy system P, we now consider the minimal closure of C^{cZ} under system P, denoted by

$$C^{P(cZ)} : \Delta \mapsto \mathrel{|\!\sim}^{P(cZ)}_{\Delta}.$$

Example 6.28. *Let Δ be the belief base from Example 6.27. We have $\overline{b}d \mathrel{|\!\sim}^{P(cZ)}_{\Delta} \overline{a}$ and $\overline{b}d \mathrel{|\!\sim}^{P(cZ)}_{\Delta} f$, as these inferences are already possible with C^{cZ}. Furthermore, we have $\overline{b}d \mathrel{|\!\sim}^{P(cZ)}_{\Delta} \overline{a}f$ because this inference is derivable with the postulate (AND) that is implied by system P.*

$C^{P(cZ)}$ is the smallest inductive inference operator that captures system Z and c-inference and additionally satisfies system P.

Proposition 6.29. *Every inductive inference operator C' that captures extended system Z and extended c-inference and that satisfies system P captures $C^{P(cZ)}$.*

Proof. C' is a closure of C^{cZ} under system P. As $C^{P(cZ)}$ is the unique minimal closure of C^{cZ} under system P, it is captured by C'. □

Extended system W captures both extended system Z and extended c-inference and additionally satisfies system P, and thus captures $C^{P(cZ)}$. The question arises whether extended system W is the smallest inductive inference operator to do this and thus coincides with $C^{P(cZ)}$. This is not the case. While $C^{P(cZ)}$ is captured by system W, it does not coincide with system W.

Proposition 6.30. *$C^{P(cZ)}$ is captured and strictly extended by extended system W.*

Proof. Extended system W captures both c-inference and system Z and additionally satisfies system P. Proposition 6.29 immediately implies that extended system W captures $C^{P(cZ)}$. It is left to show that these inductive inference operators do not coincide.

Let $\Sigma := \{a, b\}$ and $\Delta := \{(ab|a), (ab|a \vee b)\}$. The Z-ranking function $\kappa^z_\Delta = \{ab \mapsto 0, a\bar{b} \mapsto 1, \bar{a}b \mapsto 1, \bar{a}\bar{b} \mapsto 0\}$ induced by Δ is also an extended c-representation of Δ (choose the impacts $\vec{\eta} = (0, 1)$). Therefore, $\mid\!\sim^c_\Delta$ must be a subset of or equal to $\mid\!\sim_{\kappa^z_\Delta} = \mid\!\sim^z_\Delta$. This entails that $\mid\!\sim^z_\Delta = \mid\!\sim^{cZ}_\Delta = \mid\!\sim^{P(cZ)}_\Delta$. As $a\bar{b} \vee \bar{a}b \not\mid\!\sim^z_\Delta \bar{a}b$ and $a\bar{b} \vee \bar{a}b \mid\!\sim^{\mathsf{w}}_\Delta \bar{a}b$ we have that $\mid\!\sim^{P(cZ)}_\Delta \neq \mid\!\sim^{\mathsf{w}}_\Delta$. □

Hence, the inductive inference operators C^{cZ} and $C^{P(cZ)}$ strictly lie between extended c-inference and extended system Z on one side and extended system W on the other side.

In the other direction, adapted lexicographic inference captures and strictly extends extended system W (see Section 6.4). Similar to C^{cZ} and $C^{P(cZ)}$ between extended c-inference/extended system Z and extended system W, we can also find inductive inference operators that capture and strictly extend extended system W and are captured and strictly extended by adapted lexicographic inference. E.g., following a suggestion in [Tön22], we can consider the following modification of the preferred structure on worlds that induces such an inductive inference operator.

Definition 6.31 ($<^{wl}_\Delta$, $\mid\!\sim^{wl}_\Delta$). *For a belief base Δ we define the limited SPO on worlds $(\Omega^{feas}_\Delta, <^{wl}_\Delta)$ with Ω^{feas}_Δ as in Definition 5.2 and the relation $<^{wl}_\Delta \subseteq \Omega^{feas} \times \Omega^{feas}_\Delta$ given by, for any $\omega, \omega' \in \Omega^{feas}$,*

$$\begin{aligned} \omega <^{wl}_\Delta \omega' \quad \textit{iff} \quad & \textit{there exists an } m \in \{0, \dots, k\} \textit{ such that} \\ & \xi^i_\Delta(\omega) = \xi^i_\Delta(\omega') \quad \forall i \in \{m+1, \dots, k\} \textit{ and} \\ & |\xi^m_\Delta(\omega)| < |\xi^m_\Delta(\omega')| \,. \end{aligned}$$

The inductive inference operator $C^{wl} : \Delta \mapsto \mid\!\sim^{wl}_\Delta$ is the inference operator that maps every Δ to the inference relation $\mid\!\sim^{wl}_\Delta := \mid\!\sim_{(\Omega^{feas}_\Delta, <^{wl}_\Delta)}$ induced by $(\Omega^{feas}_\Delta, <^{wl}_\Delta)$.

Because C^{wl} is defined via a strict partial order on worlds it is lSPO-representable and therefore satisfies system P (see Proposition 5.15).

Proposition 6.32. *C^{wl} satisfies system P.*

The next proposition shows that C^{wl} indeed captures and strictly extends system W (and thus also c-inference and system Z) while it is captured and strictly extended by adapted lexicographic inference.

Proposition 6.33. *System W is captured and strictly extended by C^{wl}. Furthermore, C^{wl} is captured and strictly extended by adapted lexicographic inference.*

Proof. By comparing the definitions of $<^{\mathsf{w}}_{\Delta}$, $<^{wl}_{\Delta}$, and $<^{lex}_{\Delta}$ we can see that $<^{\mathsf{w}}_{\Delta} \subseteq <^{wl}_{\Delta} \subseteq <^{lex}_{\Delta}$. Observe that $A \mathrel{|\!\!\sim}^{alex}_{\Delta} B$ iff for every $\omega' \in Mod_{\Sigma}(A\overline{B}) \cap \Omega^{feas}_{\Delta}$ there is an $\omega \in Mod_{\Sigma}(AB) \cap \Omega^{feas}_{\Delta}$ such that $\omega <^{lex}_{\Delta} \omega'$. Comparing this with the definitions of C^{wl} and extended system W yields that $A \mathrel{|\!\!\sim}^{\mathsf{w}}_{\Delta} B$ implies $A \mathrel{|\!\!\sim}^{wl}_{\Delta} B$ and that $A \mathrel{|\!\!\sim}^{wl}_{\Delta} B$ entails $A \mathrel{|\!\!\sim}^{alex}_{\Delta} B$. It is left to show that the inductive inference operators strictly extend each other.

Let $\Sigma := \{a, b, c, d, e, f\}$ and $\Delta := \{(d|\top), (e|\top), (f|\top), (c|a), (\overline{c}|b), (a|b)\}$. The extended Z-partition of Δ is $EP(\Delta) = (\Delta^0, \Delta^1)$ with $\Delta^0 = \{(d|\top), (e|\top), (f|\top), (c|a)\}$ and $\Delta^1 = \{(\overline{c}|b), (a|b)\}$.

We have $abc\overline{d}ef <^{lex}_{\Delta} \overline{a}b\overline{c}\overline{d}\overline{e}f$ and therefore $abc\overline{d}ef \vee \overline{a}b\overline{c}\overline{d}\overline{e}f \mathrel{|\!\!\sim}^{lex}_{\Delta} \overline{a}b\overline{c}\overline{d}\overline{e}f$ but $abc\overline{d}ef \vee \overline{a}b\overline{c}\overline{d}\overline{e}f \mathrel{|\!\!\not\sim}^{wl}_{\Delta} \overline{a}b\overline{c}\overline{d}\overline{e}f$. Hence, lexicographic inference strictly extends C^{wl}.

Furthermore, we have $\overline{a}b\overline{c}de\overline{f} <^{wl}_{\Delta} \overline{a}b\overline{c}\overline{d}\overline{e}f$ and therefore $\overline{a}b\overline{c}de\overline{f} \vee \overline{a}b\overline{c}\overline{d}\overline{e}f \mathrel{|\!\!\sim}^{wl}_{\Delta} \overline{a}b\overline{c}de\overline{f}$ but $\overline{a}b\overline{c}de\overline{f} \vee \overline{a}b\overline{c}\overline{d}\overline{e}f \mathrel{|\!\!\not\sim}^{\mathsf{w}}_{\Delta} \overline{a}b\overline{c}de\overline{f}$. Hence, C^{wl} strictly extends system W. □

In summary, we obtain a landscape of inductive inference operators approximating system W from both sides: Extended system W lies between $C^{P(cZ)}$ on the one side and C^{wl} on the other side.

6.7. Overview of the Relations among Inductive Inference Operators

To conclude this chapter, we will summarize the relationships among the inductive inference operators covered in this chapter.

The "diamond" of relationships among p-entailment, system Z, c-inference, and system W shown in Figure 6.1 also holds for the extended versions of system Z, c-inference, and system W. Furthermore, extended system W (and thus all other mentioned inference operators) are captured and extended by adapted lexicographic inference. Furthermore, MP-closure coincides with extended system W.

To get a closer approximation of extended system W we introduced C^{cZ} as the union of extended c-inference and extended system Z. As this union does not satisfy system P we also introduced $C^{P(cZ)}$, the closure of C^{cZ} under system P, yielding the minimal inductive inference operator that captures both extended c-inference and extended system Z while also being preferential.

On the other side, the inference operator C^{wl} also approximates system W, but lies between extended system W and adapted lexicographic inference. Notably, extended system Z, extended system W, C^{wl}, and adapted lexicographic inference form a chain of inductive inference operators that are each defined based on a structure on worlds obtained from the extended Z-partition of a belief base. Along this chain, the inference relations induced by a belief base Δ become larger, and the structures on worlds become finer: For feasible worlds ω, ω' we have that $\kappa^{z+}_{\Delta}(\omega) < \kappa^{z+}_{\Delta}(\omega')$ implies $\omega <^{\mathsf{w}+}_{\Delta} \omega'$; and $\omega <^{\mathsf{w}+}_{\Delta} \omega'$ implies $\omega <^{wl}_{\Delta} \omega'$; and $\omega <^{wl}_{\Delta} \omega'$ implies $\omega <^{lex}_{\Delta} \omega'$.

Unlike extended system Z, which is induced by a ranking function, and adapted lexicographic inference, which is induced by a total preorder on worlds, extended system W and C^{wl} are induced by a limited SPO on worlds and do not satisfy (RM) in general.

The resulting landscape of universal inductive inference operators is illustrated by the upper half of Figure 6.2.

A corresponding landscape arises for the SCA versions of these inductive inference operators, i.e., system Z, c-inference, and system W. For relating SCA-inductive inference operators we only consider strongly consistent belief bases, and because system Z, c-inference, and system W yield the same inferences as their extended versions for strongly consistent belief bases, the same "captures"-relationships hold. The resulting landscape of SCA-inductive inference operators is illustrated by the lower half of Figure 6.2.

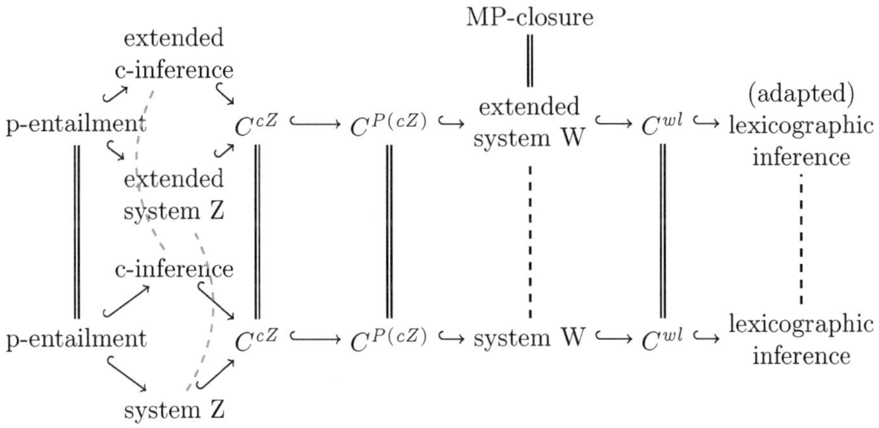

Figure 6.2. Overview of relationships among the inductive inference operators considered in this thesis. An arrow $I_1 \hookrightarrow I_2$ indicates that inductive inference operator I_1 is captured and strictly extended by I_2. Double lines $=$ indicate coinciding inference operators. Dashed lines --- indicate that two inference operators coincide for strongly consistent belief bases.

Chapter 7

Rational Closure Extending Inductive Inference Operators

Rational closure, which coincides with extended system Z, is a considerable inductive inference operator with some notable properties [GP90; CMV19]. Casini, Meyer, and Varzinczack investigated inference operators that capture rational closure more closely [CMV19]. For a special kind of inductive inference operators called *basic defeasible* inference operators, which are inference operators satisfying system P, (RM), and (Classic Preservation), the property of extending rational closure is characterized by a certain type of ranking functions. Note that extending rational closure is not equivalent to satisfying rational monotony (RM). There are inference operators that satisfy (RM) but do not extend rational closure, and there are other inference operators like, e.g., system W, that extend rational closure but do not satisfy (RM).

In this section we will consider a broader class of inference operators that extend rational closure. First we characterize preferential inductive inference operators that extend rational closure and satisfy (Classic Preservation) by so called Z-rank refining preferential models in Section 7.1. Then we characterize lSPO-representable inductive inference operators that extend rational closure and satisfy (Classic Preservation) by Z-rank refining limited SPOs on worlds in Section 7.2.

The results in this chapter on characterizing rational closure extending inductive inference operators origin from [Hal+23b].

7.1. Extending Rational Closure

The property that an inference relation extends rational closure is formalized by the following postulate (RC Extension). Because Rational Closure coincides with extended system Z, extending Rational Closure is equivalent to extending the extended system Z. Deviating from the formulation in [CMV19], here we use extended system Z instead of Rational Closure to formulate (RC Extension).

Postulate (RC Extension). *An inference relation* $\mid\!\sim$ *satisfies (RC Extension) (cf. [CMV19]) with respect to a belief base* Δ *if for all* $A, B \in \mathcal{L}_\Sigma$

$$A \mid\!\sim^{z+}_{\Delta} B \quad \textit{implies} \quad A \mid\!\sim B,$$

i.e., if every entailment that is in $\mid\!\sim^{z+}_{\Delta}$ *is also in* $\mid\!\sim$*. An inductive inference operator satisfies (RC Extension) if every belief base* Δ *is mapped to an inference relation satisfying (RC Extension) with respect to* Δ*.*

For an inductive inference operator, satisfying (RC Extension) is equivalent to capturing extended system Z.

In [CMV19] the postulate (RC Extension) was considered for *basic defeasible* (short *BD*) inductive inference operators, which are inference operators that satisfy system P, (RM), and (Classic Preservation). The inference relations yielded by BD inductive inference operators are induced by ranking functions because they satisfy system P and (RM) [KLM90]. This implies that BD inductive inference operator are a subclass of the lSPO-representable inductive inference operators. BD inductive inference operators satisfying (RC Extension) are characterized in different ways in [CMV19], among them the following: a BD inductive inference relation satisfies (RC Extension) with respect to a belief base Δ iff it is induced by a ranking function that is *base rank preserving* with respect to Δ [CMV19]. Base rank preserving is a property based on the rank of a formula as defined in Definition 3.31 which is closely connected to the extended Z-partition of belief bases (see Lemma 6.14).

In this section we consider the more general class of preferential inductive inference operators that satisfy (RC Extension). Analogously to the class of RC extending BD inductive inference operators we introduce the class of *RCP inductive inference operators.*

When characterizing (RC Extension) for an inductive inference operator it is useful to have (Classic Preservation). Therefore, we combine (Rational Closure) with (Classic Preservation) and call the inference operators satisfying both postulates *RCP inductive inference operators.*

Definition 7.1 (RCP inductive inference operator). *An* RCP inductive inference operator *is an inductive inference operator satisfying (**RC** Extension) and (**C**lassic **P**reservation).*

Because every BD inductive inference operators satisfies (Classic Preservation), the characterization of (RC Extension) in [CMV19] is also a characterization of RCP BD inductive inference operators. Similar to the results in [CMV19] we can provide a model-based characterization of RCP preferential inductive inference operators. We identify the following property of preferential models which we will show to characterize RCP preferential inference operators.

Definition 7.2 (Z-rank refining preferential models). *A preferential model $\mathcal{M} = \langle S, l, \prec \rangle$ is called* Z-rank refining *with respect to a belief base Δ if*

- $l(S) = \{\omega \in \Omega_\Sigma \mid \kappa_\Delta^{z+}(\omega) < \infty\}$ *and*
- *for any $\omega, \omega' \in \Omega_\Sigma$ it holds that $\kappa_\Delta^{z+}(\omega) < \kappa_\Delta^{z+}(\omega')$ implies that for every $s' \in l^{-1}(\omega')$ there is an $s \in l^{-1}(\omega)$ such that $s \prec s'$.*

If Δ is not weakly consistent, a preferential model is Z-rank refining with respect to Δ if and only if $S = \emptyset$.

Example 7.3. *Consider the belief base $\Delta := \{(\bot|\overline{c}), (\overline{a}|b)\}$ which induces the extended Z-ranking function κ_Δ^z given by*

	abc	$ab\overline{c}$	$a\overline{b}c$	$a\overline{b}\overline{c}$	$\overline{a}bc$	$\overline{a}b\overline{c}$	$\overline{a}\overline{b}c$	$\overline{a}\overline{b}\overline{c}$
κ_Δ^z :	*1*	∞	*0*	∞	*0*	∞	*0*	∞

The preferential model $\mathcal{M} = \langle S, l, \prec \rangle$ with $S := \{1, 2, 3, 4, 5\}$, $\prec := \{(2,1), (4,1), (4,2), (3,1), (5,1), (5,3)\}$ and $l : 1 \mapsto abc, 2 \mapsto \overline{a}bc$, $3 \mapsto \overline{a}bc, 4 \mapsto a\overline{b}c, 5 \mapsto \overline{a}\overline{b}c$ is Z-rank refining with respect to Δ.

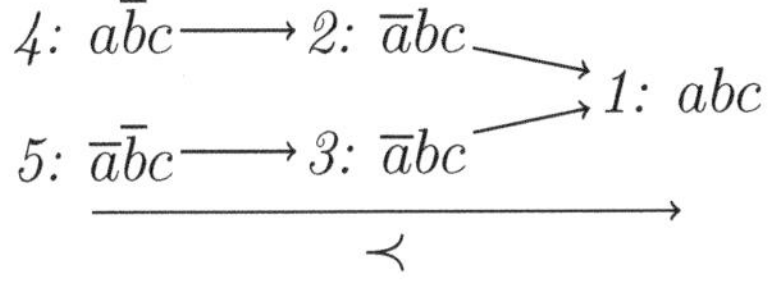

Building on the result that preferential inference relations are characterized by preferential models, we can show that RCP preferential inductive inference operators are characterized by Z-rank refining preferential models. For a preferential inference relation satisfying (Classic Preservation) and (RC Extension) there is a Z-rank refining preferential model inducing this inference relation. In the other direction, every Z-rank refining preferential model induces an inference relation satisfying (Classic Preservation) and (RC Extension).

Proposition 7.4. *Let Δ be a belief base.*

(1.) If $\mathrel{|\!\sim}$ is a preferential inference relation satisfying (Classic Preservation) and (RC Extension) with respect to Δ, then every preferential model inducing $\mathrel{|\!\sim}$ is Z-rank refining with respect to Δ.

(2.) If a preferential model $\mathcal{M} = \langle S, l, \prec \rangle$ is Z-rank refining with respect to Δ, then the inference relation $\mathrel{|\!\sim}_{\mathcal{M}}$ induced by it satisfies (Classic Preservation) and (RC Extension) with respect to Δ.

Proof. **Ad (1.):** Let $\mathrel{|\!\sim}$ be a preferential inference relation satisfying (Classic Preservation) and (RC Extension) with respect to Δ, and let $\mathcal{M} = \langle S, l, \prec \rangle$ be a preferential model inducing $\mathrel{|\!\sim}$. If Δ is not weakly consistent then $S = \emptyset$ and the proposition holds. For the remainder of *Ad (1.)* consider the case that Δ is weakly consistent. It holds that $\kappa^{z+}_{\Delta}(\omega) = \infty$ iff $\omega \mathrel{|\!\sim}^{p}_{\Delta} \bot$ (see Lemma 3.17). Because $\mathrel{|\!\sim}$ satisfies (Classic Preservation), $\omega \mathrel{|\!\sim}^{p}_{\Delta} \bot$ iff $\omega \mathrel{|\!\sim} \bot$. The inference $\omega \mathrel{|\!\sim} \bot$ occurs iff $\omega \notin l(S)$. Therefore, $l(S) = \{\omega \in \Omega_{\Sigma} \mid \kappa^{z+}_{\Delta}(\omega) < \infty\}$.

Let $\omega, \omega' \in \Omega_{\Sigma}$ with $\kappa^{z+}_{\Delta}(\omega) < \kappa^{z+}_{\Delta}(\omega')$. Then $\omega \vee \omega' \mathrel{|\!\sim}^{z+}_{\Delta} \omega$. Because $\mathrel{|\!\sim}$ satisfies (RC Extension), we have $\omega \vee \omega' \mathrel{|\!\sim} \omega$. It must hold that $\min([\![\omega \vee \omega']\!]_{\mathcal{M}}, \prec) \subseteq [\![\omega]\!]_{\mathcal{M}}$, i.e., $\min(l^{-1}(\omega) \cup l^{-1}(\omega'), \prec) \subseteq l^{-1}(\omega)$. The states in $l^{-1}(\omega')$ cannot be minimal in $l^{-1}(\omega) \cup l^{-1}(\omega')$. Therefore, for every $s' \in l^{-1}(\omega')$ there is an $s \in l^{-1}(\omega)$ with $s \prec s'$.

In summary, $\mathcal{M}$ is Z-rank refining with respect to Δ.

Ad (2.): Let $\mathcal{M} = \langle S, l, \prec \rangle$ be Z-rank refining with respect to Δ. If Δ is not weakly consistent, we have $S = \emptyset$ and thus (Classic Preservation) holds. For the remainder of *Ad (2.)* consider the case that Δ is weakly consistent. For $F \in \mathcal{L}_{\Sigma}$ we have that $F \mathrel{|\!\sim}^{p}_{\Delta} \bot$ iff $\kappa^{z+}_{\Delta}(F) = \infty$, i.e., iff $\kappa^{z+}_{\Delta}(\omega) = \infty$ for all $\omega \in \mathit{Mod}_{\Sigma}(F)$. As $\mathcal{M}$ is Z-rank refining, this happens iff $[\![F]\!]_{\mathcal{M}} = \emptyset$ which is equivalent to $F \mathrel{|\!\sim}_{\mathcal{M}} \bot$. Therefore, $\mathrel{|\!\sim}_{\mathcal{M}}$ satisfies (Classic Preservation) with respect to Δ.

Let $A, B \in \mathcal{L}_{\Sigma}$ with $A \mathrel{|\!\sim}^{z+}_{\Delta} B$. For $[\![A]\!]_{\mathcal{M}} = \emptyset$ we have $A \mathrel{|\!\sim}_{\mathcal{M}} X$ for any formula X, in this case (RC Extension) is satisfied. Now assume that $[\![A]\!]_{\mathcal{M}} \neq \emptyset$. Let $s_A \in \min([\![A]\!]_{\mathcal{M}}, \prec)$. We have to show that every $\omega_A \in l^{-1}(s_A)$ satisfies $\omega \models B$. Towards a contradiction assume there is an $\omega_A \in l^{-1}(s_A)$ with $\omega_A \models \overline{B}$. Then we have that $\omega_A \models A\overline{B}$. Because $A \mathrel{|\!\sim}^{z+}_{\Delta} B$ there must be an $\omega' \in Mod_{\Sigma}(AB)$ with $\kappa^{z+}_{\Delta}(\omega') < \kappa^{z+}_{\Delta}(\omega_A)$. As $\mathcal{M}$ is Z-rank refining, there has to be an $s' \in l^{-1}(\omega')$ with $s' \prec s_A$. Because $\omega' \models AB$ we have $s' \in [\![A]\!]_{\mathcal{M}}$. This contradicts the minimality of s_A. Hence, every $\omega_A \in l^{-1}(s_A)$ satisfies $\omega \models B$, and therefore, $\mathrel{|\!\sim}_{\mathcal{M}}$ satisfies (RC Extension) with respect to Δ. □

As a consequence of Proposition 7.4 we get the following characterization of RCP preferential inductive inference operators.

Proposition 7.5. *An inductive inference operator is RCP iff it maps each belief base Δ to an inference relation that is induced by a preferential model that is Z-rank refining with respect to Δ.*

In the next section we will focus on a subset of RCP preferential inductive operators, RCP lSPO-representable inductive inference operators.

7.2. RCP lSPO-Representable Inductive Inference Operators

In this section we consider RCP lSPO-representable inductive inference operators, i.e., RCP preferential inference operators that are also lSPO-representable. By definition these are the lSPO-representable inductive inference operators that satisfy (RC Extension) and (Classic Preservation).

While RCP preferential inductive inference operators are characterized by Z-rank refining preferential models, we can define Z-rank refining lSPOs on worlds that characterize RCP lSPO-representable inference operators.

Definition 7.6 (Z-rank refining limited SPO on worlds). *A limited SPO on worlds $(\Omega^{feas}, \prec)$ is called* Z-rank refining *with respect to a belief base Δ if*

- $\Omega^{feas} = \{\omega \in \Omega_{\Sigma} \mid \kappa^{z+}_{\Delta}(\omega) < \infty\}$ *and*
- $\kappa^{z+}_{\Delta}(\omega) < \kappa^{z+}_{\Delta}(\omega')$ *implies $\omega \prec \omega'$ for any $\omega, \omega' \in \Omega^{feas}$.*

If Δ is not weakly consistent, the only Z-rank refining limited SPO on worlds with respect to Δ is given by $(\Omega^{feas}, \prec)$ with $\Omega^{feas} = \emptyset$ and $\prec = \emptyset$.

Both Definition 7.2 of Z-rank refining preferential models and Definition 7.6 of Z-rank refining limited SPOs on worlds follow the same idea that the limited SPO in the considered structure preserves and refines the ordering on worlds that is induced by the Z-ranking function κ^{z+}_{Δ}.

Example 7.7. *Consider the belief base $\Delta := \{(b|\overline{a})\}$ over $\Sigma := \{a, b\}$ which induces the extended Z-ranking function κ^{z}_{Δ} given by*

	ab	$a\overline{b}$	$\overline{a}b$	$\overline{a}\overline{b}$
$\kappa^{z}_{\Delta}:$	*0*	*0*	*0*	*1*

The limited SPO on worlds $(\Omega^{feas}, \prec)$ with $\Omega^{feas} := \Omega_{\Sigma}$ and $\prec := \{(ab, a\overline{b}), (ab, \overline{a}\overline{b}), (\overline{a}b, \overline{a}\overline{b}), (a\overline{b}, \overline{a}\overline{b})\}$ is Z-rank refining with respect to Δ.

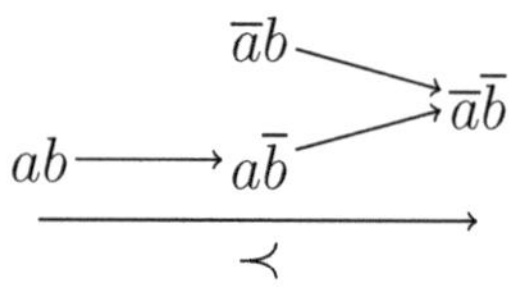

Analogously to Proposition 7.4, we can show that Z-rank refining limited SPOs on worlds characterize inference relations that satisfy (Classic Preservation) and (RC Extension).

Proposition 7.8. *Let Δ be a belief base.*

(1.) If $\mid\!\sim$ is an limited SPO representable inference relation that satisfies (Classic Preservation) and (RC Extension) with respect to Δ, then any limited SPO on worlds inducing $\mid\!\sim$ is Z-rank refining with respect to Δ.

(2.) If a limited SPO on worlds $(\Omega^{feas}, \prec)$ is Z-rank refining with respect to Δ, then the inference relation $\mid\!\sim_{(\Omega^{feas}, \prec)}$ induced by it satisfies (Classic Preservation) and (RC Extension) with respect to Δ.

Proof. **Ad (1.):** Let $\mid\!\sim$ be an inference relation satisfying (Classic Preservation) and (RC Extension) with respect to Δ and let $(\Omega^{feas}, \prec)$ be a limited SPO on worlds inducing $\mid\!\sim$. If Δ is not weakly consistent, with (Classic Preservation) we have $\Omega^{feas} = \emptyset$ and $\prec = \emptyset$, and therefore

$(\Omega^{feas}, \prec)$ is Z-rank refining. For the remainder of *Ad (1.)* consider the case that Δ is weakly consistent. It holds that $\kappa_\Delta^{z+}(\omega) = \infty$ iff $\omega \mathrel{|\!\!\sim}^p_\Delta \bot$. Because $\mathrel{|\!\!\sim}$ satisfies (Classic Preservation), $\omega \mathrel{|\!\!\sim}^p_\Delta \bot$ iff $\omega \mathrel{|\!\!\sim} \bot$. The inference $\omega \mathrel{|\!\!\sim} \bot$ occurs iff $\omega \notin \Omega^{feas}$, i.e., $\Omega^{feas} = \{\omega \in \Omega \mid \kappa_\Delta^{z+}(\omega) < \infty\}$.

Let $\omega, \omega' \in \Omega^{feas}$ be worlds such that $\kappa_\Delta^{z+}(\omega) < \kappa_\Delta^{z+}(\omega')$. In this case $\omega \vee \omega' \mathrel{|\!\!\sim}^{z+}_\Delta \omega$. As $\mathrel{|\!\!\sim}$ satisfies (RC Extension), we have $\omega \vee \omega' \mathrel{|\!\!\sim} \omega$. Because ω and ω' are feasible, this entails $\omega \prec \omega'$.

In summary, $(\Omega^{feas}, \prec)$ is Z-rank refining.

Ad (2.): Let $(\Omega^{feas}, \prec)$ be a limited SPO on worlds that is Z-rank refining with respect to Δ, and let $\mathrel{|\!\!\sim}_{(\Omega^{feas},\prec)}$ be the inference relation induced by it. If Δ is not weakly consistent, we have $\Omega^{feas} = \emptyset$ and $\prec = \emptyset$, and therefore (Classic Preservation) and (RC Extension) are satisfied with respect to Δ. For the remainder of *Ad (2.)* consider the case that Δ is weakly consistent.

For $F \in \mathcal{L}_\Sigma$ we have that $F \mathrel{|\!\!\sim}^p_\Delta \bot$ iff $\kappa_\Delta^{z+}(F) = \infty$, i.e., iff $\kappa_\Delta^{z+}(\omega) = \infty$ for all $\omega \in Mod_\Sigma(F)$. As $(\Omega^{feas}, \prec)$ is Z-rank refining, this happens iff $Mod_\Sigma(F) \cap \Omega^{feas} = \emptyset$ which is equivalent to $F \mathrel{|\!\!\sim}_{(\Omega^{feas},\prec)} \bot$. Therefore, $\mathrel{|\!\!\sim}_{(\Omega^{feas},\prec)}$ satisfies (Classic Preservation) with respect to Δ.

Let $A, B \in \mathcal{L}_\Sigma$ such that $A \mathrel{|\!\!\sim}^{z+}_\Delta B$. If $\kappa_\Delta^{z+}(A) = \infty$ there are no feasible models of A and therefore $A \mathrel{|\!\!\sim}_{(\Omega^{feas},\prec)} B$. Otherwise, we have $\kappa_\Delta^{z+}(AB) < \kappa_\Delta^{z+}(A\overline{B})$ and especially $\kappa_\Delta^{z+}(AB) < \infty$. Let $\omega \in \arg\min_{\omega \in Mod_\Sigma(AB)} \kappa_\Delta^{z+}(\omega)$. Because $\kappa_\Delta^{z+}(AB) < \infty$ we get $\kappa_\Delta^{z+}(\omega) < \infty$ and therefore $\omega \in \Omega^{feas}$. For any $\omega' \in Mod_\Sigma(A\overline{B})$ it holds that $\kappa_\Delta^{z+}(\omega) < \kappa_\Delta^{z+}(\omega')$. Because $(\Omega^{feas}, \prec)$ is Z-rank refining, we have $\omega \prec \omega'$ for any feasible $\omega' \in Mod_\Sigma(A\overline{B})$. Therefore, $A \mathrel{|\!\!\sim}_{(\Omega^{feas},\prec)} B$. Thus, $\mathrel{|\!\!\sim}_{(\Omega^{feas},\prec)}$ satisfies (RC Extension) with respect to Δ. □

From Proposition 7.8 we obtain the following characterization of RCP lSPO-representable inductive inference operators.

Proposition 7.9 (RCP lSPO-representable inference operators). *Let $C : \Delta \mapsto \mathrel{|\!\!\sim}^C_\Delta$ be an lSPO-representable inductive inference operator. C is RCP iff for each belief base Δ the inference relation $C(\Delta) = \mathrel{|\!\!\sim}^C_\Delta$ is induced by a limited SPO on worlds that is Z-rank refining with respect to Δ.*

As the lSPO-representable inductive inference operators are a subclass of preferential inductive inference operators, every RCP lSPO-representable inductive inference operator is also an RCP preferential inductive inference operator. Analogously, every BD-inductive inference operator satisfying (RC Extension) is an RCP lSPO-representable inductive inference operator. The reverse of these statements is not true, as observed by the following Lemmas 7.10 and 7.11.

Lemma 7.10. *There are RCP preferential inductive inference operators that are not lSPO-representable.*

Proof. Consider an RCP preferential inductive inference operator C that maps $\Delta = \{(\bot|\overline{c}), (\overline{a}|b)\}$ from Example 7.3 to the inference relation $\mid\!\sim_{\mathcal{M}}$ induced by the preferential model $\mathcal{M} = \langle S, l, \prec \rangle$ from Example 7.3; this mapping violates neither (RC Extension) nor (Classic Preservation) as $\mathcal{M}$ is Z-rank refining with respect to Δ.

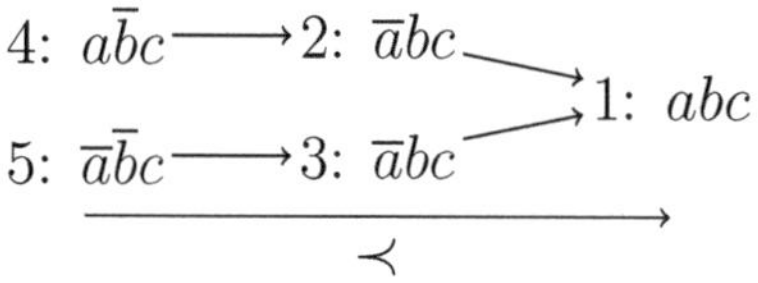

But $\mid\!\sim_{\mathcal{M}}$ is not lSPO-representable. For the worlds $\overline{a}bc, a\overline{b}c, \overline{a}\overline{b}c$ we can check that

$$\begin{array}{lll} \overline{a}bc \vee a\overline{b}c \not\mid\!\sim_{\mathcal{M}} \overline{a}bc & \overline{a}bc \vee \overline{a}\overline{b}c \not\mid\!\sim_{\mathcal{M}} \overline{a}bc & a\overline{b}c \vee \overline{a}\overline{b}c \not\mid\!\sim_{\mathcal{M}} a\overline{b}c \\ \overline{a}bc \vee a\overline{b}c \not\mid\!\sim_{\mathcal{M}} a\overline{b}c & \overline{a}bc \vee \overline{a}\overline{b}c \not\mid\!\sim_{\mathcal{M}} \overline{a}\overline{b}c & a\overline{b}c \vee \overline{a}\overline{b}c \not\mid\!\sim_{\mathcal{M}} \overline{a}\overline{b}c. \end{array}$$

By these observations, if there were a limited SPO $\prec_{\mathcal{M}}$ on worlds inducing $\mid\!\sim_{\mathcal{M}}$, the SPO $\prec_{\mathcal{M}}$ would not contain any relation among $\overline{a}bc, a\overline{b}c, \overline{a}\overline{b}c$. Therefore, $\prec_{\mathcal{M}}$ would not allow for the inference $\overline{a}bc \mid\!\sim_{\mathcal{M}} a\overline{b}c \vee \overline{a}\overline{b}c$ that is induced by $\mathcal{M}$. Hence, a limited SPO on worlds inducing $\mid\!\sim_{\mathcal{M}}$ cannot exist. □

Lemma 7.11. *There are RCP lSPO-representable inductive inference operators that are not BD inductive inference operators.*

Proof. Consider a rational lSPO-representable inductive inference operator C that maps $\Delta = \{(b|\overline{a})\}$ to the inference relation $\mid\!\sim_{(\Omega^{feas}, \prec)}$ from Example 7.7. This mapping violates neither (RC Extension) nor (Classic Preservation) because $(\Omega^{feas}, \prec)$ is Z-rank refining with respect to Δ.

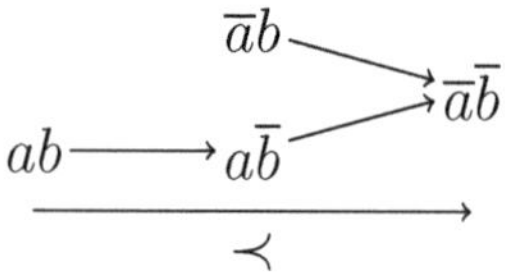

The inference relation $\mid\!\sim_{(\Omega^{feas},\prec)}$ violates (RM): for $A := \top, B := \overline{a} \vee \overline{b}, C := b$ we have $A \mid\!\sim_{(\Omega^{feas},\prec)} C$ and $A \not\mid\!\sim_{(\Omega^{feas},\prec)} \overline{B}$ but not $AB \mid\!\sim_{(\Omega^{feas},\prec)} C$. Therefore, C is not a BD inductive inference operator.

□

To conclude this section, we observe that extended system W is an RCP lSPO-representable inductive inference operator. We have already shown that extended system W captures rational closure/extended system Z (Proposition 6.2), that it satisfies (Classic Preservation) (Proposition 5.8), and that it is lSPO-representable (Proposition 5.18).

Proposition 7.12. *Extended system W is an RCP lSPO-representable inductive inference operator.*

Matching the characterization result in Proposition 7.8, the preferred structure on worlds $<^{\mathsf{w}+}_{\Delta}$ is a Z-rank refining limited SPO on worlds inducing $\mid\!\sim^{\mathsf{w}+}_{\Delta}$.

To summarize, we adapted the notion of "base rank preserving" that was defined for ranking functions in [CMV19] to preferential models and limited SPOs on worlds, calling the newly introduced property "Z-rank refining". We showed that Z-rank refining preferential models and Z-rank refining limited SPOs on worlds characterize RCP preferential inductive inference operators and RCP lSPO-representable inductive inference operators, respectively.

Compared to [CMV19], where base rank preserving ranking functions were shown to characterize (RC Extension) for BD inductive inference operators, the notion of RCP inductive inference operators captures inference operators that satisfy both (RC Extension) and (Classic Preservation). This is because (Classic Preservation) is a property that is useful to have for the characterization of (RC Extension). But while BD inductive inference operators already satisfy (Classic Preservation) by definition, preferential and lSPO-representable inference operators in general do not. Correspondingly, the definitions of Z-rank refining preferential models and Z-rank refining limited SPOs on worlds contain each a condition on the set of worlds that are considered feasible in each structure, ensuring that (RC Extension) holds.

Chapter 8

Summary and Future Work

In this thesis we addressed topics related to reasoning with defeasible conditionals. In short, we investigated the properties of the inductive inference operator system W, we showed how system W and c-inference can be extended to reason with infeasible words, and we investigated the interrelationships among different inductive inference operators.

At the beginning, we formulated five research questions for this thesis (cf. Section 1.2):

Q1 How can an agent handle plausible inference from belief bases that are not strongly consistent?

Q2 What are adequate syntax splitting postulates for reasoning with infeasible worlds?

Q3 What properties does system W have, especially with respect to syntax splitting?

Q4 How can we extend system W and c-inference to belief bases that are not strongly consistent?

Q5 How do different inductive inference operators relate to each other?

As a first step towards Q1, we contrasted strong and weak consistency in Section 2.2. In Section 5.1, we showed how weakly consistent belief bases require worlds to be infeasible. Later, in Section 5.3 we introduce limited SPOs on worlds that can be used to model weakly consistent belief bases.

In Section 3.9 we generalized the syntax splitting postulates by Kern-Isberner, Beierle, and Brewka [KBB20] to cover weakly consistent belief bases, thus answering Q2. In Section 5.4 we characterized the thus generalized syntax splitting postulates for inference operators based on limited SPOs on worlds.

Q3 is addressed in Chapter 4. We evaluated system W with respect to various postulates for inference relations and compared the results with the properties of other inductive inference operators. We introduced the class of fSPO-representable (*full* SPO-representable) inductive inference operators and showed that it contains system W. To prove that system W satisfies syntax splitting, we first introduced adapted versions of the syntax splitting postulates for fSPO-representable inference operators and then showed that these postulates are satisfied by system W. Furthermore we investigated the effect of syntax splitting on the preferred structure on worlds underlying system W, and we also showed that system W satisfies the more general conditional syntax splitting.

In Chapter 5, towards answering Q4, we extended system W and c-inference, that were previously only defined for strongly consistent belief bases, to cover also weakly consistent belief bases. Corresponding to fSPO-inductive inference operators we introduced the class of lSPO-representable (*limited* SPO-representable) inductive inference operators that contains extended system W. We then showed that extended c-inference and extended system W still satisfy desirable properties already satisfied by system W and c-inference like complying with syntax splitting.

For Q5, first, in Chapter 6 we related the inductive inference operators considered in this thesis by establishing subset relations among the inference relations induced by them. This yields a landscape of inductive inference operators consisting of (extended) c-inference, (extended) system Z, (extended) system W, and lexicographic inference [Leh95]. We showed that MP-closure [GG21] coincides with system W, and we introduced inference operators approximating extended system W. Second, in Chapter 7 we characterized preferential and lSPO-representable inductive inference operators that extend rational closure by Z-rank refining preferential models and Z-rank refining limited SPOs on worlds, respectively.

The research in this thesis on inference from weakly consistent belief bases fills a gap in the recent results on c-inference, system W, and syntax splitting for inductive inference operators. By transferring the ideas on inference with infeasible worlds presented here to other inference operators, future research in this area will benefit from our research.

The investigation of properties of system W as well as the established relations among inductive inference operators help us to understand the behaviour of different inference operators. Because of system W's central position in the landscape of inference operators we established, comparing other inductive inference operators with system W might help us to better understand their properties.

The work in this thesis can be extended in several directions.

Compliance with (conditional) syntax splittings is an important topic of this thesis. One way to continue this work is to investigate the effect of other splittings, like the ones presented in [Wil+23], on inductive inference operators. It is also left for future work to prove that extended system W complies with conditional syntax splitting. Splitting a belief base into smaller, more manageable fragments seems to be a promising approach for more efficient implementations.

In another direction, future work includes integrating other inference methods, e.g., system ARS [KR10], into our landscape of inductive inference operators.

There is a rich body of research works on the theory of nonmonotonic reasoning from conditionals, but much less attention has been paid to the actual implementations as in, e.g., [OP05; GGP07; Thi14; KB21a]. While implementation for c-inference and system W are available [BEK17; Kut19; BKS19; Bei+22; BSB23], so far implementations of extended system W and extended c-inference are missing. Future research developing efficient implementations for both inference operators can make use of the theoretical work in this thesis, e.g., the characterizations of extended c-inference by CSPs or the results on syntax splittings.

List of Postulates

Bibliography

[Ada75] Ernest W. Adams. *The Logic of Conditionals: An Application of Probability to Deductive Logic.* Synthese Library. Dordrecht: Springer Science+Business Media, 1975.

[BBS22] Christoph Beierle, Martin von Berg, and Arthur Sanin. "Realization of c-Inference as a SAT Problem". In: *Proceedings of the Thirty-Fifth International Florida Artificial Intelligence Research Society Conference, FLAIRS 2022, Hutchinson Island, Jensen Beach, Florida, USA, May 15-18, 2022.* Ed. by Roman Barták, Fazel Keshtkar, and Michael Franklin. 2022. DOI: 10.32473/FLAIRS.V35I.130663.

[Bei+18] Christoph Beierle, Christian Eichhorn, Gabriele Kern-Isberner, and Steven Kutsch. "Properties of skeptical c-inference for conditional knowledge bases and its realization as a constraint satisfaction problem". In: *Ann. Math. Artif. Intell.* 83.3-4 (2018), pp. 247–275. DOI: 10.1007/s10472-017-9571-9.

[Bei+19] Christoph Beierle, Gabriele Kern-Isberner, Kai Sauerwald, Tanja Bock, and Marco Ragni. "Towards a General Framework for Kinds of Forgetting in Common-Sense Belief Management". In: *Künstliche Intell.* 33.1 (2019), pp. 57–68. DOI: 10.1007/S13218-018-0567-3.

[Bei+21] Christoph Beierle, Christian Eichhorn, Gabriele Kern-Isberner, and Steven Kutsch. "Properties and interrelationships of skeptical, weakly skeptical, and credulous inference induced by classes of minimal models". In: *Artif. Intell.* 297 (2021), p. 103489. DOI: 10.1016/J.ARTINT.2021.103489.

[Bei+22] Christoph Beierle, Jonas Haldimann, Daniel Kollar, Kai Sauerwald, and Leon Schwarzer. "An Implementation of Nonmonotonic Reasoning with System W". In: *KI 2022: Advances in Artificial Intelligence - 45th German Conference on AI, Trier, Germany, September 19-23, 2022, Proceedings*. Ed. by Ralph Bergmann, Lukas Malburg, Stephanie C. Rodermund, and Ingo J. Timm. Vol. 13404. Lecture Notes in Computer Science. Springer, 2022, pp. 1–8. DOI: 10.1007/978-3-031-15791-2_1.

[BEK16] Christoph Beierle, Christian Eichhorn, and Gabriele Kern-Isberner. "Skeptical Inference Based on C-Representations and Its Characterization as a Constraint Satisfaction Problem". In: *Foundations of Information and Knowledge Systems - 9th International Symposium, FoIKS 2016, Linz, Austria, March 7-11, 2016. Proceedings*. Ed. by Marc Gyssens and Guillermo Ricardo Simari. Vol. 9616. Lecture Notes in Computer Science. Springer, 2016, pp. 65–82. DOI: 10.1007/978-3-319-30024-5_4.

[BEK17] Christoph Beierle, Christian Eichhorn, and Steven Kutsch. "A Practical Comparison of Qualitative Inferences with Preferred Ranking Models". In: *Künstliche Intell.* 31.1 (2017), pp. 41–52. DOI: 10.1007/S13218-016-0453-9.

[Ben+93] Salem Benferhat, Claudette Cayrol, Didier Dubois, Jérôme Lang, and Henri Prade. "Inconsistency Management and Prioritized Syntax-Based Entailment". In: *Proceedings of the 13th International Joint Conference on Artificial Intelligence. Chambéry, France, August 28 - September 3, 1993*. Ed. by Ruzena Bajcsy. Morgan Kaufmann, 1993, pp. 640–647.

[BH20a] Christoph Beierle and Jonas Haldimann. "Normal Forms of Conditional Knowledge Bases Respecting Entailments and Renamings". In: *Foundations of Information and Knowledge Systems - 11th International Symposium, FoIKS 2020, Dortmund, Germany, February 17-21, 2020, Proceedings*. Ed. by Andreas Herzig and Juha Kontinen. Vol. 12012. Lecture Notes in Computer Science. Springer, 2020, pp. 22–41. DOI: 10.1007/978-3-030-39951-1_2.

[BH20b] Christoph Beierle and Jonas Haldimann. "Transforming Conditional Knowledge Bases into Renaming Normal Form". In: *Proceedings of the Thirty-Third International Florida Artificial Intelligence Research Society Conference, Originally to be held in North Miami Beach, Florida, USA, May 17-20, 2020.* Ed. by Roman Barták and Eric Bell. AAAI Press, 2020, pp. 563–568.

[BH22a] Christoph Beierle and Jonas Haldimann. "Normal Forms of Conditional Belief Bases Respecting Inductive Inference". In: *Proceedings of the Thirty-Fifth International Florida Artificial Intelligence Research Society Conference, FLAIRS 2022, Hutchinson Island, Jensen Beach, Florida, USA, May 15-18, 2022.* Ed. by Roman Barták, Fazel Keshtkar, and Michael Franklin. 2022. DOI: 10.32473/FLAIRS.V35I.130661.

[BH22b] Christoph Beierle and Jonas Haldimann. "Normal forms of conditional knowledge bases respecting system P-entailments and signature renamings". In: *Ann. Math. Artif. Intell.* 90.2-3 (2022), pp. 149–179. DOI: 10.1007/S10472-021-09745-3.

[BHK21a] Christoph Beierle, Jonas Haldimann, and Gabriele Kern-Isberner. "Semantic Splitting of Conditional Belief Bases". In: *Logic, Computation and Rigorous Methods - Essays Dedicated to Egon Börger on the Occasion of His 75th Birthday.* Ed. by Alexander Raschke, Elvinia Riccobene, and Klaus-Dieter Schewe. Vol. 12750. Lecture Notes in Computer Science. Springer, 2021, pp. 82–95. DOI: 10.1007/978-3-030-76020-5_5.

[BHK21b] Christoph Beierle, Jonas Haldimann, and Steven Kutsch. "A Complete Map of Conditional Knowledge Bases in Different Normal Forms and Their Induced System P Inference Relations Over Small Signatures". In: *Proceedings of the Thirty-Fourth International Florida Artificial Intelligence Research Society Conference, North Miami Beach, Florida, USA, May 17-19, 2021.* Ed. by Eric Bell and Fazel Keshtkar. 2021. DOI: 10.32473/FLAIRS.V34I1.128467.

[BHS23] Christoph Beierle, Jonas Haldimann, and Leon Schwarzer. "Observational Equivalence of Conditional Belief Bases". In: *Proceedings of the Thirty-Sixth International Florida Artificial Intelligence Research Society Conference, FLAIRS 2023, Clearwater Beach, FL, USA, May 14-17, 2023.* Ed. by Michael Franklin and Soon Ae Chun. AAAI Press, 2023. DOI: 10.32473/FLAIRS.36.133269.

[BK09] Christoph Beierle and Gabriele Kern-Isberner. "Formal similarities and differences among qualitative conditional semantics". In: *Int. J. Approx. Reason.* 50.9 (2009), pp. 1333–1346. DOI: 10.1016/J.IJAR.2009.04.006.

[BK12] Christoph Beierle and Gabriele Kern-Isberner. "Semantical investigations into nonmonotonic and probabilistic logics". In: *Ann. Math. Artif. Intell.* 65.2-3 (2012), pp. 123–158. DOI: 10.1007/S10472-012-9310-1.

[BK19] Christoph Beierle and Steven Kutsch. "Systematic Generation of Conditional Knowledge Bases up to Renaming and Equivalence". In: *Logics in Artificial Intelligence - 16th European Conference, JELIA 2019, Rende, Italy, May 7-11, 2019, Proceedings.* Ed. by Francesco Calimeri, Nicola Leone, and Marco Manna. Vol. 11468. Lecture Notes in Computer Science. Springer, 2019, pp. 279–286. DOI: 10.1007/978-3-030-19570-0_18.

[BKB19] Christoph Beierle, Steven Kutsch, and Henning Breuers. "On Rational Monotony and Weak Rational Monotony for Inference Relations Induced by Sets of Minimal C-Representations". In: *Proceedings of the Thirty-Second International Florida Artificial Intelligence Research Society Conference, Sarasota, Florida, USA, May 19-22 2019.* Ed. by Roman Barták and Keith W. Brawner. AAAI Press, 2019, pp. 458–463.

[BKS11] Christoph Beierle, Gabriele Kern-Isberner, and Karl Södler. "A Declarative Approach for Computing Ordinal Conditional Functions Using Constraint Logic Programming". In: *Applications of Declarative Programming and Knowledge Management - 19th International Conference, INAP 2011, and 25th Workshop on Logic Programming, WLP 2011, Vienna, Austria, September 28-30, 2011,*

Revised Selected Papers. Ed. by Hans Tompits, Salvador Abreu, Johannes Oetsch, Jörg Pührer, Dietmar Seipel, Masanobu Umeda, and Armin Wolf. Vol. 7773. Lecture Notes in Computer Science. Springer, 2011, pp. 175–192. DOI: 10.1007/978-3-642-41524-1_10.

[BKS19] Christoph Beierle, Steven Kutsch, and Kai Sauerwald. "Compilation of static and evolving conditional knowledge bases for computing induced nonmonotonic inference relations". In: *Ann. Math. Artif. Intell.* 87.1-2 (2019), pp. 5–41. DOI: 10.1007/S10472-019-09653-7.

[BMP97] Hassan Bezzazi, David Makinson, and Ramón Pino Pérez. "Beyond Rational Monotony: Some Strong Non-Horn Rules for Nonmonotonic Inference Relations". In: *J. Log. Comput.* 7.5 (1997), pp. 605–631. DOI: 10.1093/logcom/7.5.605.

[BP96] Hassan Bezzazi and Ramón Pino Pérez. "Rational Transitivity and its Models". In: *26th IEEE International Symposium on Multiple-Valued Logic, ISMVL 1996, Santiago de Compostela, Spain, May 29-31, 1996, Proceedings*. IEEE Computer Society, 1996, pp. 160–165. DOI: 10.1109/ISMVL.1996.508354.

[BSB23] Martin von Berg, Arthur Sanin, and Christoph Beierle. "Representing Nonmonotonic Inference Based on c-Representations as an SMT Problem". In: *Symbolic and Quantitative Approaches to Reasoning with Uncertainty - 17th European Conference, ECSQARU 2023, Arras, France, September 19-22, 2023, Proceedings*. Ed. by Zied Bouraoui and Srdjan Vesic. Vol. 14294. Lecture Notes in Computer Science. Springer, 2023, pp. 210–223. DOI: 10.1007/978-3-031-45608-4_17.

[BT19] Christoph Beierle and Ingo J. Timm. "Intentional Forgetting: An Emerging Field in AI and Beyond". In: *Künstliche Intell.* 33.1 (2019), pp. 5–8. DOI: 10.1007/S13218-018-00574-X.

[Cas+14] Giovanni Casini, Thomas Meyer, Kodylan Moodley, and Riku Nortje. "Relevant Closure: A New Form of Defeasible Reasoning for Description Logics". In: *Logics in Artificial Intelligence - 14th European Conference, JELIA 2014, Funchal, Madeira, Portugal, September 24-26, 2014. Proceedings.* Ed. by Eduardo Fermé and João Leite. Vol. 8761. Lecture Notes in Computer Science. Springer, 2014, pp. 92–106. DOI: 10.1007/978-3-319-11558-0_7.

[CMV19] Giovanni Casini, Thomas Meyer, and Ivan Varzinczak. "Taking Defeasible Entailment Beyond Rational Closure". In: *Logics in Artificial Intelligence - 16th European Conference, JELIA 2019, Rende, Italy, May 7-11, 2019, Proceedings.* Ed. by Francesco Calimeri, Nicola Leone, and Marco Manna. Vol. 11468. Lecture Notes in Computer Science. Springer, 2019, pp. 182–197. DOI: 10.1007/978-3-030-19570-0_12.

[CS13] Giovanni Casini and Umberto Straccia. "Defeasible Inheritance-Based Description Logics". In: *J. Artif. Intell. Res.* 48 (2013), pp. 415–473. DOI: 10.1613/JAIR.4062.

[Del17] James P. Delgrande. "A Knowledge Level Account of Forgetting". In: *J. Artif. Intell. Res.* 60 (2017), pp. 1165–1213. DOI: 10.1613/JAIR.5530.

[DLP91] Didier Dubois, Jérôme Lang, and Henri Prade. "A Brief Overview of Possibilistic Logic". In: *Symbolic and Quantitative Approaches to Reasoning and Uncertainty, European Conference, ECSQAU, Marseille, France, October 15-17, 1991, Proceedings.* Ed. by Rudolf Kruse and Pierre Siegel. Vol. 548. Lecture Notes in Computer Science. Springer, 1991, pp. 53–57. DOI: 10.1007/3-540-54659-6_65.

[DP94] Didier Dubois and Henri Prade. "Conditional Objects as Nonmonotonic Consequence Relationships". In: *IEEE Trans. Syst. Man Cybern. Syst.* 24.12 (1994), pp. 1724–1740. DOI: 10.1109/21.328930.

[DP97] Adnan Darwiche and Judea Pearl. "On the Logic of Iterated Belief Revision". In: *Artif. Intell.* 89.1-2 (1997), pp. 1–29. DOI: 10.1016/S0004-3702(96)00038-0.

[EK19] Thomas Eiter and Gabriele Kern-Isberner. "A Brief Survey on Forgetting from a Knowledge Representation and Reasoning Perspective". In: *Künstliche Intell.* 33.1 (2019), pp. 9–33. DOI: 10.1007/S13218-018-0564-6.

[Fin37] Bruno de Finetti. "La prévision, ses lois logiques et ses sources subjectives". In: *Ann. Inst. H. Poincaré* 7.1 (1937). Engl. transl. *Theory of Probability*, J. Wiley & Sons, 1974, pp. 1–68.

[FLM91] Michael Freund, Daniel Lehmann, and Paul Morris. "Rationality, Transitivity, and Contraposition". In: *Artif. Intell.* 52.2 (1991), pp. 191–203. DOI: 10.1016/0004-3702(91)90043-J.

[Fre93] Michael Freund. "Injective Models and Disjunctive Relations". In: *J. Log. Comput.* 3.3 (1993), pp. 231–247. DOI: 10.1093/LOGCOM/3.3.231.

[Gel08] Michael Gelfond. "Answer Sets". In: *Handbook of Knowledge Representation.* Ed. by Frank van Harmelen, Vladimir Lifschitz, and Bruce W. Porter. Vol. 3. Foundations of Artificial Intelligence. Elsevier, 2008, pp. 285–316. DOI: 10.1016/S1574-6526(07)03007-6.

[GG18] Laura Giordano and Valentina Gliozzi. "Reasoning About Exceptions in Ontologies: from the Lexicographic Closure to the Skeptical Closure". In: *Proceedings of the Second Workshop on Logics for Reasoning about Preferences, Uncertainty, and Vagueness co-located with the 9th International Joint Conference on Automated Reasoning, PRUV@IJCAR 2018, Oxford, UK, July 19th, 2018.* Ed. by Thomas Lukasiewicz, Rafael Peñaloza, and Anni-Yasmin Turhan. Vol. 2157. CEUR Workshop Proceedings. CEUR-WS.org, 2018.

[GG20] Laura Giordano and Valentina Gliozzi. "Reasoning about Exceptions in Ontologies: from the Lexicographic Closure to the Skeptical Closure". In: *Fundam. Informaticae* 176.3-4 (2020), pp. 235–269. DOI: 10.3233/FI-2020-1973.

[GG21] Laura Giordano and Valentina Gliozzi. "A reconstruction of multipreference closure". In: *Artif. Intell.* 290 (2021), p. 103398. DOI: 10.1016/j.artint.2020.103398.

[GGP07] Laura Giordano, Valentina Gliozzi, and Gian Luca Pozzato. “KLMLean 2.0: A Theorem Prover for KLM Logics of Nonmonotonic Reasoning”. In: *Automated Reasoning with Analytic Tableaux and Related Methods, 16th International Conference, TABLEAUX 2007, Aix en Provence, France, July 3-6, 2007, Proceedings*. Ed. by Nicola Olivetti. Vol. 4548. Lecture Notes in Computer Science. Springer, 2007, pp. 238–244. DOI: 10.1007/978-3-540-73099-6_19.

[Gio+15] Laura Giordano, Valentina Gliozzi, Nicola Olivetti, and Gian Luca Pozzato. “Semantic characterization of rational closure: From propositional logic to description logics”. In: *Artif. Intell.* 226 (2015), pp. 1–33. DOI: 10.1016/j.artint.2015.05.001.

[GP90] Moises Goldszmidt and Judea Pearl. “On the Relation Between Rational Closure and System-Z”. In: *Proceedings of the Third International Workshop on Nonmonotonic Reasoning, May 31 – June 3*. 1990, pp. 130–140.

[GP96] Moisés Goldszmidt and Judea Pearl. “Qualitative Probabilities for Default Reasoning, Belief Revision, and Causal Modeling”. In: *Artificial Intelligence* 84.1-2 (1996), pp. 57–112. DOI: 10.1016/0004-3702(95)00090-9.

[Hal+21a] Jonas Haldimann, Kai Sauerwald, Martin von Berg, Gabriele Kern-Isberner, and Christoph Beierle. “Conditional Descriptor Revision and Its Modelling by a CSP”. In: *Logics in Artificial Intelligence - 17th European Conference, JELIA 2021, Virtual Event, May 17-20, 2021, Proceedings*. Ed. by Wolfgang Faber, Gerhard Friedrich, Martin Gebser, and Michael Morak. Vol. 12678. Lecture Notes in Computer Science. Springer, 2021, pp. 35–49. DOI: 10.1007/978-3-030-75775-5_4.

[Hal+21b] Jonas Haldimann, Kai Sauerwald, Martin von Berg, Gabriele Kern-Isberner, and Christoph Beierle. “Towards a framework of hansson’s descriptor revision for conditionals”. In: *SAC 2021*. Ed. by Chih-Cheng Hung, Jiman Hong, Alessio Bechini, and Eunjee Song. ACM, 2021, pp. 889–891. DOI: 10.1145/3412841.3442101.

[Hal+23a] Jonas Haldimann, Christoph Beierle, Gabriele Kern-Isberner, and Thomas Meyer. "Conditionals, Infeasible Worlds, and Reasoning with System W". In: *Proceedings of the Thirty-Sixth International Florida Artificial Intelligence Research Society Conference, FLAIRS 2023, Clearwater Beach, FL, USA, May 14-17, 2023.* Ed. by Michael Franklin and Soon Ae Chun. AAAI Press, 2023. DOI: 10.32473/FLAIRS.36.133268.

[Hal+23b] Jonas Haldimann, Thomas Meyer, Gabriele Kern-Isberner, and Christoph Beierle. "Rational Closure Extension in SPO-Representable Inductive Inference Operators". In: *Logics in Artificial Intelligence - 18th European Conference, JELIA 2023, Dresden, Germany, September 20-22, 2023, Proceedings.* Ed. by Sarah Alice Gaggl, Maria Vanina Martinez, and Magdalena Ortiz. Vol. 14281. Lecture Notes in Computer Science. Springer, 2023, pp. 561–576. DOI: 10.1007/978-3-031-43619-2_38.

[Hal90] Joseph Y. Halpern. "An Analysis of First-Order Logics of Probability". In: *Artif. Intell.* 46.3 (1990), pp. 311–350. DOI: 10.1016/0004-3702(90)90019-V.

[HB22a] Jonas Haldimann and Christoph Beierle. "Characterizing Multipreference Closure with System W". In: *Scalable Uncertainty Management - 15th International Conference, SUM 2022, Paris, France, October 17-19, 2022, Proceedings.* Ed. by Florence Dupin de Saint-Cyr, Meltem Öztürk-Escoffier, and Nico Potyka. Vol. 13562. Lecture Notes in Computer Science. Springer, 2022, pp. 79–91. DOI: 10.1007/978-3-031-18843-5_6.

[HB22b] Jonas Haldimann and Christoph Beierle. "Inference with System W Satisfies Syntax Splitting". In: *Proceedings of the 19th International Conference on Principles of Knowledge Representation and Reasoning, KR 2022, Haifa, Israel, July 31 - August 5, 2022.* Ed. by Gabriele Kern-Isberner, Gerhard Lakemeyer, and Thomas Meyer. 2022.

[HB22c] Jonas Haldimann and Christoph Beierle. "Properties of System W and Its Relationships to Other Inductive Inference Operators". In: *Foundations of Information and Knowledge Systems - 12th International Symposium,*

FoIKS 2022, Helsinki, Finland, June 20-23, 2022, Proceedings. Ed. by Ivan Varzinczak. Vol. 13388. Lecture Notes in Computer Science. Springer, 2022, pp. 206–225. DOI: 10.1007/978-3-031-11321-5_12.

[HB23a] Jonas Haldimann and Christoph Beierle. "Approximations of System W Between c-Inference, System Z, and Lexicographic Inference". In: *ECSQARU 2023*. Ed. by Zied Bouraoui and Srdjan Vesic. 2023, pp. 185–223.

[HB23b] Jonas Philipp Haldimann and Christoph Beierle. "Finest Syntax Splittings of Ranking Functions and Total Preorders on Worlds". In: *Proceedings of the 20th International Conference on Principles of Knowledge Representation and Reasoning, KR 2023, Rhodes, Greece, September 2-8, 2023*. Ed. by Pierre Marquis, Tran Cao Son, and Gabriele Kern-Isberner. 2023, pp. 747–751. DOI: 10.24963/KR.2023/75.

[HBK21] Jonas Haldimann, Christoph Beierle, and Gabriele Kern-Isberner. "Syntax Splitting for Iterated Contractions, Ignorations, and Revisions on Ranking Functions Using Selection Strategies". In: *Logics in Artificial Intelligence - 17th European Conference, JELIA 2021, Virtual Event, May 17-20, 2021, Proceedings*. Ed. by Wolfgang Faber, Gerhard Friedrich, Martin Gebser, and Michael Morak. Vol. 12678. Lecture Notes in Computer Science. Springer, 2021, pp. 85–100. DOI: 10.1007/978-3-030-75775-5_7.

[HBK23a] Jonas Philipp Haldimann, Christoph Beierle, and Gabriele Kern-Isberner. "Epistemic State Mappings among Ranking Functions and Total Preorders". In: *Journal of Applied Logics* 10.2 (2023), pp. 155–192.

[HBK23b] Jonas Philipp Haldimann, Christoph Beierle, and Gabriele Kern-Isberner. "Extending c-Representations and c-Inference for Reasoning with Infeasible Worlds". In: *Proceedings of the 21st International Workshop on Non-Monotonic Reasoning co-located with the 20th International Conference on Principles of Knowledge Representation and Reasoning (KR 2023) and co-located with the 36th International Workshop on Description*

Logics (DL 2023), Rhodes, Greece, September 2-4, 2023. Ed. by Kai Sauerwald and Matthias Thimm. Vol. 3464. CEUR Workshop Proceedings. CEUR-WS.org, 2023, pp. 52–63.

[HBK24] Jonas Philipp Haldimann, Christoph Beierle, and Gabriele Kern-Isberner. "Syntax Splitting and Reasoning from Weakly Consistent Belief Bases with c-Inference". In: *Foundations of Information and Knowledge Systems - 13th International Symposium, FoIKS 2024, Sheffield, UK, April 8-11, 2024, Proceedings.* Ed. by Arne Meier and Magdalena Ortiz. Lecture Notes in Computer Science. Accepted for publication. Springer, 2024.

[Hey+23] Jesse Heyninck, Gabriele Kern-Isberner, Thomas Andreas Meyer, Jonas Philipp Haldimann, and Christoph Beierle. "Conditional Syntax Splitting for Non-monotonic Inference Operators". In: *Thirty-Seventh AAAI Conference on Artificial Intelligence, AAAI 2023, Thirty-Fifth Conference on Innovative Applications of Artificial Intelligence, IAAI 2023, Thirteenth Symposium on Educational Advances in Artificial Intelligence, EAAI 2023, Washington, DC, USA, February 7-14, 2023.* Ed. by Brian Williams, Yiling Chen, and Jennifer Neville. AAAI Press, 2023, pp. 6416–6424. DOI: `10.1609/aaai.v37i5.25789`.

[HK21] Jonas Haldimann and Gabriele Kern-Isberner. "On Properties of Epistemic State Mappings among Ranking Functions and Total Preorders". In: *FCR 2021.* Ed. by Christoph Beierle, Marco Ragni, Frieder Stolzenburg, and Matthias Thimm. Vol. 2961. CEUR Workshop Proceedings. CEUR-WS.org, 2021, pp. 34–47.

[HKB20] Jonas Philipp Haldimann, Gabriele Kern-Isberner, and Christoph Beierle. "Syntax Splitting for Iterated Contractions". In: *Proceedings of the 17th International Conference on Principles of Knowledge Representation and Reasoning, KR 2020, Rhodes, Greece, September 12-18, 2020.* Ed. by Diego Calvanese, Esra Erdem, and Michael Thielscher. 2020, pp. 465–475. DOI: `10.24963/KR.2020/47`.

[HKM22] Jesse Heyninck, Gabriele Kern-Isberner, and Thomas Andreas Meyer. "Conditional Syntax Splitting, Lexicographic Entailment and the Drowning Effect". In: *Proceedings of the 20th International Workshop on Non-Monotonic Reasoning, NMR 2022, Part of the Federated Logic Conference (FLoC 2022), Haifa, Israel, August 7-9, 2022.* Ed. by Ofer Arieli, Giovanni Casini, and Laura Giordano. Vol. 3197. CEUR Workshop Proceedings. CEUR-WS.org, 2022, pp. 61–69.

[HOB20] Jonas Haldimann, Anna Osiak, and Christoph Beierle. "Modelling and Reasoning in Biomedical Applications with Qualitative Conditional Logic". In: *KI 2020: Advances in Artificial Intelligence - 43rd German Conference on AI, Bamberg, Germany, September 21-25, 2020, Proceedings.* Ed. by Ute Schmid, Franziska Klügl, and Diedrich Wolter. Vol. 12325. Lecture Notes in Computer Science. Springer, 2020, pp. 283–289. DOI: 10.1007/978-3-030-58285-2_24.

[KB17] Gabriele Kern-Isberner and Gerhard Brewka. "Strong Syntax Splitting for Iterated Belief Revision". In: *Proceedings of the Twenty-Sixth International Joint Conference on Artificial Intelligence, IJCAI 2017, Melbourne, Australia, August 19-25, 2017.* Ed. by Carles Sierra. ijcai.org, 2017, pp. 1131–1137. DOI: 10.24963/ijcai.2017/157.

[KB20] Christian Komo and Christoph Beierle. "Nonmonotonic Inferences with Qualitative Conditionals Based on Preferred Structures on Worlds". In: *KI 2020: Advances in Artificial Intelligence - 43rd German Conference on AI, Bamberg, Germany, September 21-25, 2020, Proceedings.* Ed. by Ute Schmid, Franziska Klügl, and Diedrich Wolter. Vol. 12325. Lecture Notes in Computer Science. Springer, 2020, pp. 102–115. DOI: 10.1007/978-3-030-58285-2_8.

[KB21a] Steven Kutsch and Christoph Beierle. "InfOCF-Web: An Online Tool for Nonmonotonic Reasoning with Conditionals and Ranking Functions". In: *Proceedings of the Thirtieth International Joint Conference on Artificial Intelligence, IJCAI 2021, Virtual Event / Montreal, Canada,*

19-27 August 2021. Ed. by Zhi-Hua Zhou. ijcai.org, 2021, pp. 4996–4999. DOI: 10.24963/IJCAI.2021/711.

[KB21b] Steven Kutsch and Christoph Beierle. "Semantic classification of qualitative conditionals and calculating closures of nonmonotonic inference relations". In: *Int. J. Approx. Reason.* 130 (2021), pp. 297–313. DOI: 10.1016/j.ijar.2020.12.020.

[KB22] Christian Komo and Christoph Beierle. "Nonmonotonic reasoning from conditional knowledge bases with system W". In: *Ann. Math. Artif. Intell.* 90.1 (2022), pp. 107–144. DOI: 10.1007/s10472-021-09777-9.

[KBB20] Gabriele Kern-Isberner, Christoph Beierle, and Gerhard Brewka. "Syntax Splitting = Relevance + Independence: New Postulates for Nonmonotonic Reasoning From Conditional Belief Bases". In: *Proceedings of the 17th International Conference on Principles of Knowledge Representation and Reasoning, KR 2020, Rhodes, Greece, September 12-18, 2020*. Ed. by Diego Calvanese, Esra Erdem, and Michael Thielscher. 2020, pp. 560–571. DOI: 10.24963/kr.2020/56.

[Ker01] Gabriele Kern-Isberner. *Conditionals in Nonmonotonic Reasoning and Belief Revision - Considering Conditionals as Agents*. Vol. 2087. Lecture Notes in Computer Science. Springer, 2001. ISBN: 3-540-42367-2. DOI: 10.1007/3-540-44600-1.

[Ker04] Gabriele Kern-Isberner. "A Thorough Axiomatization of a Principle of Conditional Preservation in Belief Revision". In: *Ann. Math. Artif. Intell.* 40.1-2 (2004), pp. 127–164. DOI: 10.1023/A:1026110129951.

[KLM90] Sarit Kraus, Daniel Lehmann, and Menachem Magidor. "Nonmonotonic Reasoning, Preferential Models and Cumulative Logics". In: *Artif. Intell.* 44.1-2 (1990), pp. 167–207.

[KM92] Hirofumi Katsuno and Alberto O. Mendelzon. "Propositional Knowledge Base Revision and Minimal Change". In: *Artif. Intell.* 52.3 (1992), pp. 263–294. DOI: 10.1016/0004-3702(91)90069-V.

[Kol21] Daniel Kollar. "Implementation and Evaluation of Nonmonotonic Inferences with System W". M.Sc. Thesis. Dept. of Computer Science, FernUniversität in Hagen, Germany, 2021.

[KR10] Gabriele Kern-Isberner and Manuela Ritterskamp. "Preference Fusion for Default Reasoning Beyond System Z". In: *J. Autom. Reason.* 45.1 (2010), pp. 3–19. DOI: 10.1007/S10817-009-9129-6.

[Kut19] Steven Kutsch. "InfOCF-Lib: A Java Library for OCF-based Conditional Inference". In: *Proceedings of the 8th Workshop on Dynamics of Knowledge and Belief (DKB-2019) and the 7th Workshop KI & Kognition (KIK-2019) co-located with 44nd German Conference on Artificial Intelligence (KI 2019), Kassel, Germany, September 23, 2019.* Ed. by Christoph Beierle, Marco Ragni, Frieder Stolzenburg, and Matthias Thimm. Vol. 2445. CEUR Workshop Proceedings. CEUR-WS.org, 2019, pp. 47–58.

[Kut21] Steven Kutsch. *Knowledge representation and inductive reasoning using conditional logic and sets of ranking functions.* PhD thesis. University of Hagen, Germany. IOS Press, 2021. ISBN: 978-3-89838-760-6.

[Leh89] Daniel Lehmann. "What Does a Conditional Knowledge Base Entail?" In: *Proceedings of the 1st International Conference on Principles of Knowledge Representation and Reasoning (KR'89). Toronto, Canada, May 15-18 1989.* Ed. by Ronald J. Brachman, Hector J. Levesque, and Raymond Reiter. Morgan Kaufmann, 1989, pp. 212–222.

[Leh95] Daniel Lehmann. "Another Perspective on Default Reasoning". In: *Ann. Math. Artif. Intell.* 15.1 (1995), pp. 61–82. DOI: 10.1007/BF01535841.

[LM92] Daniel Lehmann and Menachem Magidor. "What does a Conditional Knowledge Base Entail?" In: *Artif. Intell.* 55.1 (1992), pp. 1–60. DOI: 10.1016/0004-3702(92)90041-U.

[Mül19] Sophie Müller. "Beispiele für die Verwendung von qualitativen Konditionalen in der Wissensmodellierung und -verarbeitung in einem medizinischen Anwendungsgebiet". (in German). Bachelor Thesis. Dept. of Computer Science, FernUniversität in Hagen, Germany, 2019.

[NC02] Donald Nute and Charles B. Cross. "Conditional Logic". In: *Handbook of Philosophical Logic*. Ed. by D.M. Gabbay and F. Guenther. second. Vol. 4. Kluwer Academic Publishers, 2002, pp. 1–98. DOI: 10.1007/978-94-017-0456-4_1.

[Nil86] Nils J. Nilsson. "Probabilistic Logic". In: *Artif. Intell.* 28.1 (1986), pp. 71–87. DOI: 10.1016/0004-3702(86)90031-7.

[Nut80] Donald Nute. *Topics in Conditional Logic*. Dordrecht, Holland: D. Reidel Publishing Company, 1980. ISBN: 978-90-277-1049-9. DOI: 10.1007/978-94-009-8966-5.

[OP05] Nicola Olivetti and Gian Luca Pozzato. "KLMLean 1.0: A theorem prover for logics of default reasoning". In: *Proceedings of the 4th International Workshop on Methods for Modalities (M4M-4)*. Ed. by Holger Schlingloff. Vol. 194. Informatik-Berichte. edoc-Server der Humboldt-Universität zu Berlin, 2005, pp. 235–245. DOI: 10.18452/2459.

[Par99] Rohit Parikh. "Beliefs, Belief Revision, and Splitting Languages". In: *Logic, Language and Computation* 2 (1999), pp. 266–278.

[Pea89] Judea Pearl. *Probabilistic reasoning in intelligent systems - networks of plausible inference*. Morgan Kaufmann series in representation and reasoning. Morgan Kaufmann, 1989.

[Pea90] Judea Pearl. "System Z: A Natural Ordering of Defaults with Tractable Applications to Nonmonotonic Reasoning". In: *Proceedings of the 3rd Conference on Theoretical Aspects of Reasoning about Knowledge, Pacific Grove, CA, USA, March 1990*. Ed. by Rohit Parikh. Morgan Kaufmann, 1990, pp. 121–135.

[Poo88] David Poole. "A Logical Framework for Default Reasoning". In: *Artif. Intell.* 36.1 (1988), pp. 27–47. DOI: 10.1016/0004-3702(88)90077-X.

[Ram31] Frank P. Ramsey. "General Propositions and Causality". In: *The Foundations of Mathematics and other Logical Essays*. Ed. by R. B. Brainwhite. Kegan Paul, Trench, Trübner, 1931, pp. 237–255.

[Rei80] Raymond Reiter. "A Logic for Default Reasoning". In: *Artif. Intell.* 13.1-2 (1980), pp. 81–132. DOI: 10.1016/0004-3702(80)90014-4.

[RN20] Stuart Russell and Peter Norvig. *Artificial Intelligence: A Modern Approach (4th Edition)*. Pearson, 2020. ISBN: 978-0-13-461099-3.

[Rot01] Hans Rott. *Change, choice and inference - a study of belief revision and nonmonotonic reasoning*. Vol. 42. Oxford logic guides. Oxford University Press, 2001. ISBN: 978-0-19-850306-4.

[Sau+20] Kai Sauerwald, Jonas Haldimann, Martin von Berg, and Christoph Beierle. "Descriptor Revision for Conditionals: Literal Descriptors and Conditional Preservation". In: *KI 2020: Advances in Artificial Intelligence - 43rd German Conference on AI, Bamberg, Germany, September 21-25, 2020, Proceedings*. Ed. by Ute Schmid, Franziska Klügl, and Diedrich Wolter. Vol. 12325. Lecture Notes in Computer Science. Springer, 2020, pp. 204–218. DOI: 10.1007/978-3-030-58285-2_15.

[Spo88] Wolfgang Spohn. "Ordinal conditional functions: a dynamic theory of epistemic states". In: *Causation in decision, belief change, and statistics: Proceedings of the Irvine Conference on Probability and Causation*. Ed. by William L. Harper and Brian Skyrms. 2. Dordrecht: Kluwer, 1988, pp. 105–134. ISBN: 978-94-009-2865-7. DOI: 10.1007/978-94-009-2865-7_6.

[Sta81] Robert C. Stalnaker. "A Theory of Conditionals". In: *IFS: Conditionals, Belief, Decision, Chance and Time*. Ed. by William L. Harper, Robert Stalnaker, and Glenn Pearce. Dordrecht: Springer Netherlands, 1981, pp. 41–55. ISBN:

978-94-009-9117-0. DOI: 10.1007/978-94-009-9117-0_2.

[Tei23] Finn Teizel. "Empirische Untersuchungen zur Überprüfung von Eigenschaften einer nichtmonotonen Inferenzrelation". (in German). Bachelor Thesis. Dept. of Computer Science, FernUniversität in Hagen, Germany, 2023.

[Thi14] Matthias Thimm. "Tweety - A Comprehensive Collection of Java Libraries for Logical Aspects of Artificial Intelligence and Knowledge Representation". In: *Proceedings of the 14th International Conference on Principles of Knowledge Representation and Reasoning (KR'14)*. Vienna, Austria, July 2014.

[Tön22] Dietrich Tönnies. "Implementierung und empirische Untersuchung lexikographischer Inferenz für das nichtmonotone Schließen". (in German). Bachelor thesis. Dept. of Computer Science, FernUniversität in Hagen, Germany, 2022.

[Wil+23] Marco Wilhelm, Meliha Sezgin, Gabriele Kern-Isberner, Jonas Haldimann, Christoph Beierle, and Jesse Heyninck. "Splitting Techniques for Conditional Belief Bases in the Context of c-Representations". In: *Logics in Artificial Intelligence - 18th European Conference, JELIA 2023, Dresden, Germany, September 20-22, 2023, Proceedings.* Ed. by Sarah Alice Gaggl, Maria Vanina Martinez, and Magdalena Ortiz. Vol. 14281. Lecture Notes in Computer Science. Springer, 2023, pp. 462–477. DOI: 10.1007/978-3-031-43619-2_32.

[Zad65] Lotfi A. Zadeh. "Fuzzy Sets". In: *Inf. Control.* 8.3 (1965), pp. 338–353. DOI: 10.1016/S0019-9958(65)90241-X.

[Zim01] Hans-Jürgen Zimmermann. *Fuzzy Set Theory—and Its Applications.* Springer Dordrecht, 2001. ISBN: 978-0-7923-7435-0. DOI: 10.1007/978-94-010-0646-0.

Index